To Peter Hodgkinson, Michael Huck, Nigel Nicholson and Michael Spratt, my dear brother and friends, whose immense generosity, loving support and wise counsel, over many years, have enabled me to bring this work (and so much more) to completion

Images of Competitive Space

Other Books by the Author:

The Competent Organization: A Psychological Analysis of the Strategic Management Process
(*with P. R. Sparrow*)

Images of Competitive Space

A Study of Managerial and Organizational Strategic Cognition

Gerard P. Hodgkinson

First published 2005 by
PALGRAVE MACMILLAN
Houndmills, Basingstoke, Hampshire RG21 6XS and
175 Fifth Avenue, New York, N. Y. 10010
Companies and representatives throughout the world

PALGRAVE MACMILLAN is the global academic imprint of the Palgrave Macmillan division of St. Martin's Press, LLC and of Palgrave Macmillan Ltd. Macmillan® is a registered trademark in the United States, United Kingdom and other countries. Palgrave is a registered trademark in the European Union and other countries.

ISBN-13: 978–1–4039–0296–2   hardback
ISBN-10: 1–4039–0296–8   hardback

This book is printed on paper suitable for recycling and made from fully managed and sustained forest sources.

A catalogue record for this book is available from the British Library.

Library of Congress Cataloging-in-Publication Data
Hodgkinson, Gerard P., 1961–
    Images of competitive space: a study of managerial and organizational strategic cognition/ Gerard P. Hodgkinson.
        p. cm.
    Includes bibliographical references and index.
    ISBN 1–4039–0296–8
    1. Industrial management–Psychological aspects. 2. Competition (Psychology) 3. Strategic planning–Psychological aspects.
4. Cognition–Mathematical models. 5. Organizational behavior–Mathematical models. 6. Real estate business–Great Britain–Case studies. I. Title: Managerial and organizational strategic cognition. II. Title: Strategic cognition. III. Title.

HF5548.8.H554 2005
158.7–dc22   2004059170

10   9   8   7   6   5   4   3   2   1
14   13   12   11   10   09   08   07   06   05

Printed and bound in Great Britain by
Antony Rowe Ltd, Chippenham and Eastbourne

Contents

List of Figures

List of Tables

Foreword

Strategic management has been dominated by two disciplines, economics and organization theory. Although these are apparently different, both apply a macro lens to the central issues of strategy. Economics provides abstract, intellectual constructs from which frameworks and tools have been constructed. The world is captured as a series of black boxes that conform to general laws of economic rationality. The creation of these often elegant constructs arises from equally elegant, but essentially simplistic, assumptions about individual and collective behaviour. A critique of an economic approach is not so much that the tools are not useful (often they are although sometimes they are not, and it is difficult to know *a priori*) but rather that the roles of individuals and groups are subordinated to a dry and soulless collective. At best, economics can give us a good ex post view of what happened and why it might have happened in such a way. It is dramatically less helpful in ex ante construction of strategy and strategic processes.

Organization theory is subject to the same criticisms. It stands as the flip side of the strategy coin, so we are tempted to regard strategy as economics plus organization. Organization presents itself as the means by which the economic theory of the firm is captured in organization design and organization process. The very principles of organization design are based on two fundamental principles, the division of labour (or specialization) and co-ordination. Organization is simply the ways in which the different tasks are grouped together and the way these tasks are then coordinated. Adam Smith wrote this script and Henry Mintzberg (among others) articulated it with elegance and precision. The "content" of organization theory then fills up with the various formal and informal management processes that have attracted much research attention. For example the focus on strategy making typically pays attention to the constitution of and behaviour of top teams. Recent research shows how processes are routinized for economy and adapted through learning. But, overall the focus remains on the organization and its behaviour.

The idea of strategic thinking sits badly in economics and in organization theory. Both provide abstracts that act in stylized ways to achieve learning and adaptive behaviour. But now we have the emerging field of managerial and organizational cognition which Gerard Hodgkinson elaborates as strategic thinking and its practical consequences. The approach of the cognitive school is to focus on mental models rather than on economic models. This allows a conception of the economic environment in terms of the perceptions and beliefs of individuals and groups. This competitive enactment permits a construction of the environment in ways that make sense to the participants and through a social exchange process results in a collective social construction. Essentially, a social construction means a shared understanding which adapts over time to provide a dynamic conception. The potential power of the cognitive approach is that strategizing then becomes the province of individuals and groups, capable of being translated upwards into an organizational conception and, more importantly, providing a really substantial basis on which to base theories and explanations of strategizing and strategy formation.

There are some essential linkages to be examined in establishing these ideas as something other than mere intellectual abstractions. Is there a meaningful linkage of actors' cognitive models to elements of the economic environment and of the organizational context? This would then establish cognition as embedded in the range of other social science constructs that we know have impacts on strategy. Furthermore, we need to know whether and how the mental models of individual actors are collectively held and in what degrees of consonance with the environment. There needs to be a translation for the individual to the organization in ways that writers such as Nonaka and Takeuchi so memorably conveyed as the knowledge spiral. Finally we need to know the degree of stability of mental models and the conditions under which they adapt over time. A theory of strategy without dynamics is alarmingly incomplete (as economists know). These are all make-or-break issues for the cognitive approach.

The concept of cognition has been around for some time and the methods by which it is researched have been developing. In this volume there is a concerted attempt to bring the concepts of managerial and organizational cognition together in relation to strategic thinking and strategizing and to provide an empirical basis for understanding how mental models operate. On the basis of this kind of theoretical and empirical progress we can move towards a view of strategic management as a three-legged stool – economics, organization and cognition. And we all know how much more stable are three legs than two.

John McGee
Warwick Business School, University of Warwick, UK

Preface

During the past two decades we have witnessed a dramatic upsurge in the use of concepts and techniques from the cognitive sciences (broadly conceived) in an effort to further our understanding of a number of key processes in strategic management, ranging from the analysis of basic judgemental processes in decision making (Barnes, 1984; Das & Teng, 1999; Maule & Hodgkinson, 2002; Maule, Hodgkinson & Bown, 2003; Schwenk, 1984, 1986) and issue diagnosis, image formation and organizational identity (Dutton & Dukerich, 1991; Dutton & Jackson, 1987; Gioia & Thomas, 1996; Jackson, 1992; Jackson & Dutton, 1998), to a consideration of the determinants of executives' beliefs (Chattopadhyay, Glick, Miller & Huber, 1999; Markoczy, 1997; Sutcliffe & Huber, 1998) and the nature and role of cognitive processes in the boardroom and top teams more generally (Finkelstein & Hambrick, 1996; Forbes & Milliken, 1999; Knight et al., 1999). The nature and significance of actors' belief systems in organizational learning and strategic renewal has also been investigated (Barr, 1998; Barr & Huff, 1997; Barr, Stimpert & Huff, 1992; Huff, Huff & Thomas, 1992) and researchers have recently begun to gather systematic evidence concerning the efficacy of intervention procedures, with a view to overcoming some of the inherent cognitive limitations of organizational strategists identified through this rapidly developing body of work (Hodgkinson et al., 1999; Hodgkinson & Maule, 2002).

As Lant and Shapira (2001a, 2001b) have observed, two major perspectives have laid the conceptual foundations for recent work on managerial and organizational cognition (see also Lant, 2002). The first, which they term the computational perspective, stemming from work in the field of experimental psychology and related areas, initially made its impact on the organizational and administrative sciences through the early writings of the Carnegie School (Cyert & March, 1963; March & Simon, 1958; Simon, 1947). Work located within this tradition has demonstrated that organizational decisions – of the order of complexity that generally fall within the purview of strategic management – are rarely, if ever, taken on the basis of a purely rational, techno-economic evaluation. The extent to which organizations are able to engage in rational analysis is constrained fundamentally by the information processing limitations of actors. The fact that organizations deal with multiple and conflicting goals, acting on imperfect information, necessitates that decisions are based on an incomplete understanding of the situation. In order to cope with the myriad of stimuli impinging on the organization, actors develop a simplified understanding of reality, encoded in the form of a mental representation. These representations, variously termed 'cognitive maps' (Tolman, 1932), 'schemata'

(Bartlett, 1932) and 'mental models' (Craik, 1943), define which elements of the environment are of strategic significance and therefore should be attended to and acted upon.[1] Mental representations render the external world manageable by filtering out information which is of less importance, thereby limiting the field of vision of actors to a relatively small subset of a much wider range of environmental cues. The implications of the writings of the Carnegie School theorists for the field of strategic management are profound; if the strategic decisions of organizations are indeed shaped largely by the mental models of actors, it makes sense to study these models systematically, in order to better understand the processes and mechanisms by which strategies come to develop and change.

The primary origins of the second perspective identified by Lant and Shapira (2001a, 2001b), known as the interpretive perspective, lie in sociological literature on the social construction of reality (e.g. Berger & Luckmann, 1967) and work on social identity theory (Tajfel & Turner, 1979, 1986), self-categorization theory (Turner, 1985; Turner et al., 1987) and attribution theory (Kelley, 1967) from the field of social psychology. This perspective has been heavily influential in the writings of Weick (e.g. 1969, 1979, 1995), whose inter-related notions of enactment and the enacted environment, together with the basic mental representations notion enumerated above, are central to the empirical study reported in this book.

The central issue to be addressed concerns the role of actors' mental models of competitor definition in the development of business strategies. Why is it that within a given industry or market, groups of firms come to adopt particular strategic choices and not others? In what ways are businesses' strategies aided or impeded by the cognitions of their organization members? What are the behavioural and performance consequences of strategic cognition?

It is a truism that the environments in which many business organizations now operate have become increasingly competitive and complex. Firms are struggling to survive the rigours of competition in markets which are reaching the point of saturation on a global, let-alone domestic, scale (D'Avini, 1994; Ilinitch, Lewin & D'Avini, 1998). An important corollary of this is that the information processing burdens on organization members have increased apace. In consequence, organizational actors are having to

---

[1] Strictly speaking, these terms were originally devised for a variety of different purposes. However, organization and management theorists have tended to use them interchangeably, to convey the general idea that actors internalize reality in simplified forms, which in turn are assumed to be linked to managerial and organizational action-taking (see, e.g., Cannon-Bowers & Salas, 1998; Huff, 1990; Reger & Palmer, 1996; Rousseau, 2001; Walsh, 1995). As I have argued elsewhere (Hodgkinson, 2003; Hodgkinson & Sparrow, 2002), these notions are sufficiently similar in nature to jusify this general usage, a convention that will be followed in the present volume.

become increasingly skilled in the art of competitive sensemaking (Bogner & Barr, 2000; Weick, 1995), continuously questioning their underlying operating assumptions, in an attempt to avoid the pitfalls of cognitive bias and cognitive inertia, which, according to a growing number of theorists and empirical researchers, left unchecked lead ultimately to terminal decline, not only in the case of individual firms, but entire organizational populations (see e.g. Bogner & Barr, 2000; Hodgkinson & Sparrow, 2002; Porac & Thomas, 1990; Reger & Palmer, 1996).

In a field customarily dominated by economic analysis, this rapidly evolving social constructionist view has begun to enrich considerably our understanding of inter-organizational rivalry. Traditionally, the overwhelming majority of scholars in the field of strategic management have assumed that business environments are objective entities, waiting to be discovered through the application of analytical tools and techniques (see e.g. Oster, 1982; Porter, 1980). However, the speed with which the cognitive perspective in strategic management has developed over recent years, testifies to the growing recognition of the inadequacy of these traditional approaches. Increasingly, researchers are coming to the realization that in order to create successful competitive strategies, organizations must develop into open learning systems, in which the assessment of the competitive environment is much more than a technical exercise falling within the remit of a single functional department (Pettigrew & Whipp, 1991). Viewed from this perspective, competitive positioning strategies are seen as emerging from a number of complex social and political processes operating at various levels within and between organizations. The way in which actors both individually and collectively acquire, interpret and act upon information about their subenvironments is thus central in shaping the wider competitive landscape as well as the strategic responses of the individual firm (Easton, Burrell, Rothschild, & Shearman, 1993; Levenhagen, Porac & Thomas, 1993; Porac & Rosa, 1996).

The empirical study reported in this book was conceived and executed during the late 1980s and early 1990s in order to test the validity of a series of basic assertions, fundamental to what at the time was an emergent concept, but which has subsequently evolved into a major body of theory: the notion of competitive enactment, advanced by Porac and his colleagues (Porac & Thomas, 1990; Porac, Thomas & Baden-Fuller, 1989). In line with the above arguments, a body of theoretical knowledge and anecdotal evidence had begun to accumulate within the then embryonic literature on strategic cognition, which suggested that cognition and strategic choice are inextricably intertwined with the material conditions of the marketplace. In other words, the strategic choices confronting organizations at any given point in time are defined by the way in which firms within the industry individually and collectively interpret their competitive worlds. Theorists argued that through a variety of social processes operating within the marketplace, actors' beliefs about what it takes for a firm to be successful converge into a highly homogeneous world-view. According to this line of reasoning, this strongly-held collective mental model comes to dominate strategic thinking throughout the industry and determine the boundaries of competitive space and the range of options considered feasible by the various players. This study adds strong empirical substance to these arguments. The findings also add credence to the arguments of those writers who have drawn attention to the inertial properties of cognition in the operation of the life cycle of the organization and industry. Once a dominant world-view has become established, it is enormously difficult for firms to change their way of thinking about the environment in which they are functioning, even in the face of considerable changes in market conditions.

The questions to be addressed by this study demanded that the fieldwork should be undertaken longitudinally, within the confines of a single industry. For a number of reasons, explained in detail in Chapter 3, the industry of choice was the UK residential estate agency industry. The fieldwork, conducted over two separate four-month periods, from mid-1989 to late 1990, occurred at what was a most opportune time within this industry for studying the role of competitor cognition in shaping strategic behaviour and organizational performance.

The fieldwork formed the basis of my PhD thesis, awarded by the University of Sheffield, where I was employed as a full-time lecturer from 1988 to 1995. As with any newly developing line of inquiry, most studies in strategic cognition at that time had been limited both in scale and scope. This was a healthy state of affairs, only to be expected as scholars sought to establish the viability of new research methods and techniques in an exploratory fashion. However, as I remarked at the time, this line of inquiry was clearly entering a new phase in its development. We had reached the stage where the time had come to move beyond such small-scale inductive exploratory work, towards larger scale hypothetico-deductive theory building and testing, if further progress was to be achieved and it is to this end that the work documented in my initial thesis (Hodgkinson, 1993a) and associated journal articles (Hodgkinson, 1992, 1997a, 1997b) was undertaken.

I have continued to maintain a keen interest in the expanding literature on the socio-cognitive analysis of competitive structures in industries and markets over the eleven years or so that have followed all too quickly since my thesis was completed. In fact it was the opportunity to review the various developments that have occurred during the intervening period that led me to the realization that methodological and empirical advances have not kept pace with the scale of theoretical progress that has been achieved over the ensuing years (Hodgkinson, 2001a, 2001b, 2002; Hodgkinson & Sparrow, 2002). It has been both gratifying but also something of a disappointment to discover that the large-scale dataset I began accumulating some 15 years ago, incorporating a two-wave panel design, with a wide range of measures to enable a detailed exploration of the correlates of actors' mental models of competitor definition and the extent to which these models remain stable or change over time, remains unsurpassed. Indeed, my study remains the only investigation of actors' mental models of competitor definition to date, to have incorporated a truly prospective, longitudinal design.

It is the continuing dearth of methodological advances and accompanying large-scale, longitudinal datasets – of the sort ultimately required to subject the competitive enactment notion and related theoretical arguments that have been advanced subsequently to adequate empirical scrutiny – that has motivated me to write this book. The ideas presented constitute a major revision of my original thesis, in order to engage with the various theoretical, methodological and empirical developments that have occurred since I published my first review of the relevant literature (Hodgkinson, 1997a) and reported my findings in respect of the cognitive inertia hypothesis (Hodgkinson, 1997b), which form the basis of the work reported in Chapter 7.

I am indebted to a number of people and institutions whose support enabled the research documented in this book to be completed. First, I would like to thank the various organizations and individuals who participated in the study for allowing me access and giving so generously of their time. Ian Brookes and Martyn Sadler of the School of Urban and Regional Studies at the Sheffield Hallam University and Tony Fry, formerly of Sheffield Newspapers, generously acted as the expert panellists in the performance evaluation exercise reported in Chapter 4, while the data analysis associated with this project was greatly assisted by Roz Scott-Huxley of the Manchester Computing Centre and the late Roger Richards of the Academic Computing Services Department at Sheffield University. I am also grateful to Tony Coxon of Essex University for his advice relating to the use of the multidimensional scaling techniques reported in Chapters 5–7.

Nigel Nicholson, my advisor, and Gerry Johnson and John McGee, my examiners, all now close friends and colleagues, were excellent in their respective roles. That the ideas summarized in my thesis have matured into this volume rather than withered on the vine over the intervening years, bears strong testimony both to the quality of supervision I received and the rigorous and thought provoking assessment that followed.

I would also like to acknowledge the financial support of the UK Economic and Social and Engineering and Physical Research Councils' (ESRC/EPSRC) Advanced Institute of Management Research (AIM) for the award of my Fellowship (Award Number RES-331-25-0028), which enabled this book to be completed.

Thanks are also due to a number of my current colleagues at the University of Leeds and AIM, whose patience and forbearance throughout the conversion of my thesis into this monograph have been much appreciated. In particular I would like to thank Andrew Lock and Terry McNulty, my current Dean and Head of Division respectively, for ensuring that the institutional demands placed upon me during this period have been kept to a minimum. Ian Clarke and Gail Clarkson, two of my AIM colleagues, have been especially understanding and patient as I have repeatedly re-prioritized my commitments over the past nine months and I am particularly grateful to Gail for her careful and constructive reading of my earlier drafts.

Jacky Kippenberger, my commissioning Editor at Palgrave MacMillan, has been highly supportive and strongly encouraging throughout every stage of the project, despite the numerous deadlines I missed along the way. I am also very grateful to Liam Irwin, my PA, for his meticulous attention to detail in preparing the manuscript for final publication and serving the vital gate-keeping role that enabled me to complete the task.

Once again, my final thanks go to my precious Dorothy, Benjamin, David and Rebekah, from whom I have been absent all too often.

Gerard P. Hodgkinson
ESRC/EPSRC (UK) Advanced Institute of Management Research (AIM)
Leeds University Business School
The University of Leeds
September 2004

Publisher Acknowledgements

The author and publisher are grateful to the following for permission to reproduce their copyright material.

Blackwell Publishing: for Figure 2.1, 'Mutual enactment processes within an industrial sector', taken from J. F. Porac and H. Thomas (1989), 'Competitive groups as cognitive communities: The case of Scottish knitwear manufacturers', *Journal of Management Studies*, **26**, 397-416. © Basil Blackwell Ltd.

Frank Cass: for Table 3.1, 'Losses associated with the major UK estate agency chains during the first half of 1989', taken from M. Dietrich and P. Holmes (1991), 'Financial institutions and the estate agents industry in the 1980s', *The Services Industries Journal*, **11**, 481–490. © Frank Cass Ltd.

Keynote Ltd: for Table 3.2, 'Estate agents' TV and press advertising expenditure during 1987 and 1988', Table 3.4, 'Percentage changes in home ownership in the UK, 1971–1987', and Table 3.5, 'Building society mortgage arrears and repossessions, 1979–1988', all taken from Key Note (1989), *Key Note Report: An Industry Sector Overview – Estate Agents*; and for Table 3.3, 'House price increases for various geographical regions of the UK during 1985', taken from Key Note (1986), *Key Note Report: An Industry Sector Overview – Estate Agents*. © Key Note Publication Ltd.

The material in several of the chapters in this book is drawn, in part or whole, from a number of previous publications by the author, who would like to thank the following publishers for permission to incorporate this material directly and/or in adapted form in the present work.

Hodgkinson, G. P. (1992). Development and validation of the strategic locus of control scale. *Strategic Management Journal*, **13**, 311–317. © John Wiley and Sons, Ltd. (Drawn upon in Chapter 4 and Appendix 1.)

Hodgkinson, G. P. (1997a). The cognitive analysis of competitive structures: A review and critique. *Human Relations*, **50**, 625–654. © The Tavistock Institute. (Drawn upon in Chapter 2.)

Hodgkinson, G. P. (1997b). Cognitive inertia in a turbulent market: The case of UK residential estate agents. *Journal of Management Studies*, **34**, 921–945. © Blackwell Publishers Ltd. (Drawn upon in Chapter 7.)

Hodgkinson, G. P. (1998). Points or vectors? A comment on Irwin et al.'s 'Risk perception and victim perception: The judgment of HIV cases'. *Journal of Behavioral Decision Making*, **11**, 73–78. © John Wiley and Sons, Ltd. (Drawn upon in Chapter 5.)

Hodgkinson, G. P. (2001a). The psychology of strategic management: Diversity and cognition revisited. In C. L. Cooper and I. T. Robertson (Eds.), *International Review of Industrial and Organizational Psychology Volume 16*. Chichester: Wiley, pp. 65–119. © John Wiley and Sons, Ltd. (Drawn upon in Chapter 2.)

Hodgkinson, G. P. (2001b). Cognitive processes in strategic management: some emerging trends and future directions. In N. Anderson, D. S. Ones, H. K. Sinangil and C Viswesvaran (eds), *Handbook of Industrial, Work and Organizational Psychology – Volume 2: Organizational Psychology*. London: Sage, pp. 416–440. © Gerard P. Hodgkinson. (Drawn upon in Chapter 2.)

Hodgkinson, G. P. and Johnson, G. (1994) Exploring the mental models of competitive strategists: The case for a processual approach. *Journal of Management Studies*, **31**, 525–551. © Basil Blackwell Ltd. (Drawn upon in Chapter 2.)

Hodgkinson, G. P. and Sparrow, P. R. (2002). *The Competent Organization: A Psychological Analysis of the Strategic Management Process*. Buckingham: Open University Press. © Gerard P. Hodgkinson and Paul R. Sparrow. (Drawn upon in Chapter 2.)

1
Introduction

This book reports the outcomes of an empirical investigation into the nature and role of strategic cognition in industries and markets. Specifically, it is concerned with the relationships between strategic thinking, the way in which individuals and groups who work within a particular industry construe their competitive worlds and the consequences of that thinking for the organizations and the industries and markets in which they operate.

The notion that businesses should analyze their competitive environments if they are to compete effectively is a fundamental and familiar prescription in the standard texts on strategic management (e.g. Grant, 1991; Greenley, 1989; Johnson & Scholes, 1993; Luffman, Sanderson, Lea & Kenney, 1987; Oster, 1990; Porter, 1980, 1985; Wheelen & Hunger, 1989). However, while a great many analytical frameworks and models have been put forward to assist the would-be analyst in this endeavour, surprisingly few investigations have been conducted into how individuals and groups who operate within these environments actually perceive their competitive worlds (Hodgkinson, 1997a; Stubbart, 1989). This book describes one such investigation.

It stems from a fundamental conviction shared by a growing number of scholars that traditional accounts of rivalry, accounts which tend to view competition primarily as an environmental phenomenon involving economic contingencies, are limited. Much of the literature on competitive strategy is predicated on the assumption that business environments are objective entities waiting to be discovered through formal analysis. However, over the past 15–20 years, there has been a growing recognition among strategic management and organizational behaviour researchers that, ultimately, it is actors' perceptions of competitive positioning filtered through existing mental models that form the basis for strategy formulation and, therefore, that these mental models are worthy of study (e.g. Calori, Johnson & Sarnin, 1992, 1994; Daniels, Johnson & de Chernatony, 2002; Hodgkinson & Johnson, 1994; Porac, Thomas & Emme, 1987; Porac et al.,

1989; Reger, 1990a; Reger & Huff, 1993; Spencer, Peyrefitte, & Churchman, 2003). As Porac & Thomas observe:

> From a cognitive perspective, decision makers act on a mental model of the environment. Thus any explanation for strategic responses to competitive pressures must ultimately, take into consideration the mental models of competitive strategists...before competitive strategies can be formulated, decision makers must have an image of who their rivals are and on what dimensions they will compete. Given the diverse range of organizational forms and decision makers' limited capacity to process complex inter-organizational cues, the task of defining 'the competition' is both important and problematic (Porac & Thomas, 1990, pp. 224–225).

While the cognitive approach to understanding competitive strategy has gained increasing ground in recent years, much of the empirical research to date has been small-scale and/or exploratory in nature (see e.g. de Chernatony, Daniels, & Johnson, 1993; Gripsrud & Gronhaug, 1985; Hodgkinson & Johnson, 1994; Reger, 1990a). These studies have established the viability of the cognitive approach for gaining potentially useful insights into processes of strategy formulation and led to some interesting theoretical developments. However, larger-scale empirical work, designed to test the key substantive elements of this emerging theory, have been almost nonexistent.

Research agenda and key themes

The primary purpose of the study reported in this book was to help fill this empirical vacuum. The study was designed in order to test three hypotheses derived from the emerging body theory on the social construction of competitive business environments, centred on the notion of 'competitive enactment' (Porac et al., 1989; Porac & Thomas, 1990). The concept of enactment refers to the basic process by which organization members actively go about creating their environments, which in turn act back upon them, as if they are true, objective entities, thereby imposing constraints on what is considered possible, i.e. through enactment processes organizational members socially construct key aspects of their material worlds (Weick, 1969, 1979, 1995). By importing the Weickian notion of enactment, drawing also on the work of earlier Berger and Luckmann (1967), into the domain of competitive analysis, Porac and his colleagues laid the central conceptual foundations for the subsequent, highly eclectic, theorizing that has occurred over recent years (see e.g. Abrahamson & Fombrun, 1994; Bogner & Thomas, 1993; Dandrove, Peteraf & Shanley, 1998; Lant, 1999; Lant & Baum, 1995; Lant & Phelps, 1999; Levenhagen et al., 1993; Peteraf & Shanley, 1997; Porac & Rosa, 1996). Drawing, inter-alia, on social identity theory (Ashforth & Mael, 1989; Tajfel & Turner, 1979, 1986), social learning theory (Bandura, 1986; Wood & Bandura, 1989), population ecology theory (Wholey & Brittain, 1986), institutional theory (DiMaggio & Powell, 1983; Meyer & Rowan, 1977) and situated learning theory (Wenger, 1998), these and other scholars have engaged in a concerted attempt to weave more comprehensive 'social constructionist' (Levenhagen et al., 1993) or 'socio-cognitive' (Lant & Phelps, 1999) accounts of the emergence of competitive structures in industries and markets (these developments are reviewed in Chapter 2).

Much of the traditional literature on competitive analysis has been dominated by attempts to reveal the bases of competition and the structural positions occupied by firms, using secondary accounting and financial databases [for details see McGee & Thomas (1986) and Thomas & Venkatraman (1988)]. Competitive enactment and related notions have emerged as a basis for explaining the emergence of competitive industry structures (i.e. discernible groups of organizations following similar strategies) in socio-cognitive terms, thereby complementing traditional approaches to understanding inter-organizational rivalry. According to this rapidly evolving body of theory, competitive structures both determine and are determined by strategists' perceptions of the business environment. The reason competitive structures emerge within industries and markets is because, over time, strategists from rival firms develop highly similar mental models of the competitive arena, due to the fact that they confront similar technical and material problems and frequently share information in the conduct of their business transactions. This process of social exchange, in turn, leads to the development of a shared understanding – throughout the community of firms within the marketplace – of how to gain competitive advantage. Eventually, however, this collective mental model comes to over-ride any individual differences in cognition which may have originally existed amongst members of the 'cognitive community' and the industry falls into decline as previously successful strategies become ineffective through over use, i.e. previously profitable market niches become over-populated as increasing numbers of players seek to emulate the successes of the market leaders by following the 'industry recipe' (Grinyer & Spender, 1979a, 1979b; Spender, 1989). At this stage, new strategies are not forthcoming due to the inability of strategists to break free from this dominant world-view of what it takes to be successful in the industry. In short, cognition and strategic choice become inextricably intertwined with the material conditions of the marketplace.

As we shall see, there are several fundamental elements of this theory which have yet to be subjected to empirical scrutiny or for which, upon closer inspection, the existing empirical evidence is found wanting. The present study, therefore, was designed primarily in order to subject the basic notion of competitive enactment to a number of rigorous empirical tests, in order to remedy this situation.

Three issues in particular have yet to be resolved, using adequate methods and research designs:

1. The extent to which measurable features of actors' mental models of competitor definition correlate with measurable strategic behaviours and measurable features of the organization and its environment;
2. The extent to which and in what ways actors within a given industry hold similar or diverse mental models of competitor definition;
3. The extent to which these mental models remain stable or change over time.

The study reported in this book was devised to explicitly meet the methodological challenges posed by these issues through the gathering of new data using refined techniques for the elicitation and comparison of cognitive maps. As might be expected, in any newly developing field of inquiry, a host of technical issues have emerged over the ensuing years, both in the recent literature on competitor cognition and indeed within the literature on managerial and organizational cognition more generally (cf. Daniels & Johnson, 2002; Daniels et al., 2002; Hodgkinson, 2002; Hodgkinson & Sparrow, 2002; Walsh, 1995). Nevertheless, the findings of the present work and the methods employed remain highly pertinent to a number of continuing debates: How might we best operationalize actors' mental models of competition? What constitutes most appropriate the unit(s) of analysis in cognitive studies of competitive strategy? To what extent is it meaningful to speak of 'industry-level mental models' and how might we best represent such collective beliefs? How should representations of actors' mental models be compared and contrasted within and between different levels of analysis, both at a given point in time and over multiple time periods?

This study was also designed with a view to improving the practice of strategic management. As noted earlier, there is no shortage of analytical frameworks and techniques for assisting strategists in their relentless quest to search out new and more effective strategies. However, relatively little is known about the cognitive underside of environmental analysis. Such knowledge is potentially of great value for yielding fresh insights into the problems facing particular industries and firms. Cognitive mapping techniques would seem to hold considerable promise for identifying 'blind-spots' in competitor awareness (Zajac & Bazerman, 1991), which in turn could yield practical insights into how firms might develop new strategies for competitive success (cf. Balogun, Huff, & Johnson, 2003; Huff, 1990; Johnson, Melin, & Whittington, 2003). In other words, the results of cognitive analyzes might provide a useful means for enabling actors to stand back and reflect on their fundamental operating assumptions. In turn, such reflection may act as a catalyst for strategic and organizational change (Bowman & Johnson, 1992).

The study

The study was conducted in the UK residential estate agency industry. Very few industries can have experienced the degree of turbulence experienced by the UK residential estate agency industry over the years in which the data in this study were gathered. From the mid-1980s to the early 1990s, the focal period of concern, the industry experienced a series of dramatic environmental jolts, not least the entrance of the major banks, building societies and insurance companies, and the sudden steep rise in house prices in the summer of 1988, which in turn triggered a boom in the housing market, following which the market severely stagnated – to the extent that a considerable number of firms severely contracted their operations or withdrew from the industry altogether. Added to this, the industry witnessed a number of major changes in Government policy that had a bearing directly and indirectly on the way in which the industry was forced to operate. In short, the UK residential estate agency industry experienced boom, stagnation and change over the relatively short time period covered by this study. As we shall see in Chapter 3, these particular features made the estate agency industry an ideal laboratory in which to explore empirically the various issues and themes identified above, which remain of central concern to researchers in the emerging field of managerial and organizational cognition, the recent theoretical advances in the literature on competitive analysis alluded to above notwithstanding.

The fieldwork associated with this study was carried out between mid-July 1989 and December 1990 using a two-wave panel design. The use of a longitudinal design was considered essential, since it provided a rich opportunity to explore stability and change in mental models of the competitive environment, an issue which, with one or two noteworthy but limited exceptions, has been much neglected in empirical terms. As we shall see in the next chapter, the overwhelming majority of studies of competitor cognition have tended to employ cross-sectional designs, i.e. the assessment of participants' perceptions has been restricted by and large to single occasions. Although the reluctance of researchers to engage in longitudinal fieldwork is understandable, clearly this type of study is essential, if our understanding of the role of mental models in strategy-making processes is to advance significantly beyond present levels.

Methodological approach

The issues which this study addressed are multi-level in nature, spanning individual-, group-, organizational- and industry-level cognition. The research objectives to be accomplished necessitated an approach to data collection that was suitable for use with relatively large samples, both in terms of the number of participating organizations and the number of individual research participants, and which would yield data in a form which could be subsequently analyzed at a variety of levels. Consequently, the research method of choice was the questionnaire survey.

The primary advantage of questionnaire based approaches is in terms of the relative ease with which they can be administered to large numbers of participants, in comparison with other methods of data collection. The sheer volume of supplementary data to be collected in the present investigation, in addition to respondents' judgements of competitors, ruled out other, more labour intensive methods, if a sufficiently large sample of participants was to be included in the study to be able to address the central research questions with adequate rigour.

Following the lead of Reger (1987), Thomas and Venkatraman (1988), and Walton (1986), a modified repertory grid approach to cognitive assessment was adopted in the present study (cf. Daniels et al., 1994, 1995, 2002; Reger & Huff, 1993; Spencer et al., 2003). As observed by Hodgkinson and Sparrow (2002) the primary strength of the repertory grid technique lies in its inherent flexibility, both from the point of view of data collection and analysis. Though originally devised as an idiographic tool of assessment for use by clinical psychologists (Fransella & Bannister, 1977; Kelly, 1955; Slater, 1976, 1977), the repertory grid technique has come to enjoy a proven track record in applied studies of social cognition across a wide variety of domains, extending well beyond its clinical roots and idiographic origins (see e.g. Dunn & Ginsberg, 1986; Forgas, 1976, 1978; Forgas, Brown & Menyhart, 1980; Fransella, Bell, & Bannister, 2004; Smith & Gibson, 1988; Smith, Hartley & Stewart, 1978; Stewart, Stewart & Fonda, 1981).

In the present study, the grids were elicited by means of a self-administered questionnaire, the Competitor Analysis Questionnaire (CAQ), devised by the author, and subjected to analysis by multidimensional scaling (MDS) techniques (Arabie, Carroll & DeSarbo, 1987; Coxon, 1982; Kruskal & Wish, 1978; Schiffman, Reynolds & Young, 1981). As will be demonstrated, this method of analysis proved to be highly suitable as a basis for exploring the major research questions identified at the outset, enabling the systematic comparison of actors' representations of competitive space, in a multi-level, multi-layered fashion.[1]

---

[1] Throughout, I use the term 'competitive space' to denote participants' individual and collective representations of competitor definition, as revealed through MDS analyses of the CAQ data. As we shall see, these representations take the form of conceptual categories of competitor definition configured within multidimensional, Euclidean spaces. It does not follow that individuals literally walk around with such spatial representations inside their heads. Rather, as with any other form of cognitive mapping device, the outputs of a MDS analysis provide one form of data which is useful for inferring important aspects of actors' understanding (cf. Hodgkinson & Clarkson, 2005).

Structure of the book

This introductory chapter has outlined the basic issues and concerns to be addressed by the book as a whole. However, before concluding it is instructive to briefly sketch out the remaining contents. Chapter 2 provides an overview of the growing literature on cognitive approaches to understanding competition, while Chapter 3 describes the relevant historical background to the UK estate agency industry, in the run up to and during the period in which the fieldwork was undertaken, in order to contextualize the findings. The design of the study and the development and validation of the various research instruments employed in the fieldwork are discussed in Chapter 4. Chapters 5, 6, and 7, report the substantive empirical findings arising from the study, each respectively addressing one of the three central questions that motivated this work. Finally, the implications of the findings for theory-building, research methodology, practice and future research in strategic management are discussed in Chapter 8.

2
The Cognitive Analysis of Competition in Industries and Markets

As noted in the previous chapter, the cognitive approach to understanding problems in strategic management, a field traditionally dominated by economic analysis, is still in its infancy. Over the past two decades or so, however, the strategy field and indeed the management and organizaton studies fields more generally have witnessed a sudden growth of interest in the use of concepts and techniques from the cognitive sciences for the advancement of theory, research and practice, as evidenced by the proliferation of scholarly journal articles, conference proceedings, books and chapters in edited volumes addressing a wide range of topics from a cognitive perspective (see e.g. Barnes, 1984; Daft & Weick, 1984; Dutton & Jackson, 1987; Eden, 1992; Eden & Ackermann, 1998; Eden, Jones & Sims, 1979, 1983; Eden & Radford, 1990; Eden & Spender, 1998; Hodgkinson, 2001a, 2001b; Hodgkinson & Sparrow, 2002; Hodgkinson & Thomas, 1997; Huff, 1990; Huff & Jenkins, 2002; Kiesler & Sproull, 1982; Lant & Shapira, 2001c; Maule & Hodgkinson, 2002; Meindl, Stubbart, & Porac, 1994, 1996; Porac & Thomas, 1989, 2002; Schwenk, 1984; Sims & Gioia, 1986; Sparrow, 1994, 2000; Weick, 1995). The purpose of this chapter is to review those elements of this rapidly developing literature that are of particular relevance to the study of business competition from a cognitive viewpoint.

The chapter is organized in four main sections, as follows: We shall begin with a relatively brief analysis of the background research which has led to the recent interest, on the part of strategy researchers, in the cognitive analysis of competitive positioning in industries and markets. This is necessary in order to provide a context within which to evaluate the various methodological, theoretical, and empirical findings arising from the cognitive literature, to be reviewed in later sections of the chapter. Next, we shall consider recent theoretical and empirical developments associated with the study of competitive positioning strategy from a cognitive perspective, focussing in particular on the notion of competitive enactment (Porac et al., 1989; Porac & Thomas, 1990) and related conceptions. As noted in the previous chapter, however, a number of technical issues have begun to emerge, with much of the research effort in cognitive studies of competition having been concerned with the refinement of techniques for data collection and analysis. The third section of this review, therefore, comprises a critical analysis of the various methodological developments in the cognitive analysis of business environments that have taken place in recent years. As we shall see, there are a number of non-trivial methodological hurdles that have yet to be overcome, if this emerging body of socio-cognitive theory is to be subjected to adequate empirical scrutiny. Finally, the concluding section draws together the key issues and themes arising from this review and sets out the research agenda of the empirical study reported in the later chapters.

Background to the development of cognitive approaches for the analysis of competitive structures

Conventional approaches to the analysis of business competition in industries and markets have been dominated by the structure → conduct → performance paradigm of industrial organization economics (Bain, 1956; Mason, 1957). The initial impetus for cognitively-oriented theory and research into managers' mental models of competition, during the mid-late 1980s (e.g. Dess & Davis, 1984; Fombrun & Zajac, 1987; Gripsrud & Gronhaug, 1985; Hodgkinson, Gunz & Johnson, 1988; Hodgkinson & Johnson, 1987; Porac et al., 1987, 1989; Reger, 1987), stemmed from a growing dissatisfaction with a body of work firmly located within this tradition, centred on the notion of strategic groups. This concept was developed by Hunt (1972) in a study that examined the differential performance of firms in the American home appliance industry (so-called 'white goods') in the 1960s, although it is Michael Porter – a Harvard Professor of Strategic Management, whose writings have contributed greatly to the literature on competitive analysis – who has provided the commonly accepted definition of the term:

> A strategic group is the group of firms in an industry following the same or a similar strategy along the strategic dimensions. An industry could have only one strategic group if all the firms followed essentially the same strategy. At the other extreme, each firm could be a different strategic group. Usually, however, there are a small number of strategic groups which capture the essential strategic differences among firms in the industry. (Porter (1980: 129)

The bulk of the conventional strategy literature on business competition has been concerned with the refinement of techniques for the analysis of competitive structures in industries, based on this notion (see e.g. Athanasso-poulos, 2003; Bogner, Thomas, & McGee, 1996; Cool & Dierickx, 1993; Cool & Schendel, 1987, 1988; Fiegenbaum & Thomas, 1990, 1993; Harrigan, 1980,

1985; Hatten & Hatten, 1987; Hatten, Schendel & Cooper, 1978; Hawes & Crittenden, 1984; Johnson & Thomas, 1987; Lewis & Thomas, 1990; Newman, 1978; Oster, 1982).

The ultimate goal of the economic theory underpinning the strategic groups notion is to account for intra-industry variations in the competitive behaviour and performance of firms – i.e. the theory seeks to explain why it is that firms within a given industry do not all follow the same strategies (conduct), nor return uniform levels of performance. In other words, why do some strategies lead to competitive success whereas others do not? According to this theory, firms within a given group resemble one another closely in terms of their strategic capabilities. Consequently, they are able to anticipate one another's likely reactions to environmental jolts and are likely to recognize their mutual dependence on one another and respond accordingly. Between strategic groups, however, a rather different scenario is predicted (Porter, 1979).

Once strategic groups have formed, the various players develop isolating mechanisms (barriers to entry and mobility) that serve to deter new entrants from stepping into the competitive arena and to deter existing players from attempting to switch membership from one group to another (Caves & Porter, 1977). Entry barriers constitute the various (largely economic) factors that prevent would-be players from entering a particular industry or market. Their effect is not uniform, however, with some strategic groups being afforded better protection than others. The concept of mobility barriers is a generalization of the concept of entry barriers, which seeks to explain the strategic behaviour of firms already operating within an industry. Mobility barriers are the various factors that prevent members of particular strategic groups from transferring or extending their membership into other groups. The theory predicts significant between-groups performance differences will accrue, over and above differences within groups, due to the fact that mobility barriers afford stable advantages to particular groups at the expense of other groups within the same industry. Hence the concept of mobility barriers provides both an explanation for inter-group performance differences and a conceptual basis for competitively positioning rival firms (Porter, 1981: 615).

Unfortunately, a number of studies have failed to yield significant between-groups performance differences (for reviews see McGee & Thomas, 1986; Thomas & Venkatraman, 1988) and the notion of strategic groups has come under increasingly critical scrutiny. Several researchers have questioned the extent to which secondary financial and accounting information derived from company records or commercially available generic databases, as typically employed by strategic groups researchers, can adequately capture bases of competition. Ultimately, the variables selected for analysis by the researcher may not necessarily be the variables that actually guide the decision making of organizations and hence drive competition (Barney & Hoskisson, 1990; Birnbaum-More & Weiss, 1990; Calori et al., 1992; Hodgkinson & Johnson, 1994; Pettigrew & Whipp, 1991; Porac et al., 1989; Porac & Thomas, 1990; Reger, 1990a; Reger & Huff, 1993). A further limitation of this predominantly economic approach is its inability to explain how or why competitive structures in industries and markets come to develop in the first place and on what basis particular strategies are chosen. Arguably, the most extreme criticisms of the strategic groups notion have come from Barney and Hoskisson (1990) and Hatten and Hatten (1987). These researchers contend that the theoretical base underpinning strategic groups is insufficiently developed to justify the notion and that in reality strategic groups are merely analytical artefacts of the multivariate analysis techniques employed to detect them (cf. Tang & Thomas, 1992).

Theoretical developments in the cognitive analysis of competitive structures

Over the past 15 years or so researchers have responded to these criticisms and challenges directly, by advancing a variety of closely inter-related explanations for the emergence of competitive structures in industries and markets, grounded in the wider cognitive and organizational sciences. The key elements of this emerging body of theory are summarized in Table 2.1.

Competitor categorization processes

As can be seen in Table 2.1, the basic starting point is the premise that strategists do not attend equally to all potential competitors. To do so would place unacceptable burdens on individuals, well beyond their basic information processing capacities (cf. Broadbent, 1958; Simon, 1947). Rather, they attend to a limited subset of rivals, identified through a basic process of categorization.

A great volume of work has accumulated within the cognitive sciences (for details see Lakeoff, 1987; Rosch, 1978) which suggests that categorical knowledge within the human mind is organized in a hierarchical fashion. It has been shown that knowledge represented hierarchically is easier to process, since the distinguishing features of cognitive sub-categories are stored at relatively high levels of abstraction, thus reducing the burden of information processing. Rosch and her associates (e.g. Rosch, Mervis, Gray, Johnson, & Boyes-Braem, 1976) have shown that these hierarchically orga-nized categories are characterized by indefinite boundary structures and that category exemplars vary in terms of their representativeness. Certain stimuli are considered to be more prototypical and these prototypes act as the 'cognitive reference points' against which other stimuli are compared (Rosch, 1975). Moreover, different levels of abstraction are not equally informative. The level known as the 'basic level' of inclusion is generally

Table 2.1 Outline summary of principal theoretical contributions to the socio-cognitive analysis of business competition

Key concept(s)	Principal contributor(s)	Theoretical origins	Key insight(s)
Competitor categorization	Porac, Thomas and Emme (1987)	Experimental psychology and cognitive anthropology)	1. Due to fundamental information-processing limitations, individuals attend only to a limited subset of potential competitors and only consider a restricted range of strategic options.
	Porac and Thomas (1990, 1994)		
	Hodgkinson and Johnson (1994)		2. Competitor categorization schemes are formed on the basis of attribute comparisons and organized hierarchically.
Competitive enactment	Porac, Thomas and Baden-Fuller (1989)	Social psychology of organizations and the sociology of knowledge	Discernible competitive structures emerge because over time strategists from rival firms develop highly similar (or 'shared') mental models of the competitive arena, due to the fact that they share similar technical and material problems and frequently exchange information in the conduct of their business transactions. This process of social exchange, in turn, leads to the development of a shared understanding – throughout the community of firms within the marketplace – of how to compete.
	Porac and Thomas (1990)		
Cognitive inertia	Porac and Thomas (1990)	Categorization theory	Once established, actors' mental representations of the competitive landscape are relatively difficult to change, due to the fact that new information is processed using extant categories. Consequently, there is a danger that major changes taking place within the business environment may go undetected until such time as the organization's capacity for successful adaptation has been seriously undermined. Left unchecked, cognitive inertia may ultimately render entire populations or subpopulations of firms extinct.
	Reger and Palmer (1996)	Schema theory	
	Hodgkinson (1997b)	Population ecology	

| The cognitive life cycle of market domains | Levenhagen, Porac and Thomas (1993) | Various, including cognitive categorization theory, competitive enactment, population ecology, and institutional theory | 1. A four-stage life cycle (concept formation → concept championing → concept appropriation → institutionalization) underpins the social construction of market domains.
2. 'Frame-making' and 'frame-breaking' entrepreneurs initiate the key processes of social construction. |
| Competitive sets and institutional isomorphism | Lant and Baum (1995) | Cognitive categorization theory, competitive enactment and institutional theory | 1. As argued by Porac et al. (1989), mutual enactment processes result in discernible groupings of competitors, i.e. 'competitive sets' (the cognitive analogue to strategic groups).
2. In turn, these shared cognitive categorization schemes of competitors act as a vital source of institutionalized behaviour among groups of rival firms, potentially giving rise to two forms of isomorphism: mimetic adoption and normative isomorphism. |

Table 2.1 Outline summary of principal theoretical contributions to the socio-cognitive analysis of business competition – *continued*

Key concept(s)	Principal contributor(s)	Theoretical origins	Key insight(s)
Relational modelling, vicarious learning, and social identification	Peteraf and Shanley (1997)	Competitor categorization theory, competitive enactment, social learning theory and social identification theory	1. The accumulated experience gained through social learning (via a combination of direct and vicarious interorganizational interactions) enables organizations to reduce their transaction costs, by promoting continued exchanges only with those firms found to be reliable interaction partners, predictable in their behaviours and providing tolerable levels of risk. In the long-run, this tendency to look to the same group of firms on repeated occasions, leads to the development of a relatively stable cognitive entity. 2. These processes of social learning are a necessary but insufficient condition for the emergence of strategic groups that have real and measurable effects, i.e. groups that will ultimately influence the conduct and performance of their individual members. In addition, social identification must occur; group members must not only perceive the fact that a group exists ('identification of the group'), but also identify with the group.

| Situated learning | Lant (1999) Lant and Phelps (1999) | Situated learning theory | Extant sociocognitive explanations for the emergence of knowledge and identity within cognitive communities represent an under-situated perspective, which underemphasizes the extent to which learning within and between competitive groups is embedded in a social milieu. Within this body of work, learning is viewed primarily as a vicarious process. In reality, however, the emergence and evolution of competitive groups is underpinned by a relatively complex, dynamic process. Ongoing interactions among the various players both central and peripheral to the group yield not only common and predictable patterns of behaviour, but also help to preserve variations in the structures, strategies and beliefs within these groups. |

Source: Hodgkinson, 2001b: 429.

more informative and consequently attended to more frequently than other levels. Categories at higher levels of abstraction tend to be characterized by relatively few attributes which tend to be very general, and consequently less informative, in nature. Conversely, categories at lower levels of abstraction possess relatively more numerous and more specific attributes; however, they tend to overlap. It is at the basic level of abstraction that categories are optimal in terms of their information content, since it is at this level that they possess the maximum proportion of unique attributes relative to the overlapping attributes of neighbouring categories. For this reason, the basic level is usually found at intermediate levels of abstraction and is said to possess 'high cue validity' relative to categories at higher and lower levels of abstraction (Rosch et al., 1976).

Drawing on this body of work, Porac and his colleagues (e.g. Porac et al., 1987, 1989; Porac & Rosa, 1996; Porac & Thomas, 1990, 1994) have argued that managers' mental representations of competitors take the form of hierarchical taxonomies, and that attention is directed primarily towards intermediate, 'basic level' categories (see also Hodgkinson & Johnson, 1994). Researchers investigating the emergence of competitive structures from a socio-cognitive perspective are also generally agreed that competitive groups are graded, as opposed to all-or-nothing, phenomena, with fuzzy boundaries and core and peripheral exemplars (see e.g. Hodgkinson, Padmore & Tomes, 1991; Hodgkinson, Tomes & Padmore, 1996; Lant & Baum, 1995; Lant & Phelps, 1999; Peteraf & Shanley, 1997; Porac et al., 1987; Porac & Thomas, 1990, 1994; Reger & Huff, 1993). According to these researchers, categorizing competitors in this way enables actors to simplify reality and hence take action within the constraints imposed by bounded rationality.

The social construction of competitive groups

It is as various basic-level cognitive categories, defining the boundaries of competition, come to be shared among rivals, through processes of social construction, that discernible competitive structures are hypothesized to emerge by a number of researchers. As noted in the previous chapter, the notion of competitive enactment advanced by Porac and his colleagues has been foundational to the development of theory and research on competitor cognition (as has their work on competitor categorization processes, summarized above). Recapping on our earlier discussion, the notion of enactment calls into question the implicit assumption underpinning much of the traditional theory and research on inter-organizational rivalry that business environments are objective environments, awaiting discovery through the application of formal analytical techniques:

Managers construct, rearrange, single out, and demolish many 'objective' features of their surroundings. When people act they unrandomize variables, insert vestiges of orderliness, and literally create their own constraints...There is a reciprocal influence between subjects and objects, not a one-sided influence such as implied by the idea that a stimulus triggers a response. This reciprocal influence is captured... by the two-way influence between enactment and ecological change. (Weick, 1979: 164–166).

Building on these fundamental insights, Porac et al. (1989) have argued that a continual objective → subjective → objective cycle underpins the development of competitive structures. According to Porac and his colleagues, over time individuals' beliefs about the identity of their competitors, suppliers, and customers become highly unified through mutual enactment processes, in which subjective interpretations of externally situated information are objectified via behaviour:

> Thus, for example, when a group of managers define their businesses as clothing stores or supermarkets, their understanding of the competitive environment is crystallized within a mental model, and their competitive focus is slanted towards organizations they perceive as members of the same competitive set. It is easy to see how such perceptions might eventually become objectified and institutionalized through such devices as trade associations, specialized publications, and a particularistic language for describing logical ecological conditions... . In this view, competitive groups are more than analytical and economic abstractions of researchers; they represent the social psychological reality for member organizations. If this subjectivist perspective is true, it will be impossible to classify and understand organizational forms, at least at the microniche level, without describing the mental models that motivate mutually adjustive competitive activities (Porac & Thomas, 1990, p. 236).

Viewed from this perspective, 'industries', 'strategic groups' and markets are socio-cognitive constructions, created through a shared interpretation of reality among business rivals, which come to define the boundaries of the competitive arena and on what bases the battles for competitive success are to be fought. The mental models of competitive strategists from rival firms become highly similar, thereby creating 'group-level' beliefs about the marketplace, because of the tendency of organizations to imitate one another, both directly and indirectly:

> Indirect imitation occurs because strategists from different firms face similar technical/material problems with a finite number of solutions. Belief similarity develops as a result of interpreting the same cues and solving the same problems. Direct imitation occurs because of both formal and informal communications among the set of competitors.

Such communications permit the mutual exchange of ideas and concepts by externalizing individual mental models in a publicly observable form. The net result of both indirect and direct imitation is that the strategic choices of individual firms take place within the context of many shared beliefs about how and with whom to engage in transactions in the marketplace (Porac et al., 1989, p. 400).

This argument is illustrated graphically in Figure 2.1. Each competitor is involved in an individual enactment process in which the mental model of

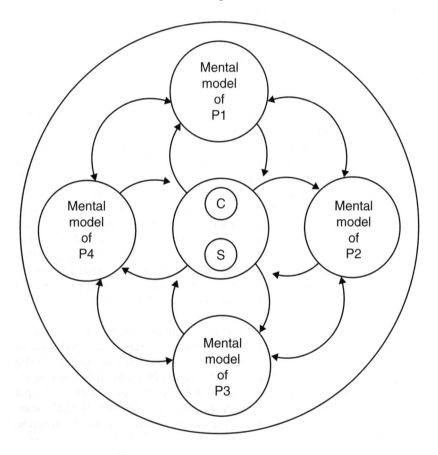

Note: C – Customers
S – Suppliers
Pn – Producers

Figure 2.1 Mutual enactment processes within an industrial sector
Source: Porac, Thomas & Baden-Fuller, 1989: 401.

its strategists is reciprocally intertwined with its strategic choices and the material conditions of the marketplace. Other parties involved in the same transactional network, however, are also enacting their beliefs, through activities within the marketplace. While the interpretations of customers, suppliers and competitors are all involved in structuring the transactional network, it is the enactment processes of the latter that are particularly important, due to the fact that they serve to link firm-level and group-level competitive activities, through the creation of socially shared belief systems.

As summarized in Table 2.1, various strands of theory from a number of sources are broadly supportive of this fundamental notion of competitive enactment. They each offer complementary insights that extend this line of reasoning. The cognitive lifecycle conception explicated by Levenhagen and his colleagues (Levenhagen et al., 1993), for example, highlights the importance of leadership as a major factor governing all elements of this social construction process, from initial concept creation and the development of category prototypes, through their wider adoption by groups of rivals within the marketplace, to the institutionalization of competitive practices and their eventual destruction by entrepreneurial agents actively seeking to overturn 'the rules of the game'.

While the lifecycle notion outlined by Levenhagen and his colleagues identifies a key role for business entrepreneurs as the engineers of new categories of competitor definition, the phenomenon known as 'cognitive inertia,' highlights one of the potential difficulties confronting would-be innovators: they must also be able to successfully challenge the legitimacy of extant categories, if their ideas are to ultimately gain credence within the wider marketplace. Cognitive inertia has been identified by a number of researchers as a major barrier to organizational learning and strategic renewal. As Porac and Thomas (1990) have observed, the literature abounds with anecdotal evidence suggesting that all too often strategists are unable to re-conceptualize the identities of their organizations sufficiently quickly in the face of radically new forms of competition (see also Abrahamson & Fombrun, 1994; Barr & Huff, 1997; Barr, Stimpert & Huff, 1992; Huff, Huff & Thomas, 1992; Rindova & Fombrun, 1999; Senge, 1990).

The work of Lant and Baum (1995) adds additional, complementary insights into this social construction process, through a consideration of 'isomorphism,' the tendency observed by institutional theorists (e.g. DiMaggio & Powell, 1983; Meyer & Rowan, 1977) for organizations to develop shared beliefs, structures, networks of relations and practices over time. Like Porac and his colleagues, Lant and Baum contend that managers *enact* a structure of strategic groups, responding to, and creating, their competitive worlds in a manner consistent with their own cognitions. Lant and Baum have identified two mechanisms of isomorphism, each underpinned by categorization processes, which potentially may play a key role in the social construction of competitive groups and the institutionalization of competitive practices: (1) *mimetic isomorphism*, resulting from firms monitoring one another; and (2) *normative isomorphism*, arising from cues taken from various normative sources, such as the parent company (if the organization is part of a wider conglomerate), and agents in the institutional environment who act as transmitters of information, including, for example, higher education institutions and industry consultants. Lant and Baum have suggested that it is managers' conceptualizations of their strategic identities, embodied in their shared categorization schemes, that ultimately give rise to the development of competitive groups within industries and the existence of isomorphic practices within these groups:

> ...homogeneous firms, typically identified post hoc as strategic groups based on objective measures, may exhibit institutionalized behavior in their causal attributions and choices of strategies and practices, as a result of the development of shared cognitions about who are members of these strategic groups and which attributes distinguish members from non-members (Lant & Baum, 1995: 36)

Each of these notions (competitive enactment, cognitive inertia, the cognitive life cycle conception, and the processes of normative and mimetic adoption associated with institutional isomorphism) highlight the importance of direct and indirect interaction in the marketplace as bases for the emergence of homogeneous and stabilized cognitions, which in turn underpin the formation of competitive structures and substructures. In another highly complementary development, Peteraf and Shanley (1997) have introduced the notions of relational modelling and vicarious learning from social learning theory (Bandura, 1986; Wood & Bandura, 1989). In common with Lant and Baum (1995) and Porac and Thomas (1990), they have also drawn attention to the importance of managers' conceptions of identity in the social construction of competitive groups, borrowing concepts from social identity theory (Ashforth & Mael, 1989; Tajfel & Turner, 1979, 1986). The more recent work of Lant (1999) and Lant and Phelps (1999), however, drawing on the work of Wenger (1998), calls into question the adequacy of this portrayal of learning as a predominantly vicarious process, in which referent others are modelled or imitated, as exemplified Peteraf and Shanley's paper, but also implicit in much of the other recent work on the socio-cognitive analysis of competitive structures.

The situated learning perspective

As summarized in Table 2.1, the situated learning perspective draws attention to the fact that the ongoing interactions among actors within the marketplace do not merely result in common and predictable patterns of behaviour within strategic groups. Additionally, they help to preserve variations in structures, strategies and beliefs within these groups. According to this view, such variations are vital to the accomplishment of learning and change, thereby enhancing the longer-term survival capabilities of the wider population of organizations. Building on this key insight, this new perspective challenges a fundamental premise of conventional strategic groups theory, the notion that mobility barriers serve as protective devices which preserve the long-term survival chances of established groups (Caves & Porter, 1977). According to Lant and Phelps (1999), strategic groups with high mobility barriers will actually have *lower* long-term survival chances, compared to groups with lower barriers, due to the fact that these barriers inhibit learning by preventing players with new beliefs and practices from entering the group. Over time, this will result in a lessening of variation in structures, strategies and beliefs, thus rendering the wider population of firms vulnerable to competency-destroying technological changes of the sort discussed by Tushman and Anderson (1990).

The situated learning perspective also calls into question the adequacy of the 'topographic' view of organizations portrayed within much of the extant body of work on the socio-cognitive analysis of competition and indeed the field of organization studies more generally. Drawing on the work of Araujo (1998), Lant and Phelps (1999), Palinscar (1998), and Tsoukas (1992) challenge two assumptions in particular implicit within this view: (1) the assumption that knowledge is localized in individual minds or other anthropomorphized entities such as organizations; and (2) the assumption that organizations are relatively self-contained, bounded entities that learn through key individuals, such as top managers.

Empirical studies of competitive enactment and related conceptions: A review and critique

Unfortunately, very few elements of this emerging body of socio-cognitive theory have been empirically tested with an acceptable degree of rigour. The basic argument that individuals attend only to a limited subset of potential competitors and competitor categories has been well established empirically (see e.g. Clark & Montgomery, 1999; de Chernatony et al., 1993; Gripsrud & Gronhaug, 1985; Hodgkinson & Johnson, 1994; Odorici & Lomi, 2001; P. Johnson, Daniels & Asch, 1998; Porac et al., 1987, 1989, 1995; Porac & Thomas, 1994; Reger & Huff, 1993). Porac and his colleagues have also uncovered empirical evidence suggesting that business strategists regard their own firms as the prototypical exemplar of the category or categories in which they locate their major source(s) of competitive threat, i.e. the 'primary competitive group'. They have also argued that the manager's own business acts as the cognitive reference point against which they evaluate potential rivals on the basis of feature comparisons; the greater the perceived similarity between a strategist's own firm and a given rival, the greater the perceived competitive threat (Porac et al., 1987; Porac & Thomas, 1994). Beyond these basic observations, however, there is very little high quality evidence to substantiate the claims of the various socio-cognitive theorists, discussed above. In the remainder of this chapter the available evidence base is critically evaluated. Three limitations in particular are identified that warrant significant methodological and empirical attention:

1. The majority of published studies have been cross-sectional, small-scale and exploratory in nature, illustrating the potential applicability of particular concepts. Furthermore, with one notable exception, the few larger-scale studies that have been undertaken to date have employed cross-sectional designs, thus limiting the insights that can be gained into what are essentially dynamic processes.

2. Excepting the present work, just three longitudinal studies have been reported, each of which is beset with research design and other methodological limitations that severely restrict the inferences that can be drawn from the data.

3. The majority of studies that have been cited in support of the evolving body of theory on the socio-cognitive construction of competitive industry structures have employed single informant, multiple organization designs, predicated on the implicit assumption that sole informants can adequately represent the views of the wider organization (or at least the dominant coalition). As will be demonstrated, this assumption is problematic on both theoretical and empirical grounds. Unfortunately, however, those studies that have revealed marked intra-organizational variations in actors' mental models of competitor definition are also beset with significant methodological limitations, pointing towards a need for further multi-informant, multi-organization investigations, using more sophisticated methods of data collection and analysis.

Ultimately what is required, if social constructionist notions such as competitive enactment, cognitive inertia, institutional isomorphism and the related cognitive life-cycle conception outlined above are to be tested with an acceptable degree of rigour, are large-scale longitudinal field studies, in which the mental representations of multiple informants, situated at differing vantage points within and between organizations in the same industrial sector are assessed repeatedly in conjunction with measurable aspects of strategic behaviour and organizational performance, over extended time periods (Hodgkinson, 1997a). Such studies would enable researchers to explore the extent to which, under what circumstances, and over what time scale and with what effect, actors' mental representations of competition converge, diverge, stabilize and change. Only then would we be able to disentangle the myriad of cause-effect relationships and potentially competing explanations for the evolution of competitive structures implied by this emerging body of socio-cognitive theory. Unfortunately, however, such high quality studies have not been forthcoming, as the following review of the relevant literature demonstrates.

The limitations of small-scale exploratory and larger-scale cross-sectional studies

As with virtually any new line of inquiry, theorizing in this area has evolved largely on an inductive basis, using studies of particular industries and markets in order to illustrate the applicability of selected focal concepts. The basic features of the competitive enactment notion, for example, were demonstrated empirically by means of a small-scale inductive study of the Scottish knitwear industry (N = 17 participants) conducted by Porac et al. (1989). This study revealed an overwhelming tendency for managers from a number of rival firms to disregard as competitors firms located outside the immediate vicinity of Scotland. Despite the fact that Scottish knitwear producers account for a mere 3 percent of the total amount of knitted outer-wear manufactured on a world-wide basis, only firms within the immediate locality and who produce a similar range of goods to one another, using similar technological processes of production and common channels of distribution, were regarded as serious competition. The cognitive lifecycle conception developed by Levenhagen and his colleagues was also grounded contextually, by drawing on occasional examples 'provided from research conducted by the authors in the software development industry' (Levenhagen et al., 1993: 76).

Building on the notion of competitive enactment, competitor categorization theory and the arguments outlined earlier concerning institutional isomorphism, Lant and Baum (1995) drew on a study of hotel managers (N = 43) in the Manhattan district of New York. Using a form of network analysis (Borgatti, Everett & Freeman, 1992) in conjunction with hierarchical cluster analysis, some 14 competitive groupings (i.e. 'competitive sets') were identified from a total of 167 hotels. As predicted, managers within each discernible group of hotels tended to regard one another as relevant competitors. Also as predicted, a number of significant differences emerged between the competitive groups in relation to the mean size, price and location (street and avenue) of the hotels, indicating that the aggregation of the competitive sets elicited from the individual managers reveals relatively homogeneous groups of hotels. Like the aforementioned Scottish knitwear study, the findings of this study offer broad support for the general proposition that competitive structures may evolve through processes of social construction involving competitive enactment. However, as the authors themselves readily acknowledge, due to limitations in the research design, this study contributes very little to our understanding of the precise mechanisms through which such managerial perceptions converge over time, thereby giving rise to institutional isomorphism. Given that this study utilized a cross-sectional design, it was not possible to discern which of the various hypothesized forms of mimetic and normative isomorphism ultimately account for the observed pattern of findings. As with the Scottish knitwear study, the findings of this research should be regarded as tentative rather than conclusive, opening the field to further lines of inquiry, with larger samples and greater controls. A larger-scale follow up investigation of the Scottish knitwear industry reported by Porac et al. (1995) and a more recent study of mimetic adoption processes (Greve, 1998) illustrate two rather differing (but nonetheless complementary) ways in which this preliminary work might inform future research in this area.

Commencing with a series of field interviews of Managing Directors (MD's) (N = 20) as a basis for capturing the 'nomenclature' of the knitwear industry, Porac and his colleagues developed a structured questionnaire which was subsequently administered to a further sample of N = 89 MD's. (A panel of three industry experts was consulted in order to help verify and interpret the information gathered during the preliminary interviews, prior to constructing the questionnaire.) The questionnaire data were submitted to a network analysis, along similar lines to the Lant and Baum (1995) study. The findings suggested a six-category model of organizational forms which seemed to capture actors' common perceptions of competition within the industry, with several attributes (principally size, technology, product style, and geographic location) forming the underlying basis of this commonly perceived structure.

In a population ecology study of the spread of new radio formats in the U.S., Greve (1998) modelled processes of innovation diffusion, using the technique of event history analysis (Tuma and Hannan, 1984), the study population being commercial radio stations. On the basis of his findings, Greve concluded that the major driver of the mimetic adoption of new market positions is managers' mental models, which in turn are informed by information access (the degree to which individuals are able to observe competitors by virtue of geographical proximity) and relevancy judgements (as measured by market size). According to Greve, differential access to information, coupled with variations in perceived relevance, has given rise to the emergence of new strategic groups within this industry, through selective mimetic adoption. These results, suggesting that managers distinguish markets using market size as a relevancy criterion for deciding which competitors' practices are worthy of imitation, represent the beginnings of a journey to discover how managers might categorize and distinguish markets.

The limitations of extant longitudinal studies

As observed earlier, if the various social constructionist notions discussed above are to be tested with an acceptable degree of rigour, large-scale longitudinal field studies are ultimately required, in order to track actors' mental representations over time. Unfortunately, however, just three studies to date have employed any form of longitudinal design, each of which is beset with significant methodological limitations.

In a study of the forest products industry, Gronhaug and Falkenberg (1989) compared senior managers' perceptions of their own and their competitors' strategies, during periods of growth and recession ('boom and bust'). However, this study focused on just seven respondents from four organizations and employed a retrospective design, i.e. the informants were required to report their cognitions for the periods of interest on the basis of recall. The organizations, selected from the Fortune 500 list of the largest US industrial firms, were pursuing strategies which emphasized wood products over pulp and paper. Multiple sources of data were used, including semi-structured interviews with top management, questionnaires, company reports and articles from relevant business periodicals. Competitive positioning strategy was operationalized in terms of Miles and Snow's (1978) four-fold typology. Within this particular framework, organizations classified as *Prospectors* attempt to pioneer product/market developments and tend to compete primarily by stimulating and meeting new market opportunities. *Defenders*, in contrast, are those organizations that attempt to control secure niches within their industry and compete primarily on the basis of price, quality, delivery and service. *Analyzers* are an intermediate type of organization, making fewer product/market innovations, over longer time periods, in comparison to their prospector counterparts, but are generally less committed to stability and efficiency than those organizations classified as defenders. Finally, *Reactors* are those organizations lacking any consistent product-market orientation, responding in an *ad hoc* fashion to environmental pressures. It is noteworthy that with the sole exception of the reactor category, Miles and Snow consider all of these strategic types to be equally viable.

Following Miles and Snow's (1978) original procedure, the participants were each presented with a basic description of the four strategic types and requested to classify their own firms and the three competitors as to type, retrospectively, over the two time periods covered by the study. Each of the four firms were also classified by the researchers for both time periods, in order to provide an additional basis of comparison. According to Gronhaug and Falkenberg, great discrepancies were observed in relation to the self-evaluations and competitors' evaluations of the firms' strategies, with no changes in strategies reported by the firms themselves, despite the fact that such changes were observed by their competitors. The reliability and validity of such retrospective recall techniques in strategy research in general, let alone on such a limited sample, has been seriously questioned in recent years and should only be used in circumstances when no feasible alternative is possible (Golden, 1992, 1997; Miller, Cardinal & Glick, 1997).

Nevertheless, this study clearly illustrates the potential value of longitudinal research in this field of inquiry and points overwhelmingly to the need for further studies using *prospective* designs, with larger sample sizes – both in terms of the number of individual participants and the number of participating organizations – and a greater sophistication of analytical methods. In this type of study, participants would be required to complete the research task on multiple occasions, so as to be able to gauge the extent of cognitive stability and change over extended time periods.

The second study (Reger & Palmer, 1996) attempted to compare longitudinally over a nine-year period executives' cognitive maps of competitive positioning in the U.S. financial services industry. The findings of this research provide broad support for the notion of cognitive inertia, outlined earlier. Considerable upheavals were experienced by the American financial services industry throughout the period encompassed by this research, following extensive de-regulation and other changes. However, according to Reger and Palmer, due to inertia, strategists' mental representations failed to keep pace with this changing environment. As with the Gronhaug and Falkenberg study, however, there are several methodological weaknesses associated with the design of this research that render the findings inconclusive. First, in order to explore the extent to which mental models altered over the nine-year period encompassed by their research, Reger and Palmer compared retrospectively the findings from three *separate* studies by means of a qualitative content analysis. While the data were gathered over differing time periods (1981, 1986 and 1989), as Reger and Palmer themselves acknowledge, there are several locational and industry segment disparities across the three studies. These potentially confound a number of outcomes which Reger and Palmer would otherwise have been able to attribute with much greater certainty to increasing environmental turbulence. Furthermore, there were several differences in the data analysis methods employed within each of the separate studies which might also have accounted for some of the outcomes. As in the case of the Gronhaug and Falkenberg study, these findings highlight a pressing need for further studies using *prospective* designs.

In an attempt to address directly the above criticisms regarding the small-scale, largely cross-sectional nature of previous empirical work investigating social constructionist explanations for the emergence and evolution of strategic groups, Osborne, Stubbart and Ramaprasad (2001) have recently reported the outcomes of a longitudinal study spanning a 20-year time period (1963–1982), in which documentary sources (Presidents' letters to shareholders) were used in order to identify cognitive strategic groups (i.e. strategic groups based on managers' mental models of competition) in the U.S. pharmaceutical industry. Previously, Cool and Schendel (1987) investigated strategic groups in this industry, using conventional, economic variables, reflecting variations in firm performance. Answering directly my earlier call for studies that seek to establish linkages between actors' mental representations of strategic groups and measures of performance (Hodgkinson, 1997a), Osborne and his colleagues triangulated the strategic groups identified through their thematic analysis of some 400 documents from 22 firms with the findings of the earlier Cool and Schendel study, covering the same 20-year time period. In total, 37,000 sentences (450,000 words) were content analyzed with the aid of computerized software. A series of complex statistical analyses suggested that there was a significant amount of convergence between the cognitive strategic groups identified by Osborne et al. and the economic strategic groups identified by Cool and Schendel. This recent study illustrates the fact that there has been a clear strengthening of research methods now being employed in an effort to enrich this field. For example, it overcomes the sample size limitations of previous cognitive studies, uses a longitudinal research design, and concerted efforts have been made to triangulate cognitive findings with economic performance data (all vital pre-requisites for ascertaining the validity of the notion of competitive enactment). There are, however, still problems associated with the retrospective use of documentary sources, in that the data they contain may be subject to bias and distortion (cf. Hodgkinson, 2001a). Moreover, as discussed next, single informant, multiple organization designs yield data that might be unrepresentative of the wider body of strategists and other key members of the organizaton.

The limitations of single informant, multiple organization designs

As noted above, the notion that competitive groups are socially constructed entities implies a strong requirement for studies in which the mental representations of multiple informants, situated at differing vantage points within and between organizations in the same industrial sector, are assessed repeatedly over time. As I have argued elsewhere (Hodgkinson, 1997a, 2001a, 2001b; Hodgkinson & Sparrow, 2002), such studies would enable researchers to explore the extent to which, under what circumstances and over what time scale, and with what effect, actors' mental representations of competition converge, diverge, stabilize and change (cf. Fiol, 2002; Lant, 2002; Porac & Thomas, 2002; Porac, Ventresca & Mishina, 2002). Thus far, however, very few studies have sought to systematically compare and contrast actors' mental representations of competitive environments on a cross-sectional basis, let alone using such sophisticated longitudinal datasets.

Virtually all of the empirical work that has been gathered as a basis for developing and/or testing the emerging body of socio-cognitive theory summarized in the earlier sections of this chapter has relied on the use of single informant (typically the owner-manager, managing director or CEO), multiple organization designs, exemplified by the Scottish knitwear (Porac et al., 1989, 1995) and Manhattan hotel industry (Lant & Baum, 1995) studies outlined above (for additional representative examples, see Dess & Davis, 1984;

Fombrun & Zajac, 1987; Porac et al., 1987; Porac & Thomas, 1994; Reger & Huff, 1993; Spencer et al., 2003). Research designs of this type suffer from a number of limitations and drawbacks, not least the fact they are predicated upon an implied level of consensus within and between organizations that is highly questionable (Floyd & Wooldridge, 2000; Wooldridge & Floyd, 1989). As will be discussed shortly, there is a growing body of evidence suggesting that there may be significant intra-organizational individual differences in competitor cognition. To the extent that such differences exist, they might have an important bearing on processes of strategy formulation and implementation. Unfortunately, however, the leading researchers who have contributed to the various theoretical developments outlined above, with the notable exception of Lant (1999) and Lant and Phelps's (1999) recent work, have implicitly or explicitly assumed away the significance of such variations in cognition, treating them as a source of unwanted error variance, and focused instead on commonly reported perceptions and beliefs. That the importance of these potentially significant intra-organizational differences for understanding the strategic management process has been 'assumed away' by this group of scholars is epitomized by the following quotation, taken from the recent paper by Peteraf and Shanley (1997). In this paper, in which they outlined their social identity theory of strategic groups, Peteraf and Shanley questioned the conditions under which it might be reasonable to apply a cognitive perspective collectively to an organization:

... When a firm is led by a single top decision maker, as many small firms are, the cognitive processes of the CEO are arguably the same as those of the firm. This is because although the firm may be composed of many individuals, the CEO has full responsibility for scanning the environment and charting a course of action for the firm. Few would dispute that a cognitive analogy from individuals to firms is applicable in such a circumstance... More often, however, a firm is managed by a top management team that exercises collective decision-making. In this case, the team may be characterized as a collective actor with cognitive capabilities if group-level processes... allow team members to reconcile their cognitive differences and make decisions in a relatively unified and consistent manner... When the top management team is relatively homogeneous and when there is continuity of management, it is even more reasonable to view the firm as a collective cognitive actor. (Peteraf & Shanley, 1997: 167–168)

This would appear to be exactly the sort of logic applied at the industry-level of analysis by Porc and his colleagues in their study of the Scottish knitwear industry:

... In our analysis of the Scottish knitwear sector we took intra-industry variation as a given. At the same time, however, we ought to distil from interview and secondary data core beliefs that seemed to be repeated by our sources and widely accepted. Our analyses suggest that certain beliefs about competitor and market identity isolate a commonly perceived competitive arena for many of the Scottish managers (Porac et al., 1989: 405).

In their larger-scale follow up investigation, while recognizing the importance of differences in perceptions, especially inter-organizational asymmetries in the classification of firms into particular categories of rival, once again the analysis conducted by Porac and his colleagues centred primarily on commonalities, with a view to identifying '... a collectively understood industry model of organizational forms... [which] ... has become part of the macro-cultural belief system of the industry participants' (Porac et al., 1995: 221).

However, the issue of consensus with regard to mental models of competitor definition within and between organizations in industries and markets is fundamentally problematic. The extent to which each of the conditions outlined in the above Peteraf and Shanley quotation actually hold in the various studies reviewed above is highly debatable. Given that none of these studies actually assessed the extent of cognitive variation or homogeneity within and between firms, let alone controlled for the various intra-organizational processes alluded to in this quotation, it is impossible to judge the extent to which the key assumptions underpinning this body of theory and research are justified. Certainly, as we saw towards the end of the previous section, the situated learning perspective on strategic groups recently advanced by Lant (1999) and Lant and Phelps (1999), openly challenges the adequacy of this viewpoint. There are, however, additional reasons for opening up the analysis of actors' mental models of competitor definition to the study of individual and sub-group differences.

The case for studying individual and subgroup similarities and differences in mental models of competitor definition

Within the strategy literature there is a growing body of work concerned with processes of strategic management and questions of how strategic decisions come about. Such research has established that the development of strategies is perhaps best explained by understanding social, political and cultural processes in organizations (e.g. Bower, 1972; Hedberg & Jonsson, 1977; Johnson, 1987, 1988; Pettigrew, 1973, 1985; Pettigrew, Ferlie & McKee, 1992; Pettigrew & Whipp, 1991; Pfeffer, 1981a, 1981b; Pfeffer & Salancik, 1974). This stream of research has important implications for the rapidly expanding number of cognitive studies of competitor definition that are seeking to further our understanding of strategy development and implementation, not least the requirement that these studies be extended to a variety of additional levels of analysis, particularly the organizational-level, functional group-level and the individual-level. The primary reason for extending cognitive research to these additional levels of analysis is that different actors, in different roles, face different environmental contingencies at least in terms of context, function and level of responsibility (Lawrence & Lorsch, 1967). Clearly, to the extent that strategists' mental models of their business environments are shaped by past experiences and material circumstances (i.e. previous interactions with the business environment), *a priori*, we would expect to find differences in the nature and characteristic features of these mental models from one research participant to another.

Furthermore, a number of writers have argued that there exist sets of relatively common assumptions related to different contexts. Strategists are likely to be influenced by, and interact with, all of these frames of reference (Huff, 1982). Figure 2.2 represents some of these different sets of assump-

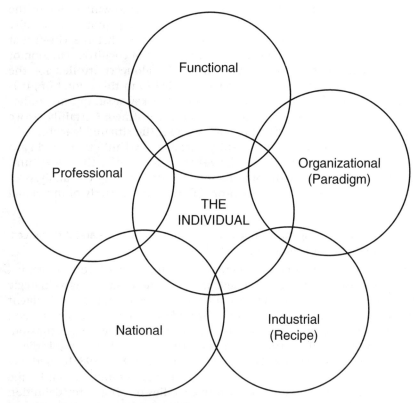

Figure 2.2   Frames of reference of strategists
Source: Hodgkinson & Johnson, 1994: 530.

tions. These exist at the organizational-level (Bartunek, 1984; Johnson, 1987, 1988; Laughlin, 1991; Pfeffer, 1981a; Prahalad & Bettis, 1986; Sheldon, 1980) and, as acknowledged above, at the industry-level (Grinyer & Spender, 1979a, 1979b; Spender, 1989). Arguably however, the diversity of frames of reference upon which strategists draw goes still wider than the organizational- or industry-level. For example, there is increasing evidence that national culture affects managers' interpretations and responses to strategic issues (Calori et al., 1992; Schneider & De Meyer, 1991), and their perceived control of the environment and strategic behaviour (Hofstede, 1980; Kagono et al., 1985). There are also within-organization influences. At the level of functional groups, for example, there are functionally specific belief systems and perceptions of issues (Dearborn & Simon, 1958; Handy, 1985). Moreover, it has been argued that managers' views of the world are shaped, at least in part, by their career backgrounds (e.g. Bouchet, 1976; Gunz, 1989; Gunz & Whitley, 1985; Hambrick & Mason, 1984; Whitley, 1987). Finally, there are various individual-level frames of reference that may influence the way in which strategists perceive their competitive environments (Markus, 1977; Markus & Nurius, 1986; Markus & Wurf, 1987).

In short, any actor, or group of actors, draws on a series of frames of reference to make sense of their world. There is a continual interplay between the individual, the context in which he or she operates, the frames of reference related to those contexts, and the political and social processes at work. Understanding the process of strategic management is therefore centrally concerned with explaining how diverse frames of reference are reconciled within and between organizations in order to formulate and implement strategies.

Studies of the nature and extent of individual and subgroup variations and homogeneity in mental models of competitor definition

In the light of the above lines of reasoning, a number of researchers have investigated individual- and group-level similarities and differences in the structure and content of mental models of competitor definition, across a range of sectors (see e.g. Bowman & Johnson, 1992; Calori et al., 1992, 1994; Daniels et al., 1994; de Chernatony et al., 1993; Hodgkinson & Johnson, 1994; P. Johnson et al., 1998; Reger, 1990a). These studies have revealed considerable individual and group variations, thus calling into question the validity of the assumption of widespread consensus which has underpinned much of the theory development that has occurred over the past decade or so, stemming from the foundational notion of competitive enactment.

In a study of competition in the Chicago banking market, for example, Reger (1990a) investigated, at the individual-level of analysis, the mental models of senior managers from a number of rival firms, in order to explore the extent to which the participants were in agreement regarding the bases of competition, and concluded as follows:

> A surprisingly low level of agreement as to the important strategic dimensions was found in this industry. ... The results shown do not support the proposition that key strategic dimensions will be widely shared by strategists in an industry. .... It may be that subgroups of strategists in the industry share more commonality of dimensions than exhibited by the group as a whole. In particular, two subgroups are likely to share more commonality. First, members of the same BHC [bank holding company] might be expected to share more common dimensions because they interact more often with each other and are more likely directly to discuss competitors' strategies and key strategic dimensions in the industry. Second, strategists who share similar functional or product backgrounds are likely to share common dimensions because their training and experiences are similar and these may have shaped their cognitive constructive systems in similar ways (Reger, 1990a, pp. 77–79).

Preliminary supporting evidence for these hypotheses has been obtained in two empirical studies by Johnson and his associates in the off-shore pumps industry (Daniels et al., 1994; de Chernatony et al., 1993) and the UK grocery retail industry (Hodgkinson & Johnson, 1994). In the former study, the revealed mental models of several managers from differing functional backgrounds and organizations were compared and, as in Reger's investigation, the findings suggested considerable variation among the participants in terms of their views of the way in which the industry was structured. However, the results also indicated that managers within particular organizations shared more similar views than managers across organizations. Furthermore, managers within particular functional areas were found to be more similar in their views than managers across functional areas.

The second study, by Hodgkinson and Johnson (1994), uncovered evidence which suggests that the degree of detail (structural complexity) associated with mental models of competitive structures may vary systematically according to the role requirements of the strategist's job. Managers whose roles require them to have a more detailed grasp of the business environment (for example those concerned with the formulation of national merchandising policy at head office), were found to have significantly more elaborate representations, in comparison with their counterparts whose roles did not require them to possess such detailed insights and knowledge concerning the actions of their competitors (for example regional area managers concerned with the implementation of head office policy in the field). Hodgkinson and Johnson contend that these differences have arisen due to the fact that differing jobs place differing demands upon individuals and subgroups, which in turn result in differing interpretations of the competitive arena (cf. Calori et al., 1994).

Another, more recent study, however, lends support to the argument that strategists' mental models are idiosyncratic in nature, as opposed to there being a meaningful socio-cognitive grouping. P. Johnson et al. (1998) reported the findings of a study of 22 managers spanning three organizations operating in the international automotive industry. On the basis of three separate sets of analysis, focussing on the competitors named by the participants, the number of constructs they employed, and a content analysis of these constructs, Johnson and her colleagues concluded that there was little evidence of industry-, organizational- or even group-level homogeneity in the knowledge structures that the managers held of their competitive environments:

> ...When considering the issue of the level to which managers' knowledge structures can be considered commonly held, the findings ... support a high degree of idiosyncrasy and therefore subscribe to the individual level perspective. That is managers failed to demonstrate sufficient homogeneity to group together at the organization level or even the functional level (P. Johnson et al., 1998, pp. 140–141).

On the basis of these findings, P. Johnson and her colleagues question the validity of the propositions advanced by social constructionist theorists such as Porac et al. (1987, 1989) and Reger and Huff (1993) concerning the idea that managers' knowledge structures converge at the strategic group- and organizational-levels of analysis. This pattern of findings also conflicts with the findings of Daniels et al. (1994) and Hodgkinson and Johnson (1994), whose work suggests that managers from the same organization and functional position tend to share similar beliefs. P. Johnson and her colleagues attribute such variations to differences in analytic focus. Hodgkinson and Johnson and Daniels et al. drew their conclusions on the basis of comparisons of the content *and* structure of their participants' cognitive maps, whereas P. Johnson et al.'s analysis focused on map content *per se*. Such debates highlight a key problem bedevilling progress in the study of managerial and organizational cognition in general. This is the difficulty of obtaining a body of empirical findings that are sufficiently robust to emerge across a range of situational contexts, using alternative methods of data collection and analysis (Hodgkinson, 1997a, 2001a), an issue to which we shall return shortly.

One other significant methodological limitation associated with this group of studies is worthy of comment at this juncture. As with the empirical studies reviewed earlier in support of competitive enactment and institutional isomorphism and related notions, with the notable exception of Bowman and Johnson's (1992) study (N = 309 individuals from N = 35 businesses), the sample sizes of studies investigating individual and sub-group differences in mental models of competitor definition, both in terms of the number of participating organizations and the number of individual research participants, have been modest to say the least, ranging from N = 22 (e.g. Hodgkinson & Johnson, 1994; P. Johnson et al., 1998; Walton, 1986) to N = 33 (Calori et al., 1992) individuals, drawn from considerably smaller numbers of organizations. Clearly these samples are too small for performing meaningful comparisons, if the findings are to be generalized to larger populations, for example at the industry-level. These problems notwithstanding, we can begin to draw some significant conclusions from this body of work as a whole.

Social constructionist notions, such as 'competitive enactment,' 'institutional isomorphism,' and the theory of strategic group identity, seem to imply that differences in actors' cognitions are of little consequence in accounting for the strategy and performance of organizations; ultimately, it is the commonalities in decision makers' cognitive maps that unite individuals and galvanize collective action, deviations from the 'norm' being little more than 'error variance'. However, when we consider the theoretical arguments regarding the nature and potential significance of intra- and inter-organizational cognitive diversity in actors' mental models of competitor definition, together with the findings of the growing number of empirical studies across a range of sectors which clearly demonstrate such diversity, it becomes clear that these notions, to say nothing of the ways in which researchers have gone about testing them, may well be too simplistic.

Towards fusion: Exploring the relative impact of task and institutional influences on actors' mental models of competitive industry structures

In the final analysis, both sets of theory and research outlined in this chapter must ultimately be reconciled, if we are to develop a truly comprehensive understanding of the nature and significance of actors' mental models of competitive industry structures (cf. Sutcliffe & Huber, 1998). To this end, a study conducted recently by Daniels et al. (2002) has sought to delineate the relative contributions of 'task and institutional influences' as determinants of managers' mental representations of competitive industry structures, in an exploration of the UK financial services industry. Building upon both streams of theory and research outlined above, Daniels and his colleagues have used the least squares dummy vectors (LSDV) approach to multiple regression (Cohen & Cohen, 1983) in order explore the relative contribution of managerial function, level of seniority, organizational membership, and the interaction effects of these variables on the overall levels of belief similarity vs. dissimilarity in their sample of participants.

Theories emphasizing the primacy of institutional forces such as mimetic adoption (e.g. Lant & Baum, 1995) suggest that managers' mental models within the same industry sector should move towards convergence at the level of the industry, strategic group, managerial function and rank. Theories asserting the primacy of the competitive or task environment (e.g. Hodgkinson & Johnson, 1994), on the other hand, predict that a divergence of cognition should emerge between organizations, between management functions, and amongst managers of differing levels of seniority. Interestingly, the overall pattern of findings in this latest study suggests that neither task nor institutional explanations are inherently superior in the context of this particular industry setting. Whilst there is some evidence that the institutional environment exerts significant influence (primarily through a convergence of mental models among middle managers across the industry as a whole) there is also evidence of significant task influences. In particular, a number of significant differences emerged across organizations, with greater differentiation among senior managers.

This study has brought together these hitherto largely disparate streams of theory and research within a unified framework. In exploring the relative contributions of task and institutional influences on managers' mental models of competition, it has undoubtedly broken new ground. Unfortunately, however, as I have argued elsewhere (Hodgkinson, 2002), the way in which Daniels and his colleagues elicited and compared the cognitive maps in this study may well have biased the results obtained in favour of the substantive hypotheses under test. However, as discussed in the next section, these problems are by no means unique to this particular investigation.

Methodological issues in analysis of competitor cognition

Within a remarkably short time period, the field of strategic management has witnessed a proliferation in the range of techniques being applied in an effort to 'map' actors' mental representations of issues and problems (see e.g. Eden & Ackermann, 1998; Eden & Spender, 1998; Fiol & Huff, 1992; Hodgkinson & Sparrow, 2002; Huff, 1990; Huff & Jenkins, 2002; J. Sparrow, 1998; Walsh, 1995). Techniques employed by researchers specifically investigating actors' mental representations of competition have ranged from relatively simple procedures that merely require a listing of competitors by name (de Chernatony et al., 1993; Gripsrud & Gronhaug, 1985), through semi-structured interviews, using taxonomic mapping procedures (Calori et al., 1992, 1994; Hodgkinson & Johnson, 1994; Porac et al., 1989, 1995; Porac & Thomas, 1994) and network analysis, using block modelling and related procedures (Lant & Baum, 1995; Odorci & Lomi, 2001; Porac et al., 1995), to repertory grid (Daniels, Johnson & de Chernatony, 1994; Reger, 1990a; Reger & Huff, 1993; Spencer et al., 2003) and related multidimensional scaling and clustering techniques (Hodgkinson, Padmore & Tomes, 1991, Hodgkinson, Tomes & Padmore, 1996; Walton, 1986), and fully structured questionnaires, based on extant typologies of competitive positioning strategy (Bowman & Ambrosini, 1997a, 1997b; Bowman & Johnson, 1992; Dess & Davis, 1984). Unfortunately, the fact that such a wide range of techniques has been applied across relatively small numbers of participants and organizations, in such highly diverse settings, renders problematic the extent to which we can generalize the findings from one study to another, thus hampering knowledge accumulation. In particular, this confounding of method with context means that we are unable to ascertain the underlying reasons for the different patterns of findings that have emerged across the various studies that have investigated the extent of homogeneity and diversity in actors' mental models of competitive positioning strategy, reviewed in the previous section.

The piecemeal adoption of such a wide array of cognitive mapping techniques is problematic for other reasons; this lack of consistency from one study to another means that we have failed to accumulate much-needed methodological knowledge to enable the refinement of procedures for the systematic elicitation, comparison and validation of maps, a vital prerequisite for the future advancement of the field. Significant methodological refinements are urgently needed in all three of these areas, if the assessment of actors' mental models of competitor definition and hence the overall scientific quality of studies in this domain are to progress beyond present levels.

The elicitation of maps

The majority of the studies that have sought to discover the extent to which actors' mental models are homogeneous or diverse – in terms of their structure and content – have tended to use idiographic methods of data collection and analysis. As I have argued elsewhere (Hodgkinson, 1997a), these techniques are inherently unsuitable for exploring this particular issue because idiographic research methods, by their very nature, tend to accentuate differences in cognition at the expense of commonalities.

A common methodological limitation associated with all idiographic cognitive mapping techniques, when used in the context of hypothetico-deductive research directed towards the discovery of variations in the structural complexity of cognition, is that the various elicitation procedures employed necessitate extensive interactions between the researcher and participant. During the course of these interactions, there is ample opportunity for a range of factors associated with the dynamics of the interview (chiefly, the length of the interview and the behaviour of the interviewer and interviewee) to influence the extent to which more or less elaborated cognitive maps are elicited. Consequently, it is difficult to ascertain the extent to which observed differences in cognition are due to the characteristics of the industry under study, the characteristics of the individual participants and participating organizations, or the research methods employed in order to gather and analyze the data.

Hodgkinson and Johnson's (1994) study, for example, used a variant of Porac and Thomas's (1987) taxonomic interview procedure (known as the 'self-entry within-subjects assessment method'), in order to elicit individuals' mental models of their competitive worlds in the UK grocery retail industry. Using this technique, informants are required to discuss the nature of their business, what class of business it is (the 'starting category'), what related classes of business there are, and what sub-classes of each there might be. The process is continued upwards, until the informant is unable to generalize usefully further, laterally, until all the related classes of business he or she can recall have been recorded, and downwards, until no further meaningful distinctions can be drawn. The process is recorded by the researcher on a whiteboard in full view of the informant, thus enabling him or her to correct or modify their responses as the session progresses. The end result is a complete hierarchical taxonomy that represents the mental model of the individual respondent. In short, this particular interview task is designed to capture individuals' personalized mental models of their competitive worlds. However, it is evident that the technique itself, by its very nature, will tend to lead participants to generate idiosyncratic responses, which are more than likely a function of the demand characteristics of the data collection task, rather than a reflection of underlying substantive differences in cognition.[1]

---

[1] An alternative approach for eliciting individual-level cognitive taxonomies, known as the 'top-down within-subjects' variant (Porac & Thomas, 1987), requires the research participant to identify the sub-categories which emanate from a starting category supplied by the researcher, known as the 'root beginner' category. In all other respects this approach is identical to the procedure employed by Hodgkinson and Johnson (1994). This particular variant was the approach adopted by Porac et al. (1989) in their study of the Scottish knitwear industry discussed earlier. A third approach, known as the 'top-down, between-subjects' variant (Porac & Thomas, 1987), was employed by Porac et al. (1987) and Porac and Thomas (1994) in their studies of American grocery retailers in rural Illinois. This version uses multiple samples of research participants in order to identify successive subordinate levels within the taxonomy, emanating from a root beginner. The result is an aggregate taxonomy representing the collective cognitive structure of the research participants. However, as Hodgkinson and Johnson (1994) observe, it is highly questionable to what extent the results of this particular procedure are meaningful. Whilst this procedure enables the researcher to represent the *collective responses* of the participants, it does not follow, indeed it seems highly unlikely, that the resulting cognitive structure reflects the viewpoint of any given individual actor or group of actors. This method, by its very nature, forces each successive group of research participants to consider the responses of previous subgroups of participants in order to generate additional levels in the resulting taxonomy. (For further discussion of the strengths and limitations of these and related techniques see Hodgkinson & Sparrow, 2002, especially Chapter 7).

This observation is equally applicable to most of the other methods that have been used to explore the extent of consensus and diversity in mental models of competitive structures. Reger (1990a), for example, employed the classic 'minimum context form' of the repertory grid technique in order to elicit separate sets of constructs from each participant, using triads of named competitors supplied by the researcher. As in the case of the taxonomic interview procedure employed by Hodgkinson and Johnson, it is highly likely that this approach, by definition, will generate idiosyncratic responses [for a related example see Walton (1986), whose data was reanalyzed by Reger & Palmer (1996), together with Reger's (1990a) data, in the aforementioned longitudinal investigation of competitor cognition in the U.S. financial services industry].

Similarly, Calori et al.'s (1992) use of 'loosely structured interviews' in order to uncover executives' strategic thinking in relation to anticipated changes in their industries and organizations may have accentuated minor differences in cognition at the expense of fundamental commonalities. In this study the participants' mental models were inferred from the interview transcripts by the researchers using content analysis. Commendably, in a later study exploring the links between the map complexity of CEOs and the scope of their organizations in terms of their business portfolios, geographic scope, and the extent of foreign links with parent companies, Calori and his colleagues controlled for the effect of the length of their interviews on map complexity (operationalized in terms of comprehensiveness and connectedness), using analysis of covariance (ANCOVA). Partial support was obtained for the hypothesis that the complexity of CEOs' cognitive structures matches the complexity of the environment. Unfortunately, however, only relatively modest amounts of variance were explained, with relatively low levels of statistical significance. This might well be due the lack of power resulting from the small sample size (N = 26 CEOs drawn from four industries, spanning two countries), as acknowledged by the authors themselves, but we cannot rule out the additional possibility that the variable length of the interview was a contributory factor.

As a final illustration, consider the work of Daniels and his colleagues (Daniels et al., 1994, 1995, 2002). In addition to a variant of the repertory grid, these researchers employed a card sort technique in their studies of managers' mental models of competition in the off-shore pumps and financial services industries. Using this procedure, participants are required to list their competitors on a series of cards (1 card per competitor) and sort the cards into 'meaningful categories', in the presence of the researcher. The participant is free to place the cards (on a table) in any order that personally makes sense. They are instructed to place cards closer together in order to denote the fact that particular firms are perceived to be in closer competition to one another. Conversely, the participant indicates that firms are in competition to a lesser extent by placing the relevant cards further apart (in any direction). Once the participant is satisfied that the cards are arranged appropriately, the researcher makes a record of the configuration. Again, there is a danger that the knowledge elicitation technique itself may yield idiosyncratic responses that accentuate surface-level differences in cognition which are more apparent than real. [For further details of the merits and limitations of this particular elicitation method see the inter-change between Daniels and Johnson (2002) and Hodgkinson, 2002.]

The comparison of maps

A further problem concerns the difficulty of comparing the cognitive maps with one another, in terms of their structure and content, a problem which intensifies with increased numbers of research participants and levels of analysis. Which particular features should form the basis of such comparisons and how should the necessary analyses be performed? The answer to this question is non-trivial and ultimately the decision as to which particular feature(s) should form the focus of analysis may prove to be the crucial deciding factor that determines the outcomes of a given study. This can be illustrated by reference to Reger's (1990a) study of the Chicago banking market.

As we saw earlier, Reger (1990a) found considerable variation in terms of the personal constructs elicited from managers from different banks within the Chicago area and (on the basis of a series of factor analyses) concluded that there were low levels of agreement amongst strategists in the banking industry regarding the important dimensions defining the bases of competition. In a later piece of work, however, Reger and Huff (1993), re-analyzing the same dataset (using a variety of cluster analysis techniques), noted considerable agreement in terms of the research participants' categories of competitors. On the basis of this re-analysis, Reger and Huff concluded that the findings of their study offered complementary support for the social constructionist arguments of Porac and his colleagues (Porac et al., 1989; Porac & Thomas, 1990) that there is, therefore, a cognitive basis for forming strategic groups. Clearly this interpretation is somewhat at variance with Reger's (1990a) initial conclusions that strategists have different cognitive frameworks and serves well to illustrate the fact that the comparative evaluation of data across individuals in cognitive studies of competitive positioning strategy is far from straightforward.

Similar conclusions can be drawn from my own study of the UK grocery retail industry (Hodgkinson & Johnson, 1994). Recall that this study revealed considerable variation in the structure and contents of the research participants' mental models of the competitive arena, and an analysis based on the degree of detail associated with each cognitive map suggested that competitor cognition varies systematically according to the role responsibilities of each individual. However, upon closer inspection, as in the Reger and Huff (1993) re-analysis, it was found that there were several categories of competitor that the participants seemed to hold in common. In particular, a content analysis suggested that the majority of participants seemed to share similar views regarding the nature and identity both of their own businesses and of their major competitors – a further illustration that the researcher's decision as to which features of actors' revealed cognitive maps/mental models should form the basis of comparison in socio-cognitive studies of competitive positioning strategy is potentially crucial to the outcomes of the study.

As a final illustration of the limitations of existing techniques for the systematic comparison of mental models let us consider again the work of Daniels and his colleagues (Daniels et al., 1994, 1995, 2002). These researchers have attempted to circumvent some of the problems I have identified in connection with the comparison of cognitive maps through the use of structured rating scales. Having elicited cognitive maps by two complementary idiographic procedures, a variant of the repertory grid technique in conjunction with the card-sorting task outlined above, Daniels et al. then faced the problem of how to ascertain the overall degree of similarity between the resulting maps (their main dependent variable). Given that the maps were each based on differing organizations and attributes, they devised a comparative rating exercise to determine the varying degrees of similarity and dissimilarity between them. This entailed the participants rating the similarity of one another's maps to their own, individual mental models that prevailed at the time the rating tasks were performed, a considerable period after the elicitation exercise had been completed.

The problem here, as we shall see in later chapters, is that it is highly questionable to what extent such assessments of similarity – based on visual comparisons of spatial representations of actors' mental models – are meaningful. In the absence of clear criteria upon which to base these comparisons, there is a very real danger that raters will focus on surface-level characteristics, which, in turn, as in the case of many of the other methods that have been employed to study similarities and differences in cognitive structures, may give rise to findings of diversity that are more apparent than real. Moreover, there is also a likelihood with this approach, particularly if large numbers of cognitive maps are to be compared, that raters may vary the bases of comparison from one judgement to another, a further factor that could potentially give rise to artificially inflated levels of cognitive diversity (Hodgkinson, 2002).

The validation of maps

As observed a decade ago by Ginsberg (1994), very little research has sought to explore directly the empirical correlates of actors' mental models of competitive space, with a view to establishing the validity of the cognitive mapping techniques employed, a necessary preliminary step for model building and theory testing. To date, the overwhelming majority of studies have been designed primarily in order to assess the efficacy of particular methodological approaches for revealing insights into how strategists view their competitive worlds. While considerable advances have been made in this respect, surprisingly few investigations have been published, thus far, which have attempted to psychometrically evaluate the various methods employed in order to represent actors' mental models of competitive structures. A notable exception, however, is the study by Daniels et al. (1995), which evaluated the convergent validity of maps elicited by means of the visual card sort procedure and the repertory grid technique, as employed in the offshore pumps and financial services industry studies reviewed above (Daniels et al., 1994, 2002). The results (based on the self-report method of map comparison, critically evaluated above) indicated that the methods yield comparable findings, to the extent that Daniels and his associates suggested that when the degree of access to research participants, for example due to time constraints, poses a problem for researchers, the visual card sort technique, which is relatively quick to administer in comparison to the grid technique, may be used in isolation, with relatively little loss of information.

Leaving aside the methodological limitations identified in respect of this study, discussed above, while such evidence of convergent validity represents a useful step forward, from the point of view of ensuring that future substantive empirical findings are not merely a by-product of the *particular* method employed in any given study (i.e. internal validity), ultimately, studies are required which explore the extent to which the data elicited through cognitive mapping techniques are correlated with exogenous variables of theoretical interest, such as the background characteristics of the participants, environmental scanning behaviours, and the strategic, structural and performance characteristics of the organization (i.e. external validity). In the absence of adequate empirical evidence that such meaningful relationships exist between measurable features of actors' mental models of competitive space and a range of contextual variables which *a priori* we would expect to be correlated with competitor cognition, the extent to which cognitive approaches for the assessment of competitive environments can significantly further understanding of intra- and inter-organizational processes of strategy development is open to question (Ginsberg, 1994; Hodgkinson, 1997a).

However, virtually no studies, to date, have explored directly the correlates of actors' mental models of competitive positioning strategies (though for notable exceptions see Bowman & Ambrosini, 1997a; Bowman & Johnson, 1992; Calori et al., 1994; McNamara, Deephouse & Luce, 2003; McNamara, Luce & Tompson, 2002). As observed by Hodgkinson (1997a), this may be due partly to the fact that there is a dearth of techniques suitable for capturing key aspects of actors' mental models in a form which will enable researchers to detect *systematically* individual and/or sub-group differences in cognitions of competitive positioning strategies and explore the extent to which these differences are related to exogenous variables of theoretical interest (see also Ginsberg, 1994).

Implications

This review has identified a number of methodological challenges that warrant immediate attention, if the competitive enactment notion and related conceptions are to be submitted to adequate empirical scrutiny. Three problems in particular are impeding our immediate progress.

First, the time has now come for researchers to move beyond the stage where actors' mental models of competitive space are studied for their own sake (on the basis of the largely untested assumption that they are somehow related to individual and collective strategic behaviours and outcomes.) While significant progress has been achieved in refining techniques for the analysis of actors' mental models competitor definition, as noted above, virtually no attempts have been made to develop indices that will enable researchers to systematically relate their representations of these models to exogenous variables of theoretical interest.

Second, there is the unresolved issue regarding how researchers should move between levels of analysis in studies of competitor cognition. Thus far, the majority of researchers have concentrated their efforts at a given level of analysis within particular studies, some at the level of the industry – with a view to identifying shared belief structures of competitor definition (e.g. Dess & Davis, 1984; Fombrun & Zajac, 1987; Lant & Baum, 1995; Odorci & Lomi, 2001; Porac et al., 1987, 1989) – others, at the level of the individual participant or subgroup (e.g. Bowman & Johnson, 1992; Daniels et al., 1994, Hodgkinson & Johnson, 1994; P. Johnson et al., 1998), with a view to exploring patterns of cognitive similarity *and* diversity. Ultimately, however, as observed earlier, if recent theory is to be subjected to adequate empirical scrutiny, we need to engage in large-scale, multi-level studies, in which actors' representations of competition are compared and contrasted systematically, over time, in a multi-layered fashion. Unfortunately, as we have seen, the methods of data collection and analysis that have been used to date are unable to meet these fundamental requirements.

The final, and arguably the most complex, set of issues is related to the problem of how actors' mental models should be compared one with another (Huff & Fletcher, 1990). Which features of the data should form the basis of such comparisons and how should the data be analyzed?

Towards a constructive alternative

One approach in particular, which, on the basis of its *prima facie* appearance and evidence from studies in other domains of investigation, would seem to hold considerable potential for developing a psychometrically acceptable method for responding effectively to the various challenges identifed above, is the repertory grid. As noted in the previous chapter, the primary strength of this approach lies in its inherent flexibility, both from the point of view of data collection and analysis. Although its origins lie within personal construct psychology (Kelly, 1955), over the years researchers in the field of social cognition have successfully adapted this approach, in conjunction with a powerful method of exploratory statistical analysis known generically as 'three-way scaling' (Arabie, et al., 1987) or, equivalently, 'weighted multidimensional scaling' (WMDS) (Schiffman, Reynolds & Young, 1981), in order to investigate aspects of individual *and* collective cognition at one and the same time (see e.g. Forgas, 1976, 1978, 1981; Forgas et al., 1980).

As will be demonstrated in later chapters, suitably modified in the form of a carefully designed semi-structured questionnaire, the repertory grid technique combined with three-way scaling offers researchers the opportunity to search systematically for meaningful patterns of cognitive homogeneity and diversity in mental models of competitor definition, but without unduly influencing the outcomes of their studies by virtue of the elicitation techniques employed. In this way, these techniques, which neither force consensus nor diversity, enable the researcher to capitalize on the strengths associated with existing idiographic and nomothetic knowledge elicitation procedures, without falling prey to either of their associated weaknesses. An additional useful feature of these hybrid techniques, is that they yield indices of differential cognition, which in turn may prove suitable for validating the approach, through the identification of correlations between these indices and theoretically meaningful variables exogenous to the mapping exercise.[2]

Research agenda

Supported by appropriately designed rigorous empirical studies, the emerging body of socio-cognitive theory of competition outlined in this chapter stands to greatly enrich the theory and practice of strategic management. To the extent that we can better understand the processes by which actors create, legitimize, destroy and recreate industries and markets this work might not only have considerable implications for the regulation of competition, but could also inform the design of interventions to facilitate organizational learning and strategic renewal at the level of the individual

---

[2] Interestingly, in a parallel development within the field of strategic management, Ginsberg (1989) has advocated a similar approach for investigating the way in which top management teams in organizations pursuing diversification strategies construe their business portfolios.

firm. Presently, however, theory building is running well ahead of supporting empirical research, with a rapid succession of concepts, frameworks and testable propositions having evolved over a relatively short time-span. Matters are not helped by the fact that differing authors have generated alternative concepts to describe essentially the same phenomena. Thus, for example, Porac et al. (1989) employ the term 'primary competitive group' as a cognitive analogue to the conventional notion of the strategic group, while Lant and Baum (1995) speak of 'competitive sets'. Peteraf and Shanley (1997), in contrast, adopt the label 'cognitive strategic groups' in the development of their theory of strategic group identity, a term which Lant and Phelps (1999) also favour. Clearly there is a need for scholars to reflect at some length before further terms are introduced into what is very rapidly becoming an over-crowded field.

As we have seen, theory development in this area has been amassed largely on the basis of reviews of the extant literature in adjacent sub-fields, in conjunction with studies based on limited research designs and/or inadequate samples. The above conceptual criticisms notwithstanding, if these promising theoretical leads are to be thoroughly investigated, the development of new procedures for the elicitation of knowledge in a form amenable to systematic, large-scale, longitudinal, multi-level comparisons is now vital. Hence, although the findings reported in later chapters of this book were amassed over a decade ago, they are as relevant now as they were then to the advancement of this rapidly expanding field of inquiry.

Three unresolved issues in particular stand out as especially pressing at the present time, as pressing now as they were at the time of data collection:

1. The extent to which measurable features of actors' mental models of competitor definition correlate with measurable strategic behaviours and measurable features of the organization and its environment;
2. The extent to which and in what ways actors within a given industry hold similar or diverse mental models of competitor definition;
3. The extent to which these mental models remain stable or change over time.

The study reported in this volume, sought to apply the modified repertory grid methods briefly outlined in the previous section, in order to address each of these substantive issues in turn. Before considering the finer details of these methods and the findings of the investigation, however, we turn to explore the important historical context in which the fieldwork was undertaken.

3
The Research Context

The purpose of this chapter is to present a brief historical overview of the UK residential estate agency industry, the industry in which the current study was undertaken, centred on the major events that occurred over the 10–15 years leading up to the period in which the fieldwork took place. This is necessary for two reasons: (1) to establish that the context in which the fieldwork took place was an appropriate setting in which to address the substantive concerns of the study; and (2) to provide a backcloth against which we can evaluate the significance of the findings to be reported in later chapters.

It is evident from the previous chapter that the diverse research objectives which the present study was designed to accomplish required an industry that had long passed through the earliest stages of its development. As we have seen, social constructionist notions, such as Porac et al.'s (1989) competitive enactment conception, and related conceptions, such as the industry recipe notion (Grinyer & Spender, 1979a, 1979b; Spender, 1989) and the notion of the cognitive life-cycle (Levenhagen et al., 1993), posit that as industries evolve beyond the initial stage of basic emergence actors' mental models of competitive space should converge to form highly unified perceptions of reality, particularly when, as in the residential estate agency industry, competitors interact with one another on a frequent basis, directly or indirectly, through common customers and/or suppliers. Should we fail to detect empirical evidence of such perceptual convergence, or conversely, should we find evidence of widespread cognitive diversity in this type of industry, we would have to reconsider afresh the boundary conditions pertaining to this rapidly developing body of socio-cognitive theory.

However, in order to explore the extent to which mental models of competitive space change or remain stable in the face of significant changes in market conditions, we require an industry characterized by considerable environmental instability or volatility, i.e. an industry with a marked tendency to suffer significant environmental jolts from time-to-time. Should it transpire – in this type of industry – that mental models were highly stable, over a significant period of time, this would be very strong supporting evidence for the argument that the reason mature businesses and/or industries fall into subsequent decline is due, at least in part, to cognitive inertia on the part of strategists, i.e. the inability of strategists to revise their mental models sufficiently quickly to be able to adapt their organizations to the changing conditions of the marketplace. Furthermore, an industry with this particular combination of features is a potentially fertile ground for exploring the empirical linkages between cognition and strategic behaviour and performance. This type of industry is a particularly interesting arena in which to explore such linkages, due to the fact that there is considerable pressure on firms to improve or maintain their competitive positions, accompanied by continual uncertainty regarding market conditions. Clearly in this type of industry there is a relatively high probability that strategic cognition is of major importance to individuals and the organizations in which they operate. Should empirical relationships between measurable features of actors' mental models of competitive space, and measurable features of strategic behaviour and organizational performance fail to emerge in a study carried out within this type of industry, it would be difficult to envisage a context in which such relationships would be detectable.

In sum, the present research objectives require an industry which has entered the later stages of its life cycle, yet also exhibits considerable volatility. Such an industry provides a critical test-bed in which to explore all three of the research questions set out in Chapter 2. Should we fail to detect in this type of industry evidence of high levels of homogeneity in actors' revealed mental models of competitive space, together with high levels of cognitive stability (in the face of significant changes in market conditions) this would imply the need to reconsider anew the nature and status of several of the key building block underpinning the body of socio-cognitive theory outlined in previous chapters.

The UK residential estate agency industry

One industry in particular, which appears to meet these criteria and would, therefore, seem to be highly appropriate for pursuing the present research agenda is the UK residential estate agency industry.[1] As we shall see, this

---

[1] For the purposes of this study, attention was confined to the residential sales sector of the industry, since it is this sector in particular that underwent a number of dramatic changes in the years leading up to the fieldwork, ones that made for such an interesting context in which to explore the substantive issues identified in Chapter 2, although of course it should be recognized that the estate agency industry as a whole encompasses several other diverse spheres of activity, not least of which are commercial and industrial lettings and the management of residential property.

well-established industry underwent some dramatic changes in the years leading up to the fieldwork reported in later chapters, ones that rendered it an ideal context in which to address the substantive concerns of this study. The origins of the modern estate agency profession can be traced back to the last century. Following the industrial revolution, patterns of land and property ownership changed dramatically from a situation in which a minority of highly privileged landowners possessed vast estates – which tended to remain within the same families from generation-to-generation – to a situation in which land and property ownership became much more widespread. Prior to this time, on the relatively few occasions such services were required, the related functions of estate agency and auctioneering were commonly undertaken by members of the legal profession. With such dramatic changes in patterns of land and property ownership, however, came the need for these activities to be undertaken formally as a specialist field of practice. In this way the practice of real estate gradually passed from being a minor task occasionally performed by lawyers, to a separate profession with its own identity (Centre for Business Research, 1986).[2]

The primary function of the modern residential estate agent is to act as an intermediary between vendors (those wishing to sell their properties) and would-be purchasers. During the process of selling a property, an estate agent will advise his or her client on an asking price, prepare written details, photographs and publicity proposals, advise prospective purchasers of the property's availability, execute an advertising programme, escort prospective purchasers over the property, assure him or herself of the purchaser's financial standing and brief his/her client's solicitor on the sale. Other services provided by residential estate agents include surveys, valuations, insurance brokerage and overseeing the letting and renting of property (Key Note, 1986, 1992). While, in principle, estate agents have a responsibility to both parties, they act on behalf of vendors, their fee-paying clients, and so would-be purchasers should be on their guard. However, it is not necessary (though perhaps advisable) for vendors to employ the services of an estate agent and Key Note (1986) – drawing on evidence from a 'Which?' survey – estimate that somewhere between 25 and 30 percent of the market is accounted for by the DIY sector.

Currently, there are very few restrictions governing the practice of estate agency within the UK and, with the notable exception of bankrupts – as specified in the Estate Agents Act 1979 – virtually anyone can set up in business.[3] Regulation of the industry is achieved mainly through three

---

[2] In the immediate years leading up to the fieldwork, however, the legal profession re-entered the estate agency industry, with a number of solicitors' offices offering a complete range of services from property sales through to auctioneering.

[3] Whilst the Estate Agents Act 1979 expressly prohibits bankrupts from setting up in business as 'estate agents', nevertheless they can work for someone who is.

professional bodies, namely, the Royal Institute of Chartered Surveyors (RICS), Incorporated Society of Valuers & Auctioneers (ISVA), and the National Association of Estate Agents (NAEA), who impose strict codes of conduct and standards of practice on their members. Membership of these associations is on an individual rather than a corporate basis, and is restricted to those meeting the criteria of admission, namely, the passing of certain examinations and/or a period of practical experience.

Key Note (1986) reported that there was a total of 28,000 members across the three professional bodies, which, allowing for some inevitable overlap of membership, left an estimated 25,000 individual estate agents in practice who did not belong to any recognized association. In view of the fact that there are so few legal restrictions imposed on estate agents, coupled with membership of professional associations being a voluntary matter, it is perhaps not too surprising that the industry had suffered something of an 'image problem' in the years leading up to this study.

According to the Centre for Business research at Manchester Business School, the industry is divided with regard to the issue of how business transactions should be conducted. Typically, members of the RICS and ISVA support a professional approach to the conduct of business trans-actions, seeking to ensure their members are sufficiently qualified by exam-ination and experience to offer a competent service. Others, however, view the industry primarily as a commercial venture in which the role of estate agents is to act in a brokerage capacity in order to secure the most profitable deal (Centre for Business Research, 1986).

Increasingly over the years, estate agency businesses have come to provide a diversified range of services, in what appears to be something of a general trend away from their traditional, relatively narrow function, towards one-stop home purchase packages. Following changes in the legis-lation governing the operation of financial services companies in the period immediately prior to the commencement of fieldwork, it was estimated that up to 25 percent of estate agency businesses' income was derived from the provision of financial services or related valuations and services (Key Note, 1987). It is evident that in order for business trans-actions to be successful within this industry, the various functional special-ists must be highly inter-dependent on one another. Properties which are under-valued – relative to the market norm – will undoubtedly sell quickly, but at a loss both to the vendor and the agent. Conversely, properties which are over-valued – relative to the market norm – will take longer to sell, particularly in periods of low activity within the housing market. In order to ensure effective sales, functional specialists such as valuers, negotiators, and surveyors must regularly maintain close contact with one another, exchanging valuable information regarding market conditions. In short, organizational and functional boundaries must be crossed frequently during the course of business transactions in this industry.

This high level of functional and organizational inter-dependence associated with the residential estate agency industry is a particularly attractive feature from the point of view of testing the validity of competitive enactment and related notions. To the extent that the central tenets of this social constructionist theory concerning the convergence of mental models of competitor definition across organizational and functional subgroups over time is valid, we would expect to find strong evidence of such belief similarity in this particular industry.

Major developments in the industry

As noted in Chapter 1, one of the potential benefits of employing cognitive methods in studies of competition is that these techniques may yield useful insights into the problems facing particular industries and firms. In the years leading up to this study the residential estate agency industry in the UK underwent some rather dramatic changes, ones that make the present investigation particularly valuable from a practitioner's perspective.

The entrance of national financial institutions

During the 1980s, the UK residential estate agency industry changed from being an industry in which large numbers of small firms – the vast majority of which were single office concerns – dominated local markets, to one in which an increasingly smaller number of large financial services institutions came to dominate the national scene. According to Dietrich and Holmes (1990) the major reason for these changes was the realization on the part of the large financial institutions (i.e. banks, building societies and insurance companies) of the increased opportunities afforded for marketing their financial services by entry into the estate agency sector.[4]

The rapid pace with which the financial institutions achieved extensive national coverage in estate agency was accomplished through merger and acquisition activity carried out on a vast scale. The first major entrant into the estate agency sector was Lloyds Bank in May 1982, through its launch of the 'Black Horse' chain. From the outset, the intention was to operate as a totally professional company, with only the best firms with the highest of reputations being acquired. Existing partners were retained to run the

---

[4] Prior to changes in legislation brought about by the Conservative Government, which came into effect in 1987, estate agents and building societies were precluded from establishing formal ties with one another, by virtue of the Building Societies Acts.

companies under contractual arrangements with Lloyds that guarantied complete professional freedom:

'Each of the agencies acquired retains its local image and reflects the requirements of the market in its particular area. The client has the benefits of local knowledge and the personal service of a compact company unit run entirely by professionals, who are also able to offer the benefits of a large group in terms of training, product development and general resources. This is in direct contrast with other organisations in similar positions, where service can be entirely self-oriented and not client based' (Centre for Business Research, 1986: 90).

During the process of establishing the Black Horse chain, Lloyds held joint consultations with both the RICS and the ISVA, in order to ensure that no conflicts of interest arose through its acquisition activities. According to the Centre for Business Research at Manchester Business School, the relationship between Black Horse Agencies and their parent organization, Lloyds bank, was strictly an arms-length arrangement, as evidenced by the fact that for every mortgage supplied by the clearing bank between ten and fifteen building society mortgages were sold in addition (Centre for Business Research, 1986).

Other large financial services institutions quickly followed the lead of Lloyds. The Prudential Assurance Company, one of the largest life assurance companies in the UK, entered the estate agency sector in June 1985, through the acquisition of Ekins, Dilley & Handley, a small 12 branch chain located throughout East Anglia. The chain was re-launched in January 1986 as Prudential Property Services (PPS). Within the relatively short period between its initial launch and the peak of the boom in the housing market, during the summer of 1988, PPS managed to amass some 800 branches, through an extensive nationwide programme of mergers and acquisitions. One of the most progressive innovations in the practice of estate agency at that time was introduced by this organization. The 'chain break' scheme was an attempt to make PPS much more attractive to potential customers than its competitors, by offering an opportunity for would-be purchasers – subject to certain conditions and an independent evaluation – to dispose of their existing properties by selling them directly to the Prudential.

Other large established financial institutions that joined the quest to dominate the estate agency industry in the 1980s included the Royal Insurance Group, General Accident, and the Nationwide Anglia, Abbey National and Halifax building societies. Unfortunately, however, as Table 3.1 shows, the large-scale entrance of the financial services institutions into the estate agency sector turned out to be nothing short of an unmitigated disaster, with annual losses running to seven and eight figure numbers.

Table 3.1 Losses associated with the major UK estate agency chains during the first half of 1989

Agency	Number of branches	£ million
Prudential	800	24.7
Royal Life	782	14.5
Halifax	709	N/A
General Accident	600	9.0
Black Horse	562	5.9
Hambros Countrywide	496	6.6
Cornerstone/Abbey National	430	9.5
Hamptons (estimated)	150	3.0

Source: Dietrich & Holmes (1991) – based on figures published in the Financial Times.
Note: (N/A = not available).

In the period following the peak in house sales experienced during the summer of 1988, the financial institutions severely contracted, both in terms of staff numbers and the number of branches, throughout the country. Royal Life Estates (at that time the largest UK estate agency business), for example, reduced the number of its offices from 760 in May 1990, to 608 in December 1991. Within the same period, Halifax Property Services and Black Horse Agencies contracted from 709 to 581 and from 559 to 398 branches, respectively. Other chains, the most notable being Prudential Property Services, which reduced the number of its offices to 700 in May 1990, subsequently withdrew from the sector altogether (Key Note, 1990, 1992).

Notwithstanding the heavy losses experienced during this period, the national chains had considerable assets at their disposal, which they were able to deploy in order to promote an enhanced image *vis-à-vis* their rivals. As Table 3.2 shows, these organizations invested major sums of money in advertising campaigns, in an attempt to establish new corporate identities in the mind of the consumer. The Halifax unveiled plans to spend an estimated £6 million in 1989 alone on a promotional campaign, with Prudential and Black Horse Agencies reputed to have spent some £6.8 million and £3.6 million, respectively. Nationwide Anglia, the first of the national chains to begin advertising on television, in early 1988, is reckoned to have spent a total of £3 million during the following year (Key Note, 1989). Irrespective of whether or not such campaigns were effective in countering the public perception of 'a pretty poor job at a very high price', the slogan which has come to be the standard trademark of estate agents over the years, these figures clearly demonstrate the fact that these, comparatively wealthier, institutions were capable of deploying considerable resources in the battle for competitive advantage, resources to which their smaller, local counterparts did not have access. The conclusion to be drawn is that the national chains (and to a lesser extent some of the

Table 3.2 Estate agents' TV and press advertising expenditure during 1987 and 1988

Agency	1987[†]	1988[†]
Hampton & Son	114	814
Knight, Frank & Rutley	177	905
Nationwide Anglia	1,461	1,339
Prudential Property Services	504	2,098
Savill	98	810
Strutt & Parker	94	687
Black Horse	–	926
GA Property Services	–	917
Humberts	–	387
Jackson-Stops & Staff	–	312
John DWood	–	399

Source: Key Note (1989) – based on data from MEAL.
Note: ([†] = moving annual totals (£000) to June.)

larger regionally based companies) amassed considerable market power in the mid-to-late 1980s, through a combination of high profile advertising campaigns and the development of extensive branch networks.

However, given that the market for estate agency services was traditionally a local one, in order to assess the true impact of these structural changes on competition, Dietrich and Holmes (1990, 1991) argued it was necessary to observe changes in the extent of market concentration within localized geographical areas, following the entrance of the national chains. Empirical research by Dietrich and Holmes (1990, 1991) into the dynamics of the market structure of the estate agency industry in the Tyneside region of north eastern England, illustrates the way in which the changes that took place nationally during the 1980s had a profound influence on local competition. According to Dietrich and Holmes, in the early 1980s there were 79 firms active in the Tyneside region, with the four largest firms accounting for 15.7 percent of the total industry. However, following the entrance into the local market of Black Horse, GA, Halifax, and Prudential, together with two additional relatively large local firms, the Northern Rock Building Society and Parks Estates, the percentage of the total industry accounted for by the four largest firms increased by a staggering 86 percent. These six companies, which did not exist within the locality of this study in 1987, accounted for 43 percent of the total industry size just one year later.[5]

---

[5] More precisely, the four firm concentration ratio, which measures the percentage of an industry's size accounted for by the largest four firms in that industry, rose by 86 percent from 15.7 percent to 36.1 percent (for technical details see Dietrich & Holmes, 1990).

The results of this study clearly indicate that the rapid and high profile entrance of the major national chains into estate agency during the mid-late 1980s had a highly significant impact on the way in which businesses were beginning to compete within this industry. One of the major consequences of the changes that took place nationally, is that the markets for estate agency services was becoming increasingly concentrated at the local level.

Estate agency co-operatives

The fact that the major national chains had attained such obvious visibility in the marketplace does not mean that the smaller, local firms were necessarily without market power, especially if they joined forces on a co-operative basis. That such cooperation can achieve dramatic results can be illustrated with reference to events in the City of Sheffield during the mid-1980s. Prior to 1985, Sheffield based estate agents advertised their properties in the Sheffield Morning Telegraph. However, when the newspaper requested that the agents maintain an agreed level of advertising – which previously had not been agreed but had been merely a threshold for cheaper rates – the agents collectively withdrew their advertising and established their own property newspaper, a factor which undoubtedly led to the closure of the Sheffield Morning Telegraph.[6]

A number of co-operative ventures were established within the estate agency industry during the period encompassed by the present study, with a view to increasing the market power of smaller businesses. Property World, for example, based in Halifax, West Yorkshire, was established as a marketing organization to give a national marketing image to smaller independent estate agencies throughout the UK. Another example is the 'national homelink service,' developed by the NAEA on a not-for-profit basis, in an attempt to expand the usage of its members' organizations by linking them up across the country, thereby enabling would-be purchasers seeking to move long distances to find suitable properties without having to search through numerous estate agents' offices in remote geographical regions. The National Homes Network (NHN) is a further example of a co-operative which was established in an effort to expand the business of smaller agencies on a national basis, involving the simple installation of a terminal by member offices, giving vendors and purchasers an instant link to the entire territory covered. Other co-operatives were formed at a local level, in an attempt to strengthen the hand of smaller estate

---

[6] At the time of the fieldwork, the Sheffield Newspapers Group – publishers of the *Sheffield Morning Telegraph* – had recently re-established the newspaper on a weekly basis and taken over production of the Sheffield property paper. Following this development, the property paper was issued as a free supplement in the *Sheffield Telegraph*.

agencies. Within the Derbyshire area, for example, several independent firms came together in order to advertise under the marketing banner of 'Stag Agencies', thereby creating greater market power with a combined total of 12 offices. Participation in co-operative ventures is potentially of great value to smaller firms, as a means of gaining increased market power by virtue of the enhanced marketing capabilities derived through membership of a larger umbrella organization. Other potential benefits which smaller agencies might gain through co-operative action include better staff training, enhanced purchasing power in the acquisition of basic office materials and greater access to much needed information.

Changes in the housing market

The performance of residential estate agency businesses is inextricably linked to the state of the housing market, a market which has proven to be highly volatile over the years. Two factors in particular that affect the income and profitability of residential estate agents are the number of properties sold and the extent to which house prices increase or decrease within a given period.

In recent years we have witnessed an unprecedented boom in the housing market. Annual increases in house prices between 15 and 20 percent have now become commonplace in many parts of the UK, but this a far cry from the state of the housing market at the time the fieldwork associated with this study was undertaken. Historically, peak periods of activity in the housing market have tended to last only a matter of months, with the laws of supply and demand creating alternately a buyer's and seller's market. At the time of the study, however, the UK housing market had experienced something of a major recession, to the extent that in many regions, most notably London and the south east of England, the market had all but collapsed.

During the 1970s and 1980s, house prices climbed to what were then record levels, with substantial increases reported annually. In 1985, for example, house prices in the UK rose by an average of 10 percent, compared with an average increase of 14 percent during the previous year. However, as Table 3.3 shows, such averages conceal considerable regional differences, particularly between areas north and south of the Home Counties. Nevertheless, these figures serve to illustrate the fact that house prices generally increased throughout the UK during this period, albeit to varying extents from one part of the country to another.

Paralleling these increases in the price of houses, the trend towards owner-occupation also increased, to the extent that Key Note concluded that the 1970s and 1980s may well go down in history as 'the age of home ownership' (Key Note, 1986: 3). By the mid-1980s, 60.1 percent of the total UK housing tenure was owner-occupied, compared with 28.5 percent rented in the public sector and 11.4 percent rented privately (Key Note,

1987). As Table 3.4 shows, home ownership grew slowly in the 1970s with rather more dramatic increases in the 1980s, not least due to the fact that local authorities engaged in a mass programme of council house sales.

However, it is evident from these data that the growth in home ownership was achieved primarily through an increase in the amount of money lent on mortgages. Research by Key Note (1989) indicated that between 1977 and 1987 building society lending (gross advances) alone increased by 41.3 percent, while overall lending rose by 578 percent. According to Key Note, records of bank lending from 1983 to 1987 reveal that mortgage investment almost trebled within this four-year period. Apparently, prior to

Table 3.3   House price increases for various geographical regions of the UK during 1985

Region	Percentage Increase
Scotland	5
Northern Ireland	56
North of England	6
Yorkshire and Humberside	7
North West	5
Wales	6
East Midlands	8
West Midlands	7
South West	8
Outer-South East	11
Outer-Metropolitan	14
Greater London	19
National Average	10

Source: Key Note (1986).

Table 3.4   Percentage changes in home ownership in the UK, 1971–1987

Year	Owned outright	Owned with mortgage	Total
1971	22	27	49
1975	22	28	50
1977	23	28	51
1979	22	30	52
1981	23	31	54
1983	24	33	57
1984	24	35	59
1985	24	37	61
1986	25	38	63
1987	24	39	63

Source: Key Note (1989) – based on figures from OPCS/General Household Survey.

1983 insurance companies had steadily been increasing their loans, but from 1983 onwards almost trebled them.

Unfortunately, however, as far too many people discovered to their personal cost, the increases in home ownership and the mortgage boom experienced during the 1980s were accompanied by dramatic increases in the number of households in arrears with their monthly payments. Worse still, the number of repossessions also escalated, as shown in Table 3.5.

All-told, the problem of the number of households in arrears with their mortgages grew seven-fold between 1979 and 1987, followed closely by a six-fold increase in the number of repossessions during the same period. While the number of repossessions appeared to be slackening somewhat during the relatively brief 18-month period from January 1988 to the end of June 1989, unfortunately, the number almost trebled in 1990, approaching 44,000 (Key Note, 1992).

During the summer of 1988, the housing market experienced a major peak in activity, following the decision of the government to abolish multiple mortgage income-tax relief. This decision, which took effect from August 1988, served to fuel yet further increases in house prices, as potential purchasers rushed to beat the deadline. The net consequence was that many home owners, especially first-time buyers in London and the south east of England, undertook financial commitments that rendered them extremely vulnerable to the effects of subsequent increases in interest rates.[7]

Table 3.5 Building society mortgage arrears and repossessions, 1979–1988

Year	Loans	In arrears	Repossessed
1979	5,264,000	8,420	2,530
1980	5,396,000	13,490	3,020
1981	5,505,000	18,720	4,240
1982	5,664,000	28,600	5,950
1983	5,949,000	32,120	7,320
1984	6,354,000	50,200	10,870
1985	6,705,000	61,020	16,770
1986	7,071,000	56,560	20,930
1987	7,197,000	61,220	22,930
1988 (mid)	7,230,000	57,880	9,770

Source: Key Note (1989) – based on data supplied by the Building Societies Association.

---

[7] At a more technical level, as reported by the Bank of England in its Quarterly Bulletin for November 1991, household income gearing (gross interest payments as a proportion of disposable income) rose from 5 percent to 13 percent in the decade from 1980 to 1990, whilst housing related capital gearing (mortgage debt as a percentage of the value of owner-occupied housing stock) increased from 15 percent to 25 percent over the same period.

House prices began to fall rapidly in the wake of rising interest rates during 1990, followed by rising unemployment in 1991. As sales fell to barely half their normal annual total, estate agents began to contract drastically, to the extent that more than 20 percent of the 20 leading estate agents offices were closed (Key Note, 1992). As noted earlier, one leading chain, the Prudential, withdrew from the sector altogether – with trading and purchase losses estimated to be somewhere in the region of £300 million.

As a result of the collapse of the housing market that followed, the financial institutions were faced with a major dilemma as to what they should do about the growing number households whose monthly mortgage payments were seriously in arrears. With many households in possession of properties valued at a price lower than the outstanding mortgage (particularly in London and the south east of England), a phenomenon known within the industry as 'negative equity', and limited prospects of a successful sale – even at a greatly reduced price – a major dilemma faced by mortgage lenders was whether to re-schedule the debt or, alternatively, repossess a dwelling for which there was relatively little market. Given this state of affairs, not surprisingly there were a number of calls for government intervention, both to assist those in serious difficulties with their mortgage re-payments and in order to police the future conduct of mortgage lenders and estate agency businesses. In December 1991, the Government agreed a 'mortgage rescue' scheme in an attempt to help stem the rising tide of repossessions.

Operating practices

As noted earlier, the estate agency industry is an industry which has suffered something of an 'image problem' over the years, a problem that greatly intensified particularly in the period of the housing market boom during the summer of 1988 and the long-term recession that subsequently ensued. Throughout the 1980s growing concerns were expressed by a variety of bodies as to whether or not it was advisable for the estate agency industry to continue to be responsible for the development and maintenance of standards, with repeated calls to bring in much tougher controls. The rising tide of mortgage arrears and repossessions following the short-term boom of the summer of 1988 brought about renewed calls for tighter legislation and stricter controls on the operating practices of estate agency businesses.[8]

---

[8] See for example: 8/2/90 *Scotsman* ('Protection from cowboy estate agents demanded' – p. 15), *Financial Times* ('Tough laws urged to curb dishonest estate agents' – p. 9), 1/3/90 *Financial Times* ('Estate agents are criticised' – p. 7), 10/3/90 *Telegraph* ('Estate agents face tougher test' – p. 29), *Financial Times* ('Borrie calls for legal curbs on estate agents' – p. 6), 16/3/90 *Investors Chronicle* ('Clamp-down on estate agents' – p. 31), 20/4/90 *Financial Times* ('Estate agents to be placed under stricter controls' – p. 9).

In the following years estate agents were legally constrained to reduce the size of their sale boards to 0.5 square metres and limit them to one per property. Furthermore, the Office of Fair Trading, *inter-alia*, recommended extensions to the Estate Agents Act 1979 to include powers to warn and/or ban serious or persistent offenders who misled in advertisements (including particulars of properties), a banning of offenders who bid up prices, a requirement that 'health warnings' be included in estate agents' contracts to explain obscure terms, a requirement that agents should make written disclosures of their involvement in buying or selling property, a suggestion that pressure on customers to take other services (e.g. the provision of finance) be discouraged, and a requirement that information about commission and other charges should always be provided in writing (Key Note, 1990). In addition, the Office of Fair Trading also recommended that the Trade Descriptions Act should be extended to cover property sales.[9] However, the Office of Fair Trading did not support calls by the main professional bodies to introduce minimum standards of competence for estate agents, on the grounds that the majority of complaints against agents are of an ethical nature rather than a question of professional competence (Key Note, 1990).

Other developments

There were three other on-going developments underway at the time the fieldwork in connection with this study was undertaken which perhaps are worthy of brief comment before concluding this overview of the industry. Firstly, there was a battle in progress regarding the future of conveyancing, the outcome of which would undoubtedly have an effect on the future practice of estate agency, particularly for businesses tied to the financial institutions. In an effort to widen the scope for competition there had been calls to extend the then recent changes to the laws relating to conveyancing, in order that the financial institutions could undertake their own conveyancing – much to the displeasure of licensed conveyancers and solicitors.[10] According to Key Note (1990), the law Society, by return, would like to have seen the introduction of a legal code for estate agents (a proposal which the Government had already rejected), stricter controls over mortgages (a proposal which would be difficult if not impossible to police),

---

[9] Subsequently this happened. Under the Property Misdescriptions Act, which came into effect during 1993, estate agents are liable to criminal prosecution by the Office of Fair Trading if they attempt to misrepresent properties through inaccurate and/or misleading information. The Act applies to whatever is shown, said or written about a property.

[10] In 1985 the Administration of Justice Act created a separate profession of 'licensed conveyancer' specifically to create a source of direct competition for solicitors, who prior to this Act had held a monopoly on this element of house purchase.

a statutory cooling-off period in order to enable borrowers to take independent legal advice (highly unlikely given the general push towards the speeding up of the exchange and completion of house sales contracts and the move towards 'one-stop shopping'), and the mandatory disclosure of insurance commissions (not required under the Financial Services Act for 'tied lenders') or other remuneration (a requirement which, ultimately may have entailed agents having to reveal to prospective purchasers their deals with vendors, an unlikely scenario). Given the Government of the day's adherence to *laissez-faire* policies, Key Note (1990) regarded it unlikely that any of these proposals mooted by the Law Society would achieve success.

The second development underway at the commencement of this study that would likely have had a bearing on the future well-being of estate agency businesses was the abandoning of the then recently introduced Community Charge, or 'poll tax', in favour of the Council Tax. Key Note (1992) warned that this change would in all probability bring about a return of the effect on house prices and saleability that used to be exercised by rateable values.[11]

Finally, it appeared that further structural changes might have been afoot. Particularly noteworthy in this respect was the apparent growth in the number of franchized independent estate agency businesses operating in the UK. Key Note (1992) reported that Century 21– an operation which originated in the USA, but highly active in several major countries – was launched in the UK in 1988. According to Key Note (1992), this organization had set itself a target to open more than 650 offices throughout the UK by 1998, although the target date was said to be flexible. Clearly an organization with such ambitious plans would require careful monitoring, particularly in the climate that prevailed at the time this study was undertaken.

Relevance of the industry to the research objectives

This brief and somewhat dated history of the development of the UK residential estate agency industry serves to identify the main events that took place in the decade leading up to the period in which the fieldwork

---

[11] Prior to 1990, local amenities were paid for by means of 'local authority rates', a system in which households were charged a set fee graded according to the area in which their property was situated. A single fee was charged per dwelling, irrespective of the number of occupants. Under the Community Charge system, in contrast, a set fee was levied to each individual over the age of 18 years dwelling within a given property. The Council Tax system, which came into effect on 1st April 1993, is something of a hybrid system, in that houses are graded according to the type of property *and* the geographical area in which the property is situated. As with the original rating system, a single fee is levied per household. However, unlike the rating system, under the present system there is a 25 percent discount for sole occupants.

associated with the study to be reported in the remaining chapters was undertaken. In order to better contextualize the findings, I have also outlined some of the more salient developments that took place over the three-year period immediately following the completion of data collection in connection with this study.

The conclusion to be drawn from this discussion is that this industry is an ideal context in which to address the substantive concerns of this study. The UK residential estate agency industry is a mature industry characterized by high levels of cross-functional and inter-organizational dependency. These features are particularly attractive for exploring the extent to which actors' mental models are homogeneous or diverse. To the extent that the social constructionist notions outlined earlier concerning the convergence of actors' mental models of competitive industry structures are correct, we would expect to find evidence that such mental models are highly homogeneous within this particular industry.

As we have seen, the UK residential estate agency industry is also an industry, which, both at the time of data collection and subsequently, has passed through some extremely turbulent times. As such, it constitutes an ideal context in which to investigate validity of the cognitive inertia hypothesis associated with the body of socio-cognitive theory outlined in the previous chapter. Given the degree of changes confronting this industry in the periods leading up to, during and immediately after the two waves of data collection, should we find that participants' mental models of competitive space remained stable from time 1 (T1) to time 2 (T2) this would be very strong supporting evidence indeed for the cognitive inertia hypothesis advanced by Porac and Thomas (1990), but which hitherto has been investigated on only a limited basis, using inadequate research designs, as discussed in Chapter 2.

Finally, to the extent that we are able to obtain meaningful correlations between measurable features of actors' mental models of competitor definition and exogenous variables of theoretical interest (especially measurable aspects of strategic behaviour and organizational performance) in this industry, this would provide strong supporting evidence for the assertion that cognition and strategic choice become inextricably intertwined with the material conditions of the marketplace in industries that have entered the later stages of their life-cycles. Clearly, if embryonic notions such as competitive enactment and the cognitive mapping tools employed to investigate them are to be validated, it is vital that researchers are able to demonstrate such linkages. Given the obvious importance of competitor awareness in the estate agency industry, the failure to find evidence of meaningful empirical linkages between cognition, strategic behaviour and organizational performance in this industry would raise uncomfortable questions concerning the (lack of) validity of the socio-cognitive theory outlined earlier and/or the research instruments employed to investigate competitor cognition. For some, it would undoubtedly add to the claim that the theory of strategic groups and associated conceptions, based on the structure-conduct performance paradigm of industrial-organization economics, is found wanting (cf. Barney & Hoskisson, 1990; Hatten & Hatten, 1987).

As noted in Chapter 1, the fieldwork associated with the present study took place during the 18-month period from July 1989 to December 1990, using a two-wave panel design. It is evident from this brief historical analysis of the industry, that this was a particularly timely period in which to gather the data. As we have seen, during the period leading up to this study the industry had experienced some major upheavals:

1. The entrance of the financial institutions (with considerable wealth at their disposal which enabled them to establish extensive branch networks on a national basis). The growth of these national chains was accomplished very rapidly, accompanied by high levels of advertising expenditure in an effort to establish market dominance. This appeared to have paid handsome dividends, with evidence to suggest that the industry had become highly concentrated at the local level.
2. A growth in co-operative ventures, particularly amongst some of the smaller firms – both on a national and local basis – in an attempt to gain greater market power.
3. A steady growth of activity in the housing market and increases in house prices, partly as a result of the extensive programme of council house sales engendered by changes in central government policy.
4. Following the entrance of the national chains, residential estate agency businesses increasingly diversified throughout the 1980s in a trend away from their traditional functions of surveying, valuation, sales, and property management towards more general one-stop house purchase packages. In turn, this led to an increase in the provision of mortgages and other financial services by estate agents (and a concomitant increase in the number of households in arrears with their payments and, worse still, those facing repossession).

In sum, the decade leading up to this study was a particularly buoyant period for the UK residential estate agency industry. At the time of data collection, however, the fortunes of this industry were in the process of change. During the first wave of data collection – which ran from mid-July 1989 to October 1989 – a major recession in the housing market was just beginning to emerge. By the time the second wave of data collection took place (September 1990 to mid-December 1990), the recession had deepened considerably and its effects were being felt throughout the whole of the UK. The period immediately subsequent to the fieldwork saw the recession deepen still further, with firms reducing the scale of their operations considerably. One major national chain withdrew from the industry altogether. Added to this, there were significant changes to the legislation governing the practices of estate agency businesses, amid increasing calls – from a variety of quarters – for the policing of the estate agency industry to be tightened, with an end to the era of self-regulation.

Conclusion

We began this chapter by establishing that in order to fulfil the research agenda outlined in Chapter 2, we required an industry passing through turbulent times, which had also entered the later stages of its life cycle. It is evident from this discussion that we have found such an industry.

4
Research Methods and Design

This chapter is concerned with the basic mechanics of the programme of empirical research reported in the remainder of the book. Its primary purpose is to describe the development and psychometric evaluation of the various research instruments employed in the study. Readers who are less interested in the precise technical details of the study may wish to by-pass or skim this chapter on first reading, returning to it for reference purposes, as and when necessary.

Several new instruments were designed for the present study, while others were adapted from previously published work. We shall begin with a brief description of each instrument in turn, together with a discussion of the rationale for its incorporation in the study.

The research instruments: Background and development

The competitor analysis questionnaire (CAQ)

If cognitive maps are to be compared systematically, as noted by Markoczy and Goldberg (1995), the maps to be subjected to the comparison process must ultimately be elicited on a systematic basis. In a development paralleling an advance made by Markoczy and Goldberg in the systematic elicitation and comparison of cognitive maps for revealing actors' causal belief systems, competitor cognition was assessed by means of a structured elicitation procedure, devised by the author, in a form that yields data amenable to such large-scale, systematic comparisons, while also ensuring that the elicitation task is personally meaningful to the individual participants (cf. Markoczy & Goldberg, 1995). As noted in Chapter 2, this procedure utilizes a modified repertory grid approach to cognitive assessment – following the lead of Reger (1987), Thomas and Venkatraman (1988), and Walton (1986) – in conjunction with 'three-way scaling' (Arabie et al., 1987) or, equivalently, 'weighted multidimensional scaling' (WMDS) (Schiffman et al., 1981) techniques for the comparison of revealed mental models or cognitive maps. These revealed models take the form of dimensional representations of competitor categories, in which the categories are ploted in multidimensional Euclidean space.

The basic data for the assessment of participants' cognitive maps were elicited by means a structured questionnaire, specifically constructed for the present study. The competitor analysis questionnaire (CAQ) comprises a series of 21 bipolar attribute rating scales (or 'constructs' in Kelly's (1955) terms) which the participants used in order to evaluate their own business organization and some 19 competitors. The competitors were elicited by means of a standard list of categories (or 'elements' in Kelly's (1955) terms), thus ensuring that the research task was personally meaningful to the participants, yet controlled, systematic comparisons could be made at various levels of analysis.

The constructs incorporated in the CAQ were derived through a pilot study in which eight volunteers from separate estate agency organizations were asked to list the attributes which immediately came to mind when differentiating various competitors. This yielded a total of 21 distinguishable attributes. These attributes were formed into a series of seven-point semantic differential scales (Osgood, Suci & Tannenbaum, 1957), as follows: service to vendors (very poor/very good); quality of staff (very poor/very good); service to purchasers (very poor/very good); training of staff (very poor/very good); operating practices (very poor/very good); quality of advertising (very poor/very good); profitability (very low/very high); location of business premises (very poor/very good); size of branch network (very small/very large); range of services (very narrow/very extensive); geographical coverage (very narrow/very extensive); scale of charges (very low-priced/very expensive); degree of personal attention (very low/very high); market share (very small/very large); marketing profile (very low/very high); degree of local knowledge (very limited/very extensive); strategic influence/power (very weak/very strong); amount of advertising (very limited/very extensive); financial resources (very limited/very extensive); links with financial services companies (very limited/very extensive); typical range of properties on sale (very poor/very good).

In order to elicit the elements, the pilot study participants were also asked to list the various types of estate agent which came to mind when thinking about competition within their industry. In addition, a search was made of advertisements placed by estate agency businesses in the Yellow Pages telephone directory and various local property newspapers, in order to ensure that no important categories of estate agent had been omitted. This yielded a total of thirteen types of estate agent, to which seven additional categories (the participant's own business, together with categories denoting major, secondary, and inferior competitors and categories denoting high, medium and low performing firms) were added by the author (see Table 4.1). These additional categories were incorporated in an effort to gain insights into factors that differentiate the successful and unsuccessful

Table 4.1   Categories used to elicit lists of contrasting organizations

1.	My Business
2.	My major competitor
3.	A Solicitor Agent
4.	An Estate Agent Owned by a Building Society
5.	A Traditional Estate Agent
6.	An Estate Agent Owned by an Insurance Company
7.	An Estate Agent Offering a Professional Service
8.	An Estate Agent with a Poor Reputation
9.	An Estate Agent with Chartered Surveyor Status
10.	An Estate Agent Specializing in Exclusive Property
11.	An Estate Agent Specializing in Commercial & Industrial Property
12.	An Estate Agent Specializing in Residential Property
13.	A Secondary Competitor
14.	An Estate Agent with a Good Reputation
15.	A Diversified Estate Agent
16.	An Independent Estate Agent
17.	An Inferior Competitor
18.	A Very Successful Estate Agent
19.	A Moderately Successful Estate Agent
20.	An Unsuccessful Estate Agent

Source: Hodgkinson, 1997b: 929.

players in the minds of the participants, i.e. as a means of revealing the bases of 'the industry recipe' (cf. Grinyer & Spender, 1979a, 1979b; Phillips, 1994; Porac et al., 1989, 1994, 1995; Spender, 1989).

Further pilot interviews were conducted with five fresh volunteers in order to decide which, if any, of the categories and/or attributes could be omitted from the main study on the grounds of redundancy. However, there was unanimous agreement that the complete set of categories and constructs/attributes should be retained in their entirety. Hence, the 20 categories and 21 bipolar rating scales were assembled into a questionnaire booklet.[1]

The participants were instructed to draw up a list of 19 competitors in response to the categories. These were then entered on a prepared strip of paper that could be readily inserted into each page of the booklet, in turn. Each page of the CAQ was devoted to a single attribute. Hence the participants evaluated their own organization and the 19 competitors on a

---

[1] Two further tasks were also incorporated in the final version of CAQ. The participants were instructed to rate the extent to which the 19 competitors elicited in response to the various estate agency categories were similar to and competed with their own business organization. Unfortunately, however, these tasks did not yield data in a form amenable to reliable analyses.

particular attribute rating scale before proceeding to additional scales. Responses to the CAQ formed the raw input data for revealing the participants' mental models of competitive space, reported in later chapters.[2]

As noted in Chapter 2, if the cognitive analysis of business competition is to advance beyond present levels, the time has now come to establish the external validity of the knowledge elicitation procedures employed by exploring the extent to which measurable features of the resulting cognitive maps are correlated with exogenous variables of theoretical interest, such as the background characteristics of participants, their environmental scanning behaviours, and the strategic, structural and performance characteristics of the organization. As we have seen, Porac et al.'s (1989) basic notion of competitive enactment and related conceptions assert that com-

---

[2] It should be noted that the adaptation of the repertory grid technique in this way, i.e. so as to incorporate the use of standardized elements and constructs, is not without its critics. This approach represents a significant departure from Kelly's (1955) *personal construct theory*, the underlying theory upon which the repertory grid technique was originally based. (Personal construct theory asserts that individuals construe the world differently from one another, i.e. they each have a set of constructs which vary from one individual to another.) Consequently, as originally formulated, repertory grid was intended purely as an idiographic technique and, in its purest form, both the elements and constructs are elicited separately for each individual participant. However, as we saw in Chapter 2, this frequently yields data of a form that is difficult to compare meaningfully from one individual to another and for this reason a number of researchers have developed alternative approaches to the construction and analysis of repertory grids (see, for example, Fransella & Bannister, 1977, 2004; Slater, 1976, 1977; Smith & Stewart, 1977). Nevertheless, critics remaining loyal to the Kellyian tradition have argued that many of these developments have, inappropriately, taken repertory grid away from its theoretical origins and are, therefore, unwelcome. The use of grids where elements and constructs are totally provided by the researcher is one such development. According to Phillips (1989, p. 196): 'this kind of grid would be more usefully supplanted by a semantic differential.' In the present case, however, as noted above, a compromise strategy was adopted whereby all of the constructs and the majority of the elements were elicited from a subsample of practising estate agents, rather than researcher imposed. Moreover, the fact that the participants each drew up their own unique list of competitors, albeit in response to a standardized list of categories, meant that they were not forced to make judgements about competitors that were unknown to them. In sum, in designing this study a number of steps were taken to ensure that not only was the knowledge elicitation task as a whole highly meaningful to the participants (or in Kelly's (1955) terms, 'within their range of convenience'), but also the resulting data were in a form that was amenable to systematic comparison at a variety of levels of analysis. In this way, the approach to the elicitation of competitor knowledge embodied in the CAQ is intended to combine the key strengths associated with both the idiographic and nomothetic variants of repertory grid, while minimizing their associated weaknesses (cf. Daniels et al., 1994, 1995, 2002; Hodgkinson, 2002; Reger, 1990a, 1990b; Reger & Huff, 1993; Reger & Palmer, 1996; Spencer et al., 2003; Walton, 1986).

petitor cognition and strategic choice are inextricably intertwined with the material conditions of the marketplace. To the extent that this proposition is valid, it should be possible to identify a number of theoretically meaningful correlates of competitor cognition and to this end a number of supplementary instruments designed to assess various characteristics of the research participants and their organizations were incorporated in the present study, which, *a priori*, we would expect to be related to the cognitive maps elicited by means of the CAQ.

The strategic locus of control scale

One variable in particular that might have a bearing upon the way in which actors view their competitive worlds is locus of control. The concept of locus of control originates with the work of Rotter (1966) and reflects the beliefs individuals have about the origin of key events in their lives. Individuals who perceive events in their lives as mainly under the control of their own actions, skills and abilities are said to be 'internals'. Conversely, those who perceive events in their lives to be under the control of external forces, such as other people, chance events or the Government, are said to be 'externals'.

Previous research has shown that externally oriented Chief Executive Officers (CEOs) are less likely to belong to organizations that engage in strategic planning or seek information about the business environment. Internal CEOs, in contrast, are more likely to belong to organizations that plan ahead (often for a period of several years hence), actively seek information about the business environment, and have a tendency to lead rather than follow competitors. Moreover, organizations led by internal CEOs are more likely to inhabit dynamic and hostile environments, to consult specialist technical staff in decision making and have a relatively differentiated organizational structure (Miller, 1983; Miller Kets DeVries & Toulouse, 1982; Miller & Toulouse, 1986). To the extent that locus of control beliefs are influenced by actors' past experiences of success and failure to attain mastery of the business environment, we would expect to find that this variable has a bearing on the way in which actors process strategic information and represent this information in their mental models. On the basis of a highly detailed review of the literature on top executives, Finkelstein and Hambrick (1996) have identified how this might occur. Locus of control beliefs influence an individual's field of vision, selective perception and interpretation in a variety of ways: for example, internals devote greater effort to environmental scanning, using a wider array of sources, and are aware of a greater proportion of the information they scan in comparison to their external counterparts. Hence, it follows that we should be able to observe empirical relationships between this variable and key features of actors' mental models of competitive space.

In general, researchers in the field of strategic management have employed the well known Rotter I-E scale (Rotter, 1966). This measure comprises 29 items, 23 of which are designed to assess the respondent's locus of control beliefs, the others being 'filler' items. Respondents are required to complete the questionnaire by choosing from a series of paired alternatives, the statements that more closely reflect their own beliefs. The scale is arranged such that the respondent receives a point each time he or she selects a statement designed to reflect external locus of control beliefs. The scale is scored by totalling the number of externally worded items so endorsed. Hence, the higher the score, the more external the respondent. Conversely, lower scores reflect greater levels of internality.

Unfortunately, Rotter's measure is beset with a number of limitations which, in my view, render it unsuitable for the study of strategic management problems (see also Boone, 1988; Spector, 1982). First, as Phares (1976) notes, the I-E scale is only a rough measure of the construct and researchers should develop their own domain-specific scales (cf. Adler & Weiss, 1988, p. 315). In line with this recommendation a number of domain-specific scales have been devised by researchers over the years, including scales for the assessment of physical and mental health (Lau & Ware, 1981; Wallston & Wallston, 1982; Wallston, Wallston, Kaplan & Maldes, 1976; Wood & Letak, 1982), political (Davis, 1983), economic (Furnham, 1986), work (Spector, 1988) and career (Trice, Haire & Elliott, 1989) locus of control beliefs.

A second limitation of Rotter's general measure concerns its tendency to correlate with social desirability response set (Spector, 1982). As Boone (1988) observes, unfortunately, strategy researchers investigating the role of locus of control beliefs have not generally controlled for social desirability response set in their studies and so it is possible that some, or indeed all, of the relationships previously observed between strategy-making, structure and environment are a function of respondents attempting to present themselves in a socially desirable manner. A secondary objective of the present study, therefore, was to develop a locus of control instrument that was domain-specific and not prone correlate with social desirability.

The strategic locus of control scale is a sixteen item Likert scale designed in order to assess respondents' generalized beliefs regarding the capacities of organizations to attain mastery of their business environments through the application of strategic management techniques, principles and processes. Responses to the sixteen items are summed, or averaged, to derive a single score along a domain-specific continuum representing the respondent's generalized strategic control expectancies. However, responses to internally worded items are reverse scored in order to render the scoring system compatible with Rotter's (1966) I-E and Spector's (1988) Work Locus of Control scales. Thus a low score on this scale implies the respondent's generalized strategic control expectancies are relatively internal. Conversely, a high score on this scale implies a relatively external orientation.

Strategic locus of control is a socio-cognitive variable that reflects the extent to which organization members' accumulated learning experiences, past reinforcement histories and current organizational circumstances have led them to view strategic management processes and activities within a relatively deterministic versus an agency-oriented framework. Respondents assessed by the strategic locus of control scale are internals to the extent that they believe organizations are generally capable of shaping their own destinies through the application of strategic management principles, techniques and processes. Conversely, to the extent that respondents believe organizations are generally at the mercy of uncontrollable environmental forces, they would be classified as externals. Responses to this scale are not presumed to reflect exclusively a personality characteristic of the respondent, nor their organizational circumstances, but an interaction between disposition, past learning experiences and reinforcement histories in other organizational contexts, combined with learning experiences and reinforcement histories accumulated within the present context. In other words, strategic locus of control is a generalized cognitive dimension through which organization members filter their experience. This generalized cognitive belief structure is partly determined by current circumstances, but more generally through accumulated past experiences of organizational successes and failures to attain mastery over the business environment.

The strategic locus of control scale represents a radical departure from other domain-specific control expectancy scales, and the I-E scale, in the sense that the items tap respondents' beliefs about the capacities of *organizations* to attain mastery over their environments, as opposed to beliefs regarding their personal capacities. The scale was developed from a larger bank of items, so as to ensure that none of the items retained in the final scale correlate significantly with social desirability response set. The scale exhibits acceptable internal consistency, as assessed by coefficient alpha (Cronbach, 1951), and construct validity in relation to Rotter's (1966) I-E scale and Spector's (1988) work locus of control scale. (For details of the development and initial validation of this scale see Appendix 1.)

Strategy making behaviour, organizational structure and environment

Perceptions of various aspects of strategy making behaviour, organizational structure and environment were assessed using slightly modified versions of the scales initially devised and employed by Miller and his colleagues in their studies of the role of CEO locus of control in strategy making behaviour (e.g. Miller et al., 1982). These scales comprise multiple items with Likert and bipolar type formats. In previous studies these scales have been found to have acceptable reliabilities, as assessed by coefficient alpha, and to exhibit acceptable construct validity. These scales have also exhibited adequate inter-rater reliability (for details see Miller et al., 1982; Miller, 1983; Miller & Toulouse, 1986).

Organizational structure was operationalized via three scales: **formal scanning practices** (a measure of the extent to which respondents perceive their organizations attempt to keep track of their business environments), **technocratization** (reflecting the extent to which respondents perceive their organizations rely on technical knowledge and expertise in decision making), and **differentiation** (a measure of the extent to which respondents perceive their organizations differentiate their products and services, technologies and customer bases). *Environmental variation* was operationalized in terms of four scales: **market diversity** (a measure of the extent to which the market is construed to be homogeneous or heterogeneous), **dynamism** (reflecting perceptions of the rate and pace of change in the environment) **complexity** (reflecting the extent to which respondents experience ease or difficulty in comprehending their environments) and **hostility** (a measure of the extent to which respondents perceive the competitive environment in which their firm operates to be relatively benign or hostile). Finally, *strategy making behaviour* was operationalized in terms of four scales: **innovation** (reflecting the extent to which respondents perceive their organizations to be relatively conservative or innovative in the development of products and services), **risk taking** (a measure of the extent to which respondents perceive their organizations take relatively cautious or risky decisions), **proactiveness** (reflecting respondents' perceptions of the extent to which their organizations follow the actions of other firms or actively attempt to innovate new ideas in order to move ahead of competitors) and **futurity** (reflecting respondents' perceptions of the extent to which their organizations are primarily concerned with short-term decision making, over a period of weeks or months, or longer-term decision making, over a period of several years).

Organizational size

Following Miller et al. (1982) organizational size was assessed in terms of the Log of the total number of employees in property and related services (Log No of employees). However, two additional indicators of organizational size were also employed in the present study, namely, the Log of total number of branches within the UK (Log No of branches), and the Log of the total number of geographical regions within the UK in which the organization had one or more branches (Log No of regions). Although, *a priori*, we would expect these indicators to be highly correlated with one another, all three were incorporated in the present study with a view to creating a latent variable with greater reliability and validity than any one indicator *per se*.

Market buoyancy

In order to assess perceived market conditions at the time of the study, market buoyancy was assessed by means of a single item with a Likert scale format, devised by the author. Respondents were required to indicate the extent to which they perceived the local property market to be buoyant at the time of data collection. Responses ranged from 'very depressed' (low score) to 'very buoyant' (high score).

Organizational performance

Self-report measures of organizational performance were used rather than objective indicators for a variety of reasons. Firstly, financial indicators of the relative performance of the larger estate agency firms, especially those tied to parent organizations within the wider financial services industry, were not readily available in a disaggregated form. Nevertheless an initial attempt was made to secure such financial data from the participating organizations, but almost all declined access.

Secondly, while a number of the participant organizations kept records of relative market share, these figures tended not to be reliable, being based on the number of new advertisements placed in local property papers over selected periods of time. Not all estate agents used the local press as their main source of advertising. Several of the larger national chains, for example, advertise extensively through their own newspapers. Furthermore, in the case of larger organizations with several branches in a given locality, it was not possible to detect from advertisements which properties were handled by which particular branches. Further problems arose owing to the fact that the participant organizations were drawn from across several counties. Several of the firms involved in the study actively traded over more than one boundary, thus advertising in disparate publications. In any case, advertising figures merely relate to the number of new properties placed on the books of particular firms within a given period, or potential sales, not the number of actual sales realized.

These problems made it difficult, if not impossible, to measure performance directly, using 'hard' indicators. For these reasons, self-report indices were preferred in the present study. Previous research has indicated that knowledgeable actors are able to estimate objective performance indicators accurately using self-report measures (Dess & Robinson, 1984) and as we shall see shortly, several of the self-report measures employed in the present study were found to correlate significantly with independent assessments of organizational performance carried out by a panel of expert judges.

Five aspects of organizational performance (**wealth, market position, adaptability to changing circumstances, working climate** and **future**

prospects for the immediate year ahead) were assessed using slightly modified versions of the scales developed by Nicholson (1991). Multiple items with a Likert type response format were devised in order to assess participants' perceptions of the performance of the operational unit of the organization for which they had responsibility or belonged to (section, branch or entire company) relative to its main external competitor(s). Response options ranged from 'very much weaker' (low score description), through 'no different' (the scale mid-point), to 'very much stronger' (high score description). In addition, a 'don't know' response option was incorporated in order to minimize the possibility of 'wild guessing' (for further details of the rationale and psychometric efficacy of these scales see Nicholson & Brenner, 1994).

Environmental scanning

Miller et al.'s (1982) formal scanning practices scale assesses participants' perceptions of the environmental scanning practices of their organizations, as opposed to their own personal scanning behaviours. However, an individual's scanning behaviours may differ considerably from the formal practices of their organization. For example, the fact that particular organizations have highly sophisticated scanning systems might mean that individual organization members are less inclined to monitor their competitors' actions. On the other hand, it is also possible that particular individuals belonging to organizations whose environmental scanning practices are relatively sophisticated may be more inclined to gather information than those individuals belonging to organizations with relatively less sophisticated environmental scanning systems. For these reasons, it was considered imperative to assess the individual research participants' environmental scanning strategies in addition to their perceptions of their organizations' formal scanning practices. The extent to which the individual scans the environment for pertinent information (*frequency*) was assessed via a thirteen item Likert scale devised by the present author. Participants were required to indicate the extent to which they sought information through a variety of sources, including relevant industry reports, personal contacts, clients and so on.

While frequency is undoubtedly one useful indicator of scanning activity, this does not inform us of the reasons as to why environmental information is being sought by individuals. There is a strong possibility that individuals with particular scanning orientations develop distinctive mental models of competitive space and *vice versa*. One factor in particular which may have a bearing on competitor cognition in this respect is the extent to which a given individual scans the business environment primarily for opportunities or threats (cf. Dutton, Walton & Abrahamson, 1989). *A priori*, we would expect to find that individuals who on balance are more inclined to actively seek information relating to opportunities rather than threats have a different outlook to those with a marked tendency towards the opposite extreme. In order to explore this possibility, an additional environmental scanning scale comprising four bipolar items was designed to assess the extent to which the participant scanned the environment primarily in order to learn of threats which they must defend their business against (low score description), versus *opportunistic scanning* (high score description) – i.e. scanning with a view to spotting new business opportunities.

Biographical data and career history

Finally, following my earlier study in the grocery retail industry (Hodgkinson & Johnson, 1987, 1994) – discussed in Chapter 2 – a number of questions relating to the research participants' biographical histories, focussing primarily on current job responsibilities, education, training, and work history, were incorporated in the present study, in order to further explore the extent to which differing work experiences were related to competitor cognition.

Sampling and data collection procedures

As noted in previous chapters, a two-wave panel design was employed in the present study, in order to facilitate the comparison of mental models of competitive space over time. The fieldwork at T1 was carried out between mid-July 1989 and October 1989, while the field work at T2 ran over a comparable period from September 1990 to mid-December 1990. With the exception of the questions relating to organizational size, and the questions designed in order to extract basic biographical information and information relating to the participants' employment histories, each of the instruments described above was administered on both occasions.

The sample was drawn from the north east Midlands region of the UK, spanning the area encompassed by West Yorkshire, South Yorkshire, the East Midlands and Humberside. The participating organizations were recruited by working systematically through all entries under the heading of 'Estate Agents' in the relevant volumes of the Yellow Pages telephone directory (1989 edition) covering this geographical area.

The participants were recruited by means of a telephone call to the most senior representative available within the organization (invariably this was a member of the senior management team). During the telephone conversation I briefly explained that the purpose of the study was to investigate competition between estate agency businesses, and that the participants would receive detailed feedback regarding the findings. Total anonymity was guaranteed to all potential participants and their organizations. In an attempt to minimize problems associated with low response rates, I also explained that the questionnaires were unavoidably lengthy and that a pilot study had indicated the research task would take each participant between one and a half and two hours to complete. With the exception of five refusals, all those contacted committed their organizations to take part in the study. Participation in the research at all stages was on an unpaid, voluntary basis. A total of 97 organizations agreed to take part in the study as a result of the telephone calls. Unfortunately, however, not all those who volunteered their organizations' services returned completed questionnaires for analysis. The final sample at T1 comprised a total of 208 research participants (various grades) from 58 organizations.

Basic descriptive statistics relating to company size are presented in Table 4.2, while descriptive statistics relating to biographical details of the individual participants are presented in Table 4.3. Table 4.4 presents a breakdown of the sample by company type, while Tables 4.5 and 4.6

Table 4.2 Descriptive statistics relating to the size characteristics of the various participating organizations

Variable[†]	Mean	SD	Median	Minimum	Maximum	Valid N
No of employees	473.20	1314.01	12.00	1.5	5782.00	56
No of branches	71.41	198.34	3.00	1.0	800.00	58
No of regions	2.83	4.41	1.00	1.0	17.00	58

† These data are presented for descriptive purposes only. All subsequent analyses are based on the Logarithmic transform of these variables, as explained earlier.

Table 4.3 Descriptive statistics relating to the basic biographical details of the initial sample

Variable	Mean	SD	Minimum	Maximum	Valid N
Age in years	33.34	9.64	18.00	62.00	206
Number of companies worked for within the property market	2.08	1.28	1.00	8.00	208
Length of service within the property market and related fields (number of years)	10.71	9.21	< 1.00	45.00	208
Total number of functions worked in	5.48	2.45	1.00	13.00	208
Education[†]	2.51	1.38	1.00	5.00	207
Training (approx. number of days of formal instruction)	161.15	378.19	0.00	2200.00	207

† This variable was assessed by a five-point Likert scale (1 = no post-secondary education; 2 = further education; 3 = higher education – non-degree; 4 = higher education – non-vocationally relevant degree; 5 = higher education – vocationally relevant degree).

provide an analysis in terms of the participants' geographical locations and functions, respectively. It is evident from these tables that a wide cross-section of estate agents is represented in the study, thus strengthening our confidence in the generalizability of the findings.

Unfortunately, as is common in longitudinal research, many individuals who took part in the study at T1 declined to continue their involvement in the study (or could not be traced) at T2. A total of 114 participants from 41 organizations took part in the second phase of the study, a sample attrition rate of 45.19 for individuals and 29.31 percent for participating organizations, respectively.

It is not possible to identify the reasons for non-response at T2, but the most likely explanation is the rapid deterioration in market conditions experienced during the period of the study – as outlined in Chapter 3. Several attempts were made to try and follow up those who failed to return

Table 4.4   Analysis of the initial sample by company type

Company type	N	Percent of total sample	Cumulative percent
Local Independent	72	34.6	34.6
Regional Operator	50	24.1	58.7
National Chain	86	41.3	100.0
Total	208	100.0	100.0

Table 4.5   Analysis of the initial sample by location

Location[†]	N	Percent of total sample	Cumulative percent
South Yorkshire	100	48.1	48.1
East Midlands	51	24.5	72.6
West Yorkshire	25	12.0	84.6
Humberside	32	15.4	100.0
Total	208	100.0	100.0

[†] Denotes the geographical location of the respondents' individual branch or office.

Table 4.6   Analysis of the initial sample by function

Function	N	Percent of total sample	Cumulative percent
Senior management	74	35.6	48.1
Management	70	33.7	69.3
Technical specialist	55	26.4	95.7
Administration and support service	9	4.3	100.0
Total	208	100.0	100.0

completed questionnaires at T2, but many firms were reluctant to discuss their reasons for dropping out of the study. Others, however, gave as a reason that large numbers of staff had been made redundant in the intervening period. This suggests that the most likely explanation for the high attrition rate is that the non-returners were either no longer with their organizations at T2, or were too busy in the wake of their firms' redundancy programmes to commit further time to the study. Fortunately, however, as we shall see later, there is much converging evidence that sample attrition has had a minimal impact on the validity of the findings.

Reliability analysis and data reduction

Reliability analysis

The means, standard deviations and reliability coefficients for the various self-report measures of environmental scanning behaviour, strategic locus of control, organizational structure, strategy, environment and performance, are presented in Table 4.7. With two notable exceptions, all the scales were found to have good reliabilities, with alpha coefficients ranging between 0.70 and 0.88. The alphas associated with the technocratization and environmental complexity scales, in contrast, were 0.53 and 0.58 respectively. In view of the fact that the technocratization scale was formed on the basis of just three items, it was deemed to be sufficiently reliable for use in the study. In the case of the environmental complexity, however, the reliability was considered unacceptable, given the relative large number of items (six) forming this scale (cf. Nunnally & Bernstein, 1994: 264–265). Consequently, this scale was excluded from further analysis.

Data reduction

In order to reduce the number of variables in the study to a manageable number for the purposes of further analysis, several of the instruments were submitted to principal components analysis. A conceptual analysis of the various strategy, structure and environmental variation scales suggested that these scales are closely related to one another, to the extent that they could probably be meaningfully combined to form three general scales, reflecting participants' perceptions of proactive/innovative strategy-making behaviour, structural sophistication and environmental variability, respectively.

In order to explore the feasibility of this proposal, the various strategy-making, organizational structure and environment scales were submitted to principal components analysis, with varimax rotation. Separate analyses were performed on each group of indicators, in turn. The results of these analyses are presented in Tables 4.8 to 4.10, respectively. In each case a single component was extracted with high loadings associated with the various indicators. On the basis of these findings the scales were combined in order to create a reduced set of variables. This was accomplished by

Table 4.7   Means, standard deviations, and reliability coefficients for the various scales completed by the initial sample

Scale†	N	Number of items	Mean	SD	Alpha
Strategic locus of control	208	16	2.52	0.46	0.77
Env scanning (Frequency)	208	13	4.20	0.75	0.74
Env scanning (Threat Vs Opportunity)	208	4	5.15	1.03	0.78
Strategy making					
Innovation	208	4	4.15	1.31	0.74
Risk taking	208	2	3.59	1.40	0.84
Proactiveness	208	2	5.08	1.58	0.87
Futurity	207	5	4.30	1.35	0.84
Environmental variation					
Dynamism	207	7	4.40	1.02	0.79
Hostility	208	6	4.43	1.04	0.77
Market diversity	208	8	3.97	0.96	0.75
Complexity	208	6	4.27	0.84	0.58
Organizational structure					
Env scanning	208	4	4.03	1.39	0.77
Technocratization	208	3	4.05	1.13	0.53
Differentiation	208	3	3.69	1.35	0.70
Organizational performance					
Wealth	188	4	4.43	1.30	0.81
Markets	197	4	4.48	1.10	0.81
Adaptability	203	5	4.91	1.04	0.85
Climate	205	4	5.61	1.14	0.88
Future growth	208	4	5.00	0.94	0.84
Market buoyancy	208	1	3.12	0.96	N/A

† The scores for these scales were computed by averaging across the items for each respondent.

Table 4.8   Principal components analysis of the various strategy-making scales (N = 207)

Variable	Component loading
Innovation	0.87
Risk taking	0.71
Proactiveness	0.89
Futurity	0.82
Eigen value	2.71
% Variance	67.70
MEAN	4.27
SD	1.16

Table 4.9   Principal components analysis of the various organizational structure scales (N = 208)

Variable	Component loading
Environmental scanning	0.76
Technocratization	0.84
Differentiation	0.50
Eigen value	1.53
% variance	50.90
MEAN	3.92
SD	0.91

Table 4.10   Principal components analysis of the various environmental variation scales (N = 207)

Variable	Component loading
Dynamism	0.86
Hostility	0.72
Market diversity	0.66
Eigen value	1.70
% Variance	56.50
MEAN	4.27
SD	0.76

deriving a mean score for each participant based on their scores associated with the various component sub-scales.

The three indicators of organizational size (Log No of employees, Log No of branches and Log No of regions) were also submitted to a principal components analysis. As expected, a single component was extracted with very high loadings for all three indicators. The results of this analysis are presented in Table 4.11. On the basis of these findings a single score was derived for each participant organization, i.e. the mean Z-score of the three indicators.[3]

In order to further reduce the number of variables to be employed in subsequent analyses, the items designed to elicit information about the participants' basic biographical details and work histories, were also submitted to principal components analysis, with varimax rotation. The results of this analysis are presented in Table 4.12.

---

[3] The organizational performance scales were not submitted to a principal components analysis, nor formed into a composite scale, because, notwithstanding the fact they are significantly inter-correlated, they are conceptually distinct and, as such, should not be aggregated into a general indicator.

Table 4.11   Principal components analysis of the various organizational size
indicators (N = 56)

Variable	Component loading
Log No of branches	0.98
Log No of employees	0.97
Log No of regions	0.95
Eigen value	2.80
% Variance	93.40

Table 4.12   Principal components analysis of the various biographical items
(N = 206)

Variable	Component	
	I	*II*
Age in years	0.85	0.09
Number of companies worked for within the property market	0.61	0.00
Length of service within the property market and related fields	0.91	0.19
Total number functions worked in	0.43	0.51
Education	–0.25	0.85
Training	0.32	0.61
Eigen value	2.46	1.19
% Variance	41.00	19.90

Two components were extracted with eigen values greater than unity,
accounting for a total of 60.9 percent of the variance. The first component
seems to reflect general maturity and on the job experience, as evidenced
by high loadings for the items tapping age, number of companies worked
for within the property market, length of service within the property
market and related fields, and total number of functions worked in (within
estate agency). The second component seems to reflect education and off
the job training, as evidenced by the high loadings for these two items on
this component, together with a high loading for the total number of functions worked in. It is clearly evident that breadth of functional experience
is an important indicator of both general maturity/on the job experience
and education/training.

On the basis of these findings, factor based scale scores were calculated
for each participant by computing the mean Z-score of the various indicators with loadings in excess of 0.4 on each component. As would be
expected, given the fact that breadth of functional experience is more or
less evenly loaded across both components, these scales are significantly
correlated with one another ($r = 0.49$, df = 206, $P < 0.001$, 2-tailed).
Nevertheless, with an overlapping variance of approximately 25 percent,

they are sufficiently distinct to be retained as separate scales for the purposes of subsequent analyses.

Construct validity of the scales

Several analyses were performed in order to assess the construct validity of the scales at the individual- and organizational-levels.

Individual-level analyses

First, the scale inter-correlations were computed at the individual-level. Following the work of Miller and his associates outlined earlier, and on the basis of the theory underlying the development of the strategic locus of control scale, discussed earlier, it was predicted that the strategy-making, organizational structure, environmental variation, organizational performance, and environmental scanning scales would all be positively inter-correlated with one another, but negatively correlated with the strategic locus of control scale.

The results of these analyses are presented in Tables 4.13 and 4.14 for the T1 and T2 datasets respectively. As expected, the majority of the scale inter-correlations were highly significant in the predicted directions, strongly indicating that the various scales are valid in terms of their relationships to one another. On the whole, the pattern of relationships observed at T1 appears to have been replicated at T2, suggesting the findings are reliable. (As would be expected with a greatly reduced sample size, several of the relationships found to be relatively substantial at T1 were attenuated at T2, but the overall pattern of relationships has remained stable over time.)

Organizational-level analyses

The results of the previous analyses established that the various scales exhibit acceptable construct validity at the level of the individual participant. The pattern of scale inter-correlations over both time periods was generally as predicted.

However, according to Boone and De Brabander (1993), this approach to the assessment of construct validity is limited by the fact that the participants completed all sections of the questionnaire, thus giving rise to the possibility that the significant scale inter-correlations are, at least in part, a result of shared method variance. While it is commonly assumed by many social scientists that shared method variance is a serious problem that results in inflated correlations, a number of methodological investigations (reviewed in Spector, 1992) suggest that the situation is far from straightforward. In the final analysis, the effects of shared method variance may be neither as widespread, nor as serious, as is commonly believed. Spector cites evidence which, contrary to popular belief, suggests that shared

Table 4.13 Scale inter-correlations (Pearson product-moment) for the environmental scanning, strategic locus of control, strategy-making, structure, environmental variation and organizational performance scales completed by the research participants at T1 (decimal points omitted)[†]

Variable	1	2	3	4	5	6	7	8	9	10
1. Strategic locus of control										
2. Env scanning (Frequency)	−25****									
3. Env scanning (Threat–opp)	−43****	35****								
4. Strategy	−38****	20***	43****							
5. Structure	−31****	29****	30****	51****						
6. Environmental variation	−18***	23****	26****	43****	46****					
7. Wealth	−18***	14**	37****	52****	39****	25****				
8. Markets	−26****	17***	36****	45****	29****	17***	66****			
9. Adaptability	−28****	17***	39****	57****	37****	22****	64****	59****		
10. Climate	−16***	08	19***	24****	21****	09*	34****	37****	58****	
11. Future growth	−40****	18***	30****	38****	23****	18***	23****	24****	37****	27****

* $P < 0.10$, ** $P < 0.05$, *** $P < 0.01$, **** $P < 0.001$ (1-tailed)
[†] N = 208–188; variation is due to missing data.

Table 4.14 Scale inter-correlations (Pearson product-moment) for the environmental scanning, strategic locus of control, strategy-making, structure, environmental variation and organizational performance scales completed by the research participants at T2 (decimal points omitted)†

Variable	1	2	3	4	5	6	7	8	9	10
1. Strategic locus of control										
2. Env scanning (frequency)	-27***									
3. Env scanning (Threat–opp)	-42****	34****								
4. Strategy	-50****	29****	37****							
5. Structure	-27***	32****	28****	50****						
6. Environmental variation	-43****	29****	15*	33****	38****					
7. Wealth	-22***	16*	23***	32****	37****	12*				
8. Markets	-14*	17**	16**	23***	38****	00	74****			
9. Adaptability	-37****	13*	33****	46****	22***	17**	57****	44****		
10. Climate	05	-06	-03	18**	15*	-13	22***	28****	33****	
11. Future growth	-11	19**	10	22***	15*	-09	16*	18**	28****	23***

* $P < 0.10$, ** $P < 0.05$, *** $P < 0.01$, **** $P < 0.001$ (1-tailed)
† $N = 114$–108; variation is due to missing data.

method variance may actually attenuate rather than inflate correlation coefficients. Nevertheless we must be mindful of the fact that there is a possibility that shared method variance has inflated the observed correlations, though it would be difficult to explain (given the wide variations in the correlations) why some are more inflated than others, and the pattern is repeated over two separate occasions distant in time.

One way of overcoming this criticism, and thereby strengthening the claim of construct validity, is to assess the extent to which self-report indicators correlate with some external criterion (or criteria), derived objectively from independent sources. Two variables that would be particularly suitable for this purpose are organizational size and organizational performance. To the extent that the various self-report measures of environmental scanning, strategy-making behaviour, organizational structure, environmental variation and performance employed in this study are valid indicators of the constructs they purport to assess, we would expect to find that these variables are positively correlated with organizational size and objective indicators of organizational performance. To the extent that the strategic locus of control scale is a valid indicator, we would expect this variable to correlate negatively with these objective variables.

Unfortunately, however, for reasons which we noted earlier, 'hard' indicators of organizational performance are neither readily available nor easily constructed in the estate agency industry and so a compromise strategy was adopted. In order to further assess the construct validity of the various self-report measures, an independent panel of three judges, each highly knowledgeable about the estate agency industry, assessed the relative performance of the 58 organizations that participated in this study.

The panel members independently evaluated the performance of all 58 organizations on six criteria: (1) market share; (2) sales performance; (3) breadth of coverage of the range of property types; (4) general quality of customer service; (5) ability to adapt to changing market conditions; and (6) profitability. The criteria were derived by the author on the basis of a conceptual analysis of organizational effectiveness in the estate agency industry. This analysis was informed by consulting recent industry sector reports, for example as reviewed in the previous chapter. Each criterion was assessed by means of a single item with a seven-point Likert scale response format, ranging from 'very much below average' (low score description), through 'average' (mid-point description), to 'very much above average' (high score description). As in the case of the self-report measures of organizational performance administered to the individual participants in the main study, an additional response category, 'don't know', was also included, in an attempt to minimize the possibility that panel members lacking sufficient knowledge to make meaningful judgements were responding by 'wild guessing'. Fortunately, however, none of the three judges employed for the purposes of this particular exercise returned 'don't know' responses to any of the questions.[4]

In order to assess the inter-rater reliabilities of these performance criteria, the panel members' independent judgements were analysed using Kendall's coefficient of concordance (Siegel, 1956). Table 4.15 presents the results of these analyses which indicate an acceptable degree of consensus between the raters on all six of the criteria. The coefficients are all highly significant, suggesting that there was sufficient overall agreement between the raters to aggregate their judgements into composite evaluations of the organizations on each criterion. (The coefficients associated with the general quality of customer service, adaptability to changing market conditions, and profitability items were low, but marginally acceptable).

The aggregated ratings of the assessors were submitted to a principal components analysis. The results of this analysis are presented in Table 4.16. A single component was extracted with very high loadings for each item. On the basis of these findings, the six sets of aggregated ratings were combined to form a composite measure of organizational performance. This composite indicator, together with the composite indicator of organizational size, derived earlier, formed the basis for assessing the construct validity of the various self-report measures of environmental scanning, strategic locus of control, strategy, organizational structure, environmental variation and performance.

In order to form a comparable unit of analysis to the expert panel ratings and the organizational size scores, the responses associated with particular

Table 4.15 Inter-rater reliabilities (Kendall's coefficient of concordance) for the various expert panel assessments (N = 3 judges)

Performance indicator	W	Chi-square	DF	Significance
Market share	0.75	129.00	57	0.0000
Sales performance	0.75	127.80	57	0.0000
Range of property types	0.72	123.76	57	0.0000
General quality of customer service	0.64	108.95	57	0.0000
Adaptability to changing market conditions	0.66	113.70	57	0.0000
Profitability	0.55	93.48	57	0.0017

[4] Each panel member had a minimum of 15 years practical experience in the estate agency industry. At the time of the data collection, two of the panel members were involved in the full-time training and education of estate agents in a specialist university department with an international reputation for excellence in this field. The third member of the panel was a journalist specializing in the estate agency industry. All three had extensive first-hand knowledge of the industry within the geographical area encompassed by the study.

Table 4.16 Principal components analysis of the aggregated expert panel's assessments of organizational performance

Variable	Component loading
Market share	0.96
Sales performance	0.95
Range of property types	0.92
General quality of customer service	0.94
Adaptability to changing market conditions	0.97
Profitability	0.83
Eigen value	5.17
% Variance	86.20

individuals for the various self-report measures were aggregated at the organizational-level. These aggregated (mean) scores, were correlated, in turn, with the composite judgements of the expert panel and organizational size. The results of this analysis are presented in Table 4.17. Before considering the significance of these findings, however, a brief note of explanation is in order.

For this particular analysis, Spearman rank-order correlations were used in preference to Pearson product-moment correlations owing to the fact that the mean values derived for the various participating organizations are based on unequal sample sizes, thus giving rise to the likelihood of heteroscedasticity amongst the variances distributed around the observations (means). Under these circumstances parametric statistical tests are clearly inappropriate since there is a high probability that any parameters estimated will be biased.

As expected, the correlations are generally in the predicted direction and a number are found to be statistically significant, both in relation to organizational size and the expert panel's ratings of organizational performance. Particularly noteworthy are the correlations between the self-report measures of wealth and markets with the expert panel's evaluations of overall performance. These correlations are found to be moderately large and significant over both time periods, thus providing strong evidence that the participant organizations' self-assessments of these particular dimensions of performance have an objective basis.

Several of the correlations between the self-report measures and organizational size are also worthy of comment. In particular, the correlations between size and strategic locus of control, threat vs opportunity scanning, strategy, structure, environment, wealth and markets are found to be substantial and, on the whole, highly significant for both time periods. As would be expected, given the historical events which took place in this industry in the period leading up to the study (reviewed in the previous chapter), this pattern of results confirms that the larger firms, with greater numbers of employees, branches and national or near national coverage are

Table 4.17 Spearman rank-order correlations between the organizational-level self-report ratings of strategy, organizational structure, environmental variation and performance with organizational size, and the independent expert panel's ratings of organizational performance[†]

Variable	Correlations with self-report ratings at time one[§]		Correlations with self-report ratings at time two[#]	
	Expert panel's ratings of overall performance	Organizational size	Expert panel's ratings of overall performance	Organizational size
Strategic locus of control	-0.11	-0.32***	-0.30**	-0.48****
Env scanning (Frequency)	0.14	-0.04	0.05	0.32**
Env scanning (Threat-opp)	0.15	0.37***	-0.02	0.37**
Strategy	0.20*	0.36***	0.30**	0.45****
Structure	0.28**	0.53****	0.36**	0.46****
Environmental variation	0.19*	0.49****	0.34**	0.50****
Wealth	0.62****	0.47****	0.29**	0.46****
Markets	0.51****	0.51****	0.36**	0.31**
Adaptability	0.14	0.19*	0.08	0.17
Climate	0.09	-0.13	-0.12	-0.15
Prospects for growth	-0.07	0.01	0.01	0.11

* $P < 0.10$, ** $P < 0.05$, *** $P < 0.01$, **** $P < 0.001$ (1-tailed)

[†] The correlation (Pearson product-moment) between organizational size and the expert panel's ratings of organizational performance is $r = 0.62$, $df = 56$, $P < 0.001$ (2-tailed).

[§] N = 58–56; variation is due to missing data.

[#] N = 41–40; variation is due to missing data.

relatively internal in terms of their strategic locus of control orientations, with a marked tendency to scan the environment primarily for opportunities rather than threats, in comparison with their smaller counterparts. Furthermore, the larger organizations tend to be relatively innovative/ proactive in their strategy making behaviour with relatively sophisticated organizational structures, their environments are generally perceived to be relatively more changeable and varied, and these organizations are found to be generally more successful in terms of their wealth and standing in the marketplace. The overall conclusion to be derived from these findings is that the participants' responses to the various self-report scales are correlated with objective/independently derived criteria in the predicted directions adding substantial support to the claim of construct validity for these instruments.

For the sake of completeness the organizational-level scale inter-correlations associated with the various self-report measures of environmental scanning behaviour, strategy, structure, environmental variation and organizational performance for the T1 and T2 datasets are reported in Tables 4.18 and 4.19, respectively. Once again, the relationships are generally in the predicted directions, and many statistically significant at the 5 percent level or less.

Having established that the various indicators to be employed in the main analyses demonstrate acceptable reliability and validity, in terms of their relationship to one another and the independently derived criteria, it remains to be ascertained to what extent sample attrition from T1–T2 poses a threat, or otherwise, to the validity of the findings.

Comparison of returners and non-returners

Two statistical procedures were employed in order to assess the extent to which the relatively high attrition rates associated with this study might pose a threat to the validity of the findings at T2. The initial responses of those participants who returned completed questionnaires on the second occasion were compared with the responses of those participants who subsequently dropped out of the study, using the unrelated t-test. In addition, the ratios of the variances associated with the stayers and leavers were compared for each variable using the *F*-test. These procedures were employed in order to determine whether the two groups of participants differed significantly in their mean scores and variances on each variable, due to sample attrition. The results of these analyses are presented in Table 4.20.

The results clearly demonstrate that, in general, sample attrition appears to have had a minor impact on the variances associated with the various indicators. Only two of the 14 *F*-ratios (organizational structure and market buoyancy) are found to be statistically significant, at the 5 percent level,

Table 4.18 Scale inter-correlations (Spearman rank-order) at T1 for the environmental scanning, strategic locus of control, strategy-making, structure, environmental variation and organizational performance scales, at the organizational-level of analysis (decimal points omitted)†

Variable	1	2	3	4	5	6	7	8	9	10
1. Strategic locus of control										
2. Env scanning (Frequency)	−28**									
3. Env scanning (Threat-opp)	−38***	39****								
4. Strategy	−37***	32***	61****							
5. Structure	−33***	38***	34***	52****						
6. Environmental variation	−18*	20*	31***	41****	51****					
7. Wealth	−09	02	33***	35***	38***	19*				
8. Markets	−33***	29**	49****	53****	40****	31***	63****			
9. Adaptability	−18*	38***	57****	63****	37****	20*	48****	57****		
10. Climate	01	11	21*	18*	09	01	24**	29**	46****	
11. Future growth	−33***	32***	39****	39****	25**	23**	−03	09	28**	29**

* P < 0.10, ** P < 0.05, *** P < 0.01, **** P < 0.001 (1-tailed)

† N = 58–55; variation is due to missing data.

Table 4.19 Scale inter-correlations (Spearman rank-order) at T2 for the environmental scanning, strategic locus of control, strategy-making, structure, environmental variation and organizational performance scales, at the organizational-level of analysis (decimal points omitted)†

Variable	1	2	3	4	5	6	7	8	9	10
1. Strategic locus of control										
2. Env scanning (Frequency)	-38***									
3. Env scanning (Threat-opp)	-55****	45***								
4. Strategy	-73****	31**	47****							
5. Structure	-43***	46****	33**	65****						
6. Environment	-42***	42***	22*	49****	66****					
7. Wealth	-24*	08	03	33**	37***	19				
8. Markets	-22*	24*	-01	26*	41***	20	74****			
9. Adaptability	-51****	12	37***	48****	17	09	54****	47****		
10. Climate	10	-16	03	16	-05	-15	21*	27**	42***	
11. Future Growth	-30**	20	23*	39***	32**	06	10	33**	38***	21*

* P < 0.10, ** P < 0.05, *** P < 0.01, **** P < 0.001 (1-tailed)
† N = 41–39; variation is due to missing data.

Table 4.20 Comparison of the initial responses of the returners with the responses of those research participants who subsequently dropped out of the study at T2

Variable	Stayers[†]		Leavers[§]			
	Mean	SD	Mean	SD	F-value	T-value
On the job experience/ maturity	0.20	0.75	–0.25	0.67	1.26	4.48***
Education and training	0.06	0.65	–0.08	0.71	1.19	1.49
Environmental scanning (Frequency)	4.23	0.74	4.17	0.76	1.04	0.63
Environmental scanning (Threat vs opportunity)	5.08	1.01	5.24	1.05	1.08	–1.09
Strategic locus of control	2.56	0.45	2.48	0.48	1.17	1.33
Strategy	4.14	1.17	4.44	1.13	1.07	–1.86
Organizational structure	3.90	1.00	3.95	0.80	1.57*	–0.38
Environmental variation	4.21	0.77	4.33	0.74	1.08	–1.13
Wealth	4.39	1.33	4.48	1.27	1.11	–0.47
Markets	4.36	1.13	4.63	1.05	1.16	–1.71
Adaptability	4.86	1.05	4.97	1.04	1.02	–0.80
Organizational climate	5.63	1.06	5.58	1.22	1.33	0.34
Prospects for future growth	4.84	0.88	5.20	0.98	1.23	–2.78**
Market buoyancy	3.09	0.85	3.16	1.08	1.63*	–0.54

* P < 0.05, ** P < 0.01, *** P < 0.001
[†] N = 114–106; variation is due to missing data.
[§] N = 94–82; variation is due to missing data.

with no other significant results. In view of the fact that as many as fourteen *F*-tests have been performed on the data, there is a strong possibility that either or both of these significant results has occurred due to chance factors. (For every twenty statistical tests performed on a given sample, we would expect to obtain at least one significant result on the basis of chance alone, taking the conventional five percent cut-off level as the criterion.)

Turning to the results of the *t*-tests, we find that with two notable exceptions, none of the t-values was significant, indicating that there are very few differences between the stayers and leavers on the variables measured at T1. The notable exceptions are the prospects for future growth and on the job experience/maturity scales, which are highly significant at the P < 0.01 and P < 0.001 levels, respectively. It is clearly evident from these findings that those participants who dropped out of the study at T2 were generally over-optimistic about their organizations' prospects for future growth in the immediate year ahead and/or considerably less experienced/occupationally mature, in comparison to their counterparts who returned completed questionnaires on the second occasion, supporting the explanation for T2 refusal tendered above.

Summary and conclusions

This chapter has described the development and validation of the research instruments that were devised and/or adapted for use in the main empirical study. The various self-report measures used to assess the participants' background characteristics, strategic control expectancies, environmental scanning behaviours, and their perceptions of environmental variation and the strategic, structural and performance characteristics of their organizations have been shown to be both reliable, in terms of their internal consistency assessed by coefficient alpha, and valid, as assessed by the pattern of scale inter-correlations at both the individual- and organizational-level of analysis. Further evidence for the construct validity of the scales was obtained by correlating the aggregated, organizational-level responses to the self-report measures with two independent criteria: organizational size and organizational performance. Finally, we considered the extent to which sample attrition from T1–T2 posed a threat to the validity of the findings, by comparing the initial responses of those participants who returned completed questionnaires on a second occasion with those who subsequently dropped out of the study. Despite the relatively high drop-out rate, we concluded that there was very little evidence to suggest that sample attrition posed a threat to the validity of the findings.

5
Mental Models of Competitive Space and their Correlates

As noted in Chapter 1, this study was conceived primarily to gather data that would enable a rigorous empirical examination of a number of the central claims of the emerging body of socio-cognitive theory concerning the evolution of competitive structures in industries and markets, centred on Porac et al.'s (1989) embryonic notion of competitive enactment. The next three chapters present the substantive findings arising from the study. In Chapter 2 we identified three issues in particular that remain of enduring concern, notwithstanding the theoretical developments that have occurred over the ensuing years, namely, the extent to which key features of actors' mental models of competitive space correlate in theoretically meaningful ways with strategic behaviours and outcomes, the extent to which these mental models converge or diverge within and between organizations in the same industrial sector, and the extent to which they remain stable over time, notwithstanding significant environmental jolts. In the next three chapters we shall address each of these issues in turn.

In the present chapter we are concerned with the basic proposition that competitor cognition and strategic choice are inextricably intertwined with the material conditions of the marketplace. If this key premise is tenable, it should be possible to detect theoretically meaningful relationships between measurable features of actors' mental models of competitive space and the various supplementary self-report measures – reflecting the participants' background characteristics, strategic control expectancies and environmental scanning behaviours and their perceptions of environmental variation and the strategic, structural and performance characteristics of their organizations, outlined in the previous chapter.

Assessing actors' mental models of competitive space

How then shall we begin the search for these empirical relationships? As noted in Chapter 2, previous studies of competitor cognition have employed mapping procedures that tend to yield either a representation of the collective cognitive structure of the sample of participants as a whole, but fail to capture variation at lower levels of analysis (e.g. Porac et al., 1989, 1995), or emphasize differences in cognition, but do so in a fashion that renders the resulting representations of actors' mental models methodologically non-comparable (e.g. Daniels et al., 1994, 1995, 2002; Spencer et al., 2003). The knowledge elicitation and data analysis procedures adopted in the present study were carefully chosen in an attempt to overcome these limitations. As observed in the previous chapter, the competitor analysis questionnaire (CAQ) was purposefully designed to be an adaptive instrument so as to ensure that the research participants were as knowledgeable as possible about each of the particular firms upon which they based their individual judgements. However, the knowledge elicitation task, a variant of the repertory grid technique, was framed in a way that would enable the researcher to make meaningful comparisons across particular individuals and/or subgroups of respondents (using a standardized list of competitor categories as the elements, in conjunction with a set list of constructs).

Three-way scaling for the assessment of mental models

Fortunately, there are a number of analytical procedures readily available, which, when used in conjunction with the CAQ, would appear to overcome the basic methodological limitations of previous work, identified in Chapter 2. Three-way scaling/WMDS techniques such as the INdividual Differences SCALing (INDSCAL) approach devised by Carroll and Chang (1970) and closely related procedures, including, for example, Takane, Young and DeLeeuw's (1977) ALSCAL and Ramsey's (1978) MULTISCALE, are particularly suitable for addressing the methodological and empirical issues to be addressed by this study. The main feature of these techniques that makes them particularly useful in the present context is their ability to represent individual *and* collective cognition simultaneously. The basic underlying assumption of these techniques is that a given group of actors share a common set of underlying dimensions in their mental models of a particular domain. However, at the individual (or subgroup) level, they differ in terms of the extent to which a given dimension is of relevance in their 'private cognitions', including the possibility of zero relevance.

Basic two-way scaling techniques and principal components analysis (as employed by Reger (1990a) and Walton (1986), for example, in their studies of competitor cognition in the USA financial services industries), are capable of representing particular individuals' mental models, or the collective mental model of a given group of research participants, but not both. Three-way scaling procedures, in contrast, yield an aggregate perceptual map, known as the *group space*, and a series of weights reflecting sources of variation in cognition at the individual- or subgroup-level. These *source weights* (Arabie et al., 1987) reflect the salience of the various dimensions of the group space in relation to each source's input data and *vice versa*, i.e. the extent to which a particular dimension is salient in the judgements of a given individual or subgroup, or, alternatively, the extent to which a particular condition imposed by the researcher acts as a source of variation in cognition.

The basic input to a three-way scaling analysis comprises a series of $k = 1.....$ K matrices (1 matrix per participant or other source of input data). These matrices, known as 'source matrices' (Arabie et al., 1987) represent the distances or *proximities* between a series of $i = 1.....$ I objects (i.e. the stimuli or, in Kellyian terms, the 'elements'). In general, the smaller the distance between a given pair of stimuli, the greater their overall similarity. Conversely, the greater the distance, the less similar the stimuli. These input proximities may be direct judgements of perceived similarity, or, alternatively, as in the case of repertory grid applications, derived similarities, constructed on the basis of an analysis of responses to the various bipolar attribute rating scales (i.e. constructs) associated with each stimulus/element.

In general terms, three-way scaling routines seek to optimize the fit between the input proximity values (δ_{ijk}) and corresponding output distances (d_{ijk}) for each of the $k = 1.....$ K sources. The primary aim is to capture the information contained in the input source/proximity matrices in as few dimensions as possible without unduly distorting the data. The relationships to be optimized by the analysis can be specified more formally, in general form, by the following equation:

$$f_k(\delta_{ijk}) \approx d_{ijk}; \tag{5.1}$$

The precise technical way in which this process is accomplished varies considerably from one computer algorithm to another. (For technical details of the ALSCAL routine, the procedure to be employed in the present study, see Takane et al., 1977.)

In general, as noted above, a three-way scaling analysis yields two sets of results of substantive interest to researchers, namely, a *group space*, of *r* dimensions, in which the stimuli (in this case elements depicting various categories of business competitors) are located as points, and a series of weights reflecting sources of variation in cognition at the individual- or subgroup-level. In the words of Schiffman and her colleagues:

> Geometrically, the weights stretch and shrink the dimensions of the group stimulus space to yield each [participant's] personal space. The stretching and shrinking is done separately for each [participant] according to that [participant's] own idiosyncratic weighting scheme. If the [participant] has a heavy weight on a dimension, then that dimension is stretched. If a dimension has a low weight, the dimension is shrunk. Thus, the [participant's] personal stimulus space is just like the group

stimulus space, except that the dimensions of the personal space have been stretched or shrunk according to the [participant's] pattern of weights (Schiffman et al., 1981, p. 71).

In essence, these weights, ranging between zero and unity, inform researchers of the extent to which particular individuals, or subgroups, deviate from the collective cognitive representation (i.e. the group space) in their private views. The configuration of stimuli represented in the group space is effectively a compromise between the various individuals' personal configurations. Consequently, it does not necessarily correspond to the configuration of any particular individual.

More formally, the distances between the points in the group stimulus space are defined by the following algebraic formula:

$$d_{ij} = \sqrt{\sum_{a=1}^{r} \left(x_{ia} - x_{ja} \right)^2}$$

(5.2)

where d_{ij} is the Euclidean distance between points i and j, and x_{ia} is the coordinate of point i on dimension a. This formula is directly comparable to the formula for Euclidean distances used in standard two-way multidimensional scaling (MDS) programs. However, as noted above, basic two-way scaling techniques and related procedures are incapable of capturing the interplay between individual and collective cognition. Three-way scaling procedures constitute a significant advance in this respect, enabling researchers to capture shared aspects of cognition, represented as the group stimulus space configuration, and subtle variations, represented by the personal spaces derived separately for each individual participant or subgroup.

More formally, these personal spaces are defined algebraically as follows:

$$d_{ijk} = \sqrt{\sum_{a=1}^{r} \left(x_{kia} - x_{kja} \right)^2}$$

(5.3)

where x_{kia} is an element of matrix $\mathbf{X}_k$. This is the coordinate of point i on dimension a of participant k's personal stimulus space. The personal spaces $\mathbf{X}_k = 1\ldots\ldots K$ are related to the group space $\mathbf{X}$ and the participant weights, $\mathbf{w}_k$, by means of the following equation, the fundamental equation for the WMDS model:

$$d_{ijk} = \sqrt{\sum_{a=1}^{r} w_{ka} \left(x_{ia} - x_{ja} \right)^2}$$

(5.4)

where w_{ka} is an element of matrix $\mathbf{W}$, the source weight matrix, denoting the salience of dimension a for individual k, and x_{ia} is the coordinate of stimulus i on the corresponding dimension of the group stimulus space.

The extent to which the group space adequately represents the judgements of the stimuli associated with particular sources is captured by two goodness of fit indices (stress and RSQ). As a general rule, the lower the stress level, the greater the goodness of fit. (A stress value = 0.00 would denote the fact that the derived model captures perfectly all the information contained in the input dataset.) In a standard, *matrix conditional* three-way scaling analysis, of the sort reported in this chapter, the sum of the source weights associated with a given source varies in approximate proportion to the percentage of variance accounted for (RSQ) in the input dataset associated with that particular source by the group space. The greater the RSQ value, the greater the goodness of fit. Poor average diagnostics (i.e. high stress, low RSQ) relating to the various proximity matrices suggest errorful data and/or the need for a group space of higher dimensionality in order to better represent the information contained in the input dataset as a whole, while poor diagnostics associated with particular input proximity matrices indicate errorful data and/or the need for separate models of higher dimensionality in order to represent adequately the judgements of the stimuli associated with the individual sources in question.

In sum, the development of three-way scaling/WMDS procedures such as Carroll and Chang's (1970) INDSCAL approach and related techniques for fitting the weighted Euclidean distances model represents a powerful breakthrough within the field of psychometrics that has considerable potential to contribute to the development of a reliable and valid technique for representing actors' mental models of competitive space. As the following analysis demonstrates, three-way scaling procedures provide researchers with a convenient basis for validating data elicited through the mass application of repertory grid techniques. To the extent that these methods yield valid insights into actors' mental models of competitor definition, we would expect to find significant correlations between participant source weights – reflecting individual differences in the salience of the group space dimensions – and responses to the various instruments designed to assess the background characteristics of the participants, their strategic behaviours and their perceptions of key contextual features of the organization and its environment, including aspects of its strategy and performance.

Basic analytical strategy

The basic analytical strategy to be adopted in the search for empirical correlates of competitor cognition will proceeed in four key stages, as follows. First, we shall derive an overall group space configuration, based on the T1 sample as a whole. This aggregate cognitive structure will be taken, tentatively, to represent the mental model of competitive space of the entire UK residential estate agency industry – in much the same way that Porac and his colleagues regarded the structure that emerged from the application of their taxonomic interview procedure in their studies of Scottish knitwear manufacturers (reviewed in Chapter 2) as reflecting an industry view (Porac et al., 1989, 1995). Next, a series of source weights will be derived for each of the research participants. Separate weights will be derived for the T1 and T2 datasets, adopting the T1 group space as the reference configuration. Following this, for reasons to be explained in due course, the two sets of participant source weights will be mathematically transformed. Finally, the transformed participant source weights will be subjected to an exploratory correlational analysis, along the lines indicated above. To the extent that these transformed weights are found to vary systematically with responses to the various supplementary self-report measures of strategic behaviour and outcomes outlined in the previous chapter, this will provide firm evidence in support of the validity of the CAQ as well as strengthening empirically the basic notion of competitive enactment.

Multidimensional scaling analysis

In total, 206 of the 208 questionnaires returned from the 58 organizations at T1 and all 114 questionnaires returned from the 41 organizations at T2 were usable in the present analyses. It is evident from the previous chapter that a good cross-section of estate agency firms (including small partnerships, regional operators and national chains) and a wide range of specialist functions are represented in the study. Consequently, it seems reasonable to assume that the sample is sufficiently heterogeneous to derive a group space configuration that will be representative of the industry as a whole, at least within the geographical area encompassed by the study.

Responses to the CAQ were submitted to Takane et al.'s (1977) ALSCAL procedure, a general purpose multidimensional scaling programme available within the SPSS system, which includes a three-way scaling option for operationalizing Carroll and Chang's (1970) INDSCAL model (SPSS, 1990). Firstly, however, the raw data were converted into a series of proximities matrices (Euclidean distances) via the SPSS Proximities procedure, which in turn served as the basic input data to the three-way scaling analysis. Three sets of proximities matrices were derived, reflecting different sources of variation in the participants' judgements.

Initially, a set of proximities matrices corresponding to the various bipolar rating scales/constructs was computed using the T1 dataset, by averaging over the individual respondents' judgements, using a formula derived from the generalized distance score proposed by Cronbach and Gleser (1953), Osgood and Suci (1952) and Wish, Deutsch and Kaplan (1976) for forming profile distances between stimuli, viz.:

$$\delta_{ki(s)} = \sqrt{\frac{1}{n} \sum_{k=1}^{n} \left(x_{ki(s)} - x_{kj(s)} \right)^2}$$

(5.5)

where $x_{ki(s)}$ and $x_{kj(s)}$ are respondent k's ratings of the estate agency categories i and j on scale s, and n is the total number of participants. The application of this formula results in a dissimilarity matrix which represents an aggregation of *all* the participants' judgements on a given bipolar rating scale/construct. A set of 21 proximities matrices (hereinafter referred to as 'construct source proximity matrices') was derived using this formula, i.e. one matrix per attribute/construct. When this type of proximity matrix serves as the basic input data in a three-way scaling analysis, the resulting source weights can be used directly in order to interpret the meaning and psychological significance of the group space configuration, much as factor loadings are employed in a conventional principal components or factor analysis, i.e. the greater the magnitude of a given source weight associated with a given dimension, the greater the relevance of the corresponding attribute/construct for conceptualizing that particular dimension (see e.g. Forgas, 1981; Forgas et al., 1980; Kruskal & Wish, 1978; Wish et al., 1976).

Following this, a second set of proximities matrices was derived, again using the T1 dataset, by averaging over all the scales separately for each individual participant in turn (for further details of this procedure see Kruskal & Wish, 1978, pp. 70–73). This yielded an additional 206 proximities matrices (hereinafter referred to as 'participant source proximity matrices') which subsequently provided the basis for computing a set of source weights (hereinafter referred to as participant weights) reflecting individual differences in the saliences of the dimensions of the T1 group space.

Finally, a third set of proximities matrices was computed, using the T2 dataset, again by averaging over all the scales separately for each individual participant. In turn, this set of matrices was used to derive a set of participant weights reflecting individual differences in dimensional salience at T2 in respect of the T1 group space; i.e. the TI group space served as the reference configuration. These T2 participant weights were employed in conjunction with the corresponding weights drived from the T1 dataset in the basic correlational analysis/validation exercise involving the various supplementary measures of environmental scanning behaviour, strategic control expectancies, education and training, work experience and perceptions of the organization's strategy, structure, environmental variation and performance.

Results and discussion

The industry-level mental model

The ALSCAL routine was set to compute solutions from six down to two dimensions, using the model = indscal, level = ordinal (untie), level = ordinal (tied) and level = interval options. Similar configurations were obtained across each level of measurement. However, an analysis of the diagnostic measures (stress and RSQ) suggested the level = ordinal (untie) option to be the most appropriate. Taking into account both the diagnostic criteria (average Stress = 0.212; RSQ = 0.846) and the substantive inter-pretability of the output, a two-dimensional solution was strongly indicated. This solution, which accounted for 84.6 percent of the variance in the input proxomities matrices, was considered sufficient to represent the participants' judgements both statistically and conceptually. The addition of further dimensions did not increase substantially the variance accounted for (a third dimension added a mere 1.7 percent and as many as six dimensions a mere 5.5 percent to the explained variance). Moreover, no convincing interpretation was obtained for additional dimensions.

Interpretation of the stimulus space was accomplished by examining the source weights calculated by the computer programme for each of the 21 construct source proximity matrices (see Table 5.1). As noted above, these weights (hereinafter referred to as the 'dimension weights'), ranging between zero and unity, are analogous to factor loadings in a conventional principal components or factor analysis, in the sense that the greater the magnitude of a given dimension weight, the greater the relevance of the associated attribute for conceptualizing that particular dimension.

The results in Table 5.1 strongly indicate that the first dimension represents the overall market dominance or 'power' of various types of estate agent, in terms of their sheer visibility in the marketplace, as reflected by the relatively high dimension weights for the 'size of branch network' (0.94), 'geographical coverage' (0.93), 'amount of advertising' (0.90), 'marketing profile' (0.94), 'market share' 0.83), 'financial resources' (0.93), 'links with financial services companies' (0.93), and 'strategic influence/power' (0.90) constructs. The second dimension, in contrast, seems to represent the general quality of service associated with each type of estate agent, as reflected by the relatively high dimension weights for the 'service to vendors' (0.96), 'service to purchasers' (0.94), 'quality of staff' (0.96), 'degree of personal attention' (0.94) and 'operating practices' (0.96) constructs. It is noteworthy that several of the constructs appear to be of significance for the interpretation of both dimensions. Given the pattern of dimension weights, it is clear that 'staff training', 'quality of advertising', 'profitability', 'location of business premises', 'range of services', 'scale of charges', 'degree of local knowledge' and 'typical range of properties on sale', are of some importance in relation to both market power and quality.

The aggregate judgements of the respondents with respect to each estate agency category are plotted along the two dimensions of the group space configuration in Figure 5.1. The results suggest that within the residential estate agency industry there is a general consensus that successful businesses are ones that have established dominance in the marketplace *and* offer a high quality of service to vendors and purchasers alike. Such organizations tend to gravitate towards the upper right hand quadrant of

Table 5.1   Dimension weights for the ratings of the attributes aggregated across the full sample of respondents at T1 (N = 206)

	Dimension	
Attribute	*1*	*2*
Service to vendors	0.10	0.96
Quality of staff	0.12	0.96
Service to purchasers	0.18	0.94
Training of staff	0.54	0.78
Operating practices	0.13	0.96
Quality of advertising	0.55	0.72
Profitability	0.45	0.76
Location of business premises	0.58	0.67
Size of branch network	0.94	0.00
Range of services	0.69	0.56
Geographical coverage	0.93	0.01
Scale of charges	0.64	0.50
Degree of personal attention	0.12	0.94
Market share	0.83	0.29
Marketing profile	0.94	0.15
Degree of local knowledge	0.37	0.78
Strategic influence/power	0.90	0.29
Amount of advertising	0.90	0.22
Financial resources	0.93	0.08
Links with financial services companies	0.93	0.10
Typical range of properties on sale	0.75	0.39

Source: Hodgkinson, 1997b: 934.

the figure. Unsuccessful businesses, in contrast, tend to be located in the bottom left hand quadrant of the figure, reflecting the generally held view that they are considerably less powerful than their successful counterparts and offer a poorer quality of service.

The general pattern of results arising from this analysis suggests that at the time of initial data collection within this particular industry a highly simplified mental model of competitive space had come to prevail. As in Porac et al.'s (1989) Scottish knitwear study, it is evident that only a very limited portion of the competitive space potentially available was considered strategically feasible by the vast majority of participants.

The two-dimensional solution presented in Figure 5.1 suggests that within this particular industry, establishing dominance in the marketplace *and* offering a relatively high quality of service were the order of the day. Those organizations that were perceived to be meeting these requirements (e.g. 'successful agents', 'major competitors', 'building society agents', and 'insurance company agents') are positioned towards the upper right hand quadrant of the figure, with their less successful counterparts (e.g. 'unsuccessful

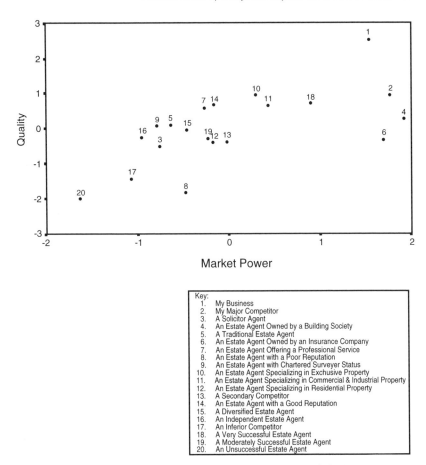

Figure 5.1 The two-dimensional group space representation of the 20 estate agency categories for the full sample of respondents at T1 (N = 206; Stress = 0.212; RSQ = 0.846)
Source: Hodgkinson, 1997b: 935.

agents', 'inferior competitors' and 'agents with a poor reputation') located in the bottom left hand quadrant of the figure. To the extent that this perceptual map is a true reflection of the wider industry's collective mental model of competitive space that had come to prevail during the late 1980s, the range of strategic options considered feasible by the vast majority of estate agents during that period was very narrow indeed. Within the confines the competitive arena as construed here, generally only the larger, more powerful organizations could enjoy the benefits of competitive success, by virtue of their access to greater material resources, which in turn was presumably seen to inform a better quality of service through the acquisition of higher calibre staff, better quality advertising and so on.

The results suggest that differentiating a larger number of dimensions in order to emphasize particular attributes, such as scale of charges, quality of advertising or marketing profile, with a view to impressing on the consumer the distinctive competences of the various firms, was not considered by the vast majority of estate agents. Rather, on the basis of these results, it would appear that estate agents throughout the industry had come to consider the strategies being pursued by national chains and larger regional operators, of attaining high levels of market power and providing a high quality service in general, as the industry recipe for the attainment of competitive success. However, when we consider the objective reality confronting industry at the time the data associated with this analysis was collected, it is clear that this image of the national and quasi-national chains as the embodiment of competitive success, was fundamentally misplaced. The more lucrative regions of the competitive space were not to be found in the zone occupied by these organizations, as clearly demonstrated by the trading figures reviewed in Chapter 3, figures that culminated in the eventual decision of the Prudential to withdraw from the sector altogether and the dramatic downscaling of operations by the majority of the other corporate players.

These findings add to a growing body of evidence concerning the constraining role of *bounded rationality* (March & Simon, 1958) in the development of competitive strategies in industries and markets (see also Calori et al., 1992; Clark & Montgomery, 1999; de Chernatony et al., 1993; Gripsrud & Gronhaug, 1985; Hodgkinson & Johnson, 1994; P. Johnson et al., 1998; Porac et al., 1987, 1989, 1995; Porac & Thomas, 1994; Reger, 1990a; Reger & Huff, 1993). Due to limited information processing capacity, organization members do not attend equally to all available environmental cues (Sims & Gioia, 1986). Rather, attributes and competitors are grouped into a much smaller subset of dimensions and categories, in an effort to reduce the information processing burden. In the present case, it would appear that the entrance of the major institutional estate agents was a highly visible stimulus, representing a competitive threat of major proportions, which in turn greatly narrowed actors' attention and in so doing came to dominate the thinking of the larger and smaller firms alike.

Validation of the CAQ

While the aggregation of judgements over participants in order to derive construct source proximity matrices greatly aids the interpretation of the group space configuration, this type of input proximities matrix does not represent the data in a form suitable for parameterizing individual differences in the relative salience or importance of the group space dimensions. The latter requires that judgements are aggregated over all of the scales, separately, for each participant in turn. As noted above, 206 and 114 such participant source proximity matrices were respectively derived from the T1 and T2 datasets by adopting this procedure. In turn, these proximities matrices were employed as a basis for estimating the source weights reflecting individual differences in the saliences of the dimensions of the T1 group space configuration. This was accomplished by using the two-dimensional solution derived from the construct-based source matrices (reported above) as a reference configuration, i.e. a pair of source weights was estimated separately in turn for each of the 206 T1 participants and the 114 T2 returners, by reference to the previously derived group space configuration. As with the dimension weights discussed above, these participant weights range between zero and unity. In this case, however, larger values denote greater dimensional salience for the individuals concerned.

A note on the meaning and significance of participant source weights

Before reporting the results of the validation exercise alluded to above, a further note of explanation is called for, regarding the nature and role of participant weights in a three-way scaling analysis. While the meaning and significance of the group space configuration in WMDS is relatively straightforward and well understood, unfortunately, the question as to how participant weights should be employed by applied researchers with substantive interests in the analysis of differential cognition has proven to be both complex and controversial (see e.g. Borg & Groenen, 1997; Coxon, 1982; Hodgkinson, 1998; Irwin & Jones, 1998; Jones, 1983; MacCallum, 1977; Schiffman et al., 1981). The reason for this becomes apparent when the source weights are used as a basis for constructing a 'source space', of identical dimensionality to the corresponding group stimulus space, in which the relative positions of the individual participants are plotted using the source weights as coordinates.

As noted earlier, in a standard three-way scaling analysis, of the sort reported in this chapter, the sum of the source weights associated with a given source varies in approximate proportion to the percentage of variance accounted for (RSQ) in the input dataset associated with that particular source by the group space. As I have argued elsewhere (Hodgkinson, 1998), this matrix conditionality has important implications that have often been overlooked, or misunderstood, by researchers applying these techniques (see e.g. Irwin & Jones, 1998; Irwin, Jones & Mundo, 1996). Whereas stimuli/elements are represented in a group space configuration (or 'private' space configuration, derived by multiplying the coordinates of the group space by a set of corresponding source weights) as a set of *data points*, the psychological significance of which are determined on the basis of location, source weights are more appropriately construed as *vectors* emanating from the origin of the source space, the lengths of which vary as a monotonic function of the proportion of variance accounted for in the 'private' cognitions of a given source by the group space. Arguably, it is the relative directionality of these vectors that is most useful for exploring differential cognition, rather than their absolute magnitude (see e.g. C. L. Jones, 1983; Coxon, 1982; MacCallum, 1977).

Perhaps this reasoning is best illustrated diagrammatically. Figure 5.2 presents the source space associated with a basic two-dimensional solution involving six hypothetical participants. This figure has been formed by plotting the position of each participant as a point using the raw source weights as co-ordinates. A cursory examination of this figure suggests that with respect to dimension 1, participants A and B attach equally great importance to this dimension, as evidenced by the fact that they are positioned toward the far right of the 'X' axis, with participant C occupying a position somewhere in the middle of the continuum, and participants D, E and F equally attaching almost no importance to this dimension. With

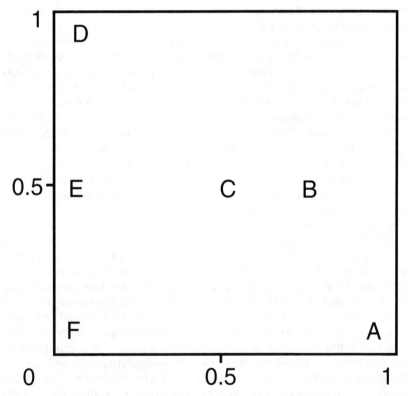

Figure 5.2   Hypothetical example illustrating the effect of using the source weights in a two-dimensional WMDS analysis in order to plot the relative positions of six individual informants
Source: Hodgkinson, 1998: 75.

respect to dimension 2, participant D seems to attach the most importance to this dimension as evidenced by his relatively extreme position along the 'Y' axis, with participants B, C and E occupying a mid-way position, and participants A and F showing the least interest.

While this interpretation is correct, it is incomplete and easily leads to misleading conclusions, as becomes evident when this figure is re-drawn, with the positions of the participants depicted more accurately as the termini of a series of vectors emanating from the origin, rather than the less accurate depiction as points (see Figure 5.3). When viewed from this perspective, it becomes clear that the nature and significance of the source weights takes on a very different form.

The 45 degree diagonal line, known as the 'line of equal weighting' (C. L. Jones & Coxon, 1980, p. 58) signifies the general orientation of par ticipants attaching equal importance to both dimensions (i.e. participants

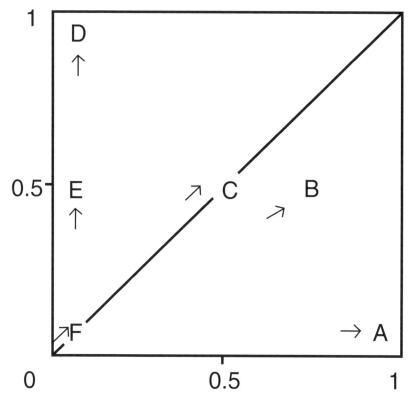

Figure 5.3   Vector representation of the source weights associated with the hypothetical two-dimensional WMDS analysis
Source: Hodgkinson, 1998: 76.

C and F). Travelling in a clockwise direction away from the line of equal weighting, the closer a given participant, or group of participants, is located to the 'X' axis, the greater the importance of dimension 1, relative to dimension 2, in accounting for their judgements of the stimuli. Conversely, travelling in an anti-clockwise direction away from the line of equal weighting towards the 'Y' axis, the greater the importance of dimension 2, relative to dimension 1, in accounting for a given individual or subgroup's judgements of the stimuli.

The basic point is that weights should be plotted as the termini of vectors emanating from the origin of the source space, rather than as points in this space. This depiction as vectors emphasizes that the relative direction of the vectors is the crucial information to be interpreted, whereas the depiction as points misleads one to interpret location. In all cases, regardless of the directionality, the lengths of the vectors vary in approximate proportion to the variance accounted for by the group space representation of the stimuli. However, it is the directionality of these vectors that provides researchers with the greatest insights concerning variation in cognition, not their relative length or magnitude.[1]

The implication of this observation is that it is inappropriate to apply ordinary linear statistical procedures, such as correlation, to the individual source weights associated with each dimension, in the search for systematic variation in cognition. Several alternatives for the proper treatment of participant source weights have been proposed in the psychometrics literature, a detailed consideration of which is beyond the scope of this book (for a review see Jones, 1983). One approach in particular, however, which is relatively straightforward in the context of a two dimensional case, simply entails computing the ratio of the weights for each participant in turn, logarithmically transformed in order to correct for positive skew [for a justification of this procedure see Coxon & Jones (1978, 1979)]. In effect,

---

[1] Not all commentators agree that such a stringent interpretation is always strictly necessary. For example, while expressing agreement that it is the direction of these vectors that contains the *primary* information concerning differences in cognition, Arabie et al. (1987, p. 34) contend that there are instances where the secondary information yielded from an examination of the relative lengths of the vectors has proven useful. In these studies systematic differences have been observed amongst subgroups in terms of the lengths of the vectors, as revealed by the relative magnitude of the source weights. According to Arabie et al., such a finding implies either that the data associated with certain sources (i.e. those with smaller source weights) is less well fitted and therefore these particular sources require a solution of higher dimensionality, or that the data associated with these sources contain greater error. Regardless of which of these interpretations turns out to be correct for a given study, in the final analysis it is difficult to see how such data (i.e. raw source weights) can be correlated meaningfully with external variables in the search for empirical relationships of *substantive* significance.

this ratio concentrates attention on the directionality of the participants' source vectors, as opposed to their magnitude, or 'goodness of fit', by capturing information regarding the angular separation of these vectors from the line of equal weighting. As noted by Coxon:

> The tangent of the angle which the... [participant source]...vector makes with the first dimension (tan θ_1) is defined as the ratio of the weight on dimension II to the weight on dimension I. Tan ($\theta_1 - 45°$) measures this predominance of dimension II over dimension I as a deflection (angular departure) from the line of equal weighting (Coxon, 1982, p. 196).

The ratios of each pair of participant source weights were logarithmically transformed using the following formula:

$$Log(dim\ II/dim\ I) \hspace{6cm} (5.6)$$

where dim I and dim II are the participant source weights associated with the market power and quality dimensions, respectively. These transformed ratios reflect the *relative* extent to which market power and quality are salient in the judgements of the participants. The greater the magnitude of this ratio for a given individual, the greater the salience of the quality dimension relative to the market power dimension. Conversely, the smaller the magnitude of this ratio for a given individual, the greater the salience of the market power dimension relative to the quality dimension. These transformed ratios provide a potentially useful index of differential cognition, in a form amenable to conventional statistical analysis (MacCallum, 1977), and therefore provide a suitable basis for investigating the extent to which the research participants' 'private' cognitions of competitive space are correlated with the exogenous variables incorporated in this study.

Correlational analysis of the participant weights at T1

The correlations between the logaritmically transformed participant source weight ratios and responses to the self-report instruments measuring the participants' background characteristics, strategic control expectancies, and environmental scanning behaviours and their perceptions of the strategy, structure, and performance of their organizations and the wider business environment, based on the T1 dataset, are presented in Table 5.2. A number of these correlations are found to be statistically significant.

Before embarking upon an interpretation of these findings, however, it is important to note that, strictly speaking, formal hypothesis testing is inappropriate, due to the fact that the source weights associated with three-way scaling procedures lack true independence. For any given analysis, the source weights (even following logarithmic transformation in ratio form) are only independently distributed from one another *conditional* upon a

Table 5.2   Pearson product-moment correlations between the logarithmically transformed ratios of the participant source weights and the various self-report measures of the participants' individual and organizational characteristics at T1[†]

Variable	Correlation with Log (dim II/dim I)
On the job experience/maturity	– 0.21**
Education and training	0.06
Environmental scanning (Frequency)	0.23**
Environmental scanning (Threat vs. Opportunity)	0.20**
Strategic locus of control	– 0.20**
Strategy	0.35***
Structure	0.27**
Environmental variation	0.31***
Wealth	0.17*
Markets	0.16*
Adaptability	0.10
Organizational climate	0.09
Prospects for growth	0.08

* $P < 0.05$, ** $P < 0.01$, *** $P < 0.001$ (2-tailed)
[†] $N = 206$–186; variation is due to missing data.

given, unchanging stimulus configuration (see e.g. Borg & Groenen, 1997; Coxon, 1982).[2] Consequently, it is advisable that any statistical procedures applied to these weights should be used for descriptive purposes only (Coxon, 1982). Bearing this restriction firmly in mind we may proceed with due caution, treating the reported significance levels merely as a basic indication of the relative magnitude of the relationships observed.

The majority of the correlations reported in Table 5.2 are statistically significant at the conventional 5 percent level or less, reflecting small-to-moderately substantial relationships, thus providing much needed evidence for the validity of the three-way scaling analysis of the CAQ. Particularly noteworthy are the relatively large correlations between the logarithmically transformed source weight ratios and the strategy, structure and environmental variation scales. The correlations between these ratios and strategy-making behaviour ($r = 0.35$) and environmental variation ($r = 0.31$) are significant at

---

[2] It is for this reason that the group space configuration derived from the T1 dataset was adopted as the reference configuration for estimating both the T1 and T2 participant weights. Since source weights are always *conditionally dependent* on the group space from which they have been derived, this strategy has the distinct advantage of enabling the researcher to make meaningful comparisons over time. In deriving the reference configuration for the present study, the complete T1 dataset was employed rather than restricting the analysis to the subsample who returned completed questionnaires on both occasions, in order to make maximum use of the available data, thereby increasing the generalizability of the findings to the wider industry.

the P < 0.001 level (2-tailed), indicative of sizeable relationships, while the correlation with organizational structure (structural sophistication) (r = 0.27) is also of a considerable magnitude, as evidenced by conventional statistical significance (P < 0.01, 2-tailed). Also noteworthy are the correlations between these ratios and frequency of environmental scanning (r = 0.23), scanning for threats versus opportunities (r = 0.20), on the job experience/maturity (r = –0.21), and strategic locus of control (r = –0.20), again highly significant by conventional standards (P < 0.01 level, 2-tailed). Finally, perhaps it is also worth noting that the correlations with two of the measures of organizational performance, wealth (r = 0.17) and markets (r = 0.16), are also significant in conventional terms, albeit at the P < 0.05 level (2-tailed).

As might be expected, the general pattern of results emerging from this analysis suggests that individuals who perceived themselves to be working within relatively proactive/innovative organizations, with relatively long-term planning horizons and sophisticated structural design features were paying considerably more attention to the quality dimension relative to the market power dimension in their competitor assessments. As we saw in the previous chapter, these organizations tended to be the larger, relatively successful companies, staffed in the main by employees characterized by relatively internal strategic control expectancies, and a marked tendency to scan the environment more frequently than their counterparts working in smaller organizations, primarily for opportunities rather than threats. This may explain the modest correlations between the logarithmically transformed source weight ratios and strategic locus of control, environmental scanning, wealth and markets. The negative correlation with on the job experience/maturity (P < 0.05) suggests that the older and more experienced participants tended to pay less attention to the quality dimension relative to the market power dimension.

A detailed consideration of the possible causal mechanisms underpinning these relationships is beyond the scope of this investigation. Given the statistical limitations associated with source weights, noted above, it would be most unwise, however tempting, to undertake a causal modelling exercise, using techniques of structural equation modelling, such as Joreskog and Sorbom's (1993) LISREL, or related techniques for the modelling of multilevel datasets (e.g. Bryk & Raudenbush, 1992; Goldstein, 1995). For now, we must content ourselves with the fact that a number of moderately-sized correlations have been detected, offering much-needed empirical support for the competitive enactment notion (and related conceptions outlined in Chapter 2) and for the validity of the CAQ at the individual-level of analysis.

Correlational analysis of the participant weights at T2

The correlations between the logarithmically transformed source weight ratios estimated using the T2 dataset and the various exogenous variables of interest, as measured at T2, are presented in Table 5.3. In rather marked contrast to the findings at T1, almost none of the relationships are found to be statistically significant.

Virtually all of the contemporaneous relationships observed at T1 have attenuated considerably at T2, to the point of statistical insignificance in conventional terms. Only the correlations with structural sophistication, organizational wealth and market dominance have remained significant across the two sets of analyses. Moreover, while the correlation with organizational structure remains significant, it has reduced in magnitude from 0.27 to a mere 0.19, indicating that the relationship at this point in time is very weak indeed.

Clearly the fact that the highly significant correlations observed at T1 have failed to materialize at T2, suggests that these relationships are time sensitive, and therefore dynamic rather than contemporaneous. Alternatively, sample attrition may have restricted the variances associated with the various measures at T2, to the extent that the relationships observed previously have atrophied – an unlikely prospect, given our observations in the previous chapter. As we have seen, sample attrition appears to have had only a minimal impact on the variances associated with the various exogenous indicators, as evidenced by the fact that there are very few statistically significant differences between those participants who returned questionnaires on the second occasion (stayers) and those who exited the study at T1 (leavers) on the variables measured at T1 (for details see Table 4.20 in the previous chapter).

Table 5.3 Pearson product-moment correlations between the logarithmically transformed ratios of the participant source weights and the various self-report measures of the participants' individual and organizational characteristics at T2[†]

Variable	Correlation with Log (dim II/dim I)
On the job experience/maturity[§]	N/a
Education and training[§]	N/a
Environmental scanning (Frequency)	0.17
Environmental scanning (Threat vs. opportunity)	0.12
Strategic locus of control	– 0.11
Strategy	0.18
Structure	0.19*
Environmental variation	0.15
Wealth	0.22*
Markets	0.19*
Adaptability	0.10
Organizational climate	– 0.08
Prospects for growth	0.05

* P < 0.05 (2-tailed)
[†] N = 114–110; variation is due to missing data.
[§] These variables were measured at T1 only

Cross-lagged analysis

While a detailed consideration of the potential causal mechanisms underpinning the links between the exogenous variables incorporated in this study and competitor cognition is beyond the scope of this investigation, nevertheless, it is highly instructive to explore the pattern of relationships that emerges dynamically, across the two time periods. If the significant correlations observed at T1 were found to be replicated dynamically, this would greatly strengthen the case for the competitive enactment notion. It would also point towards the necessity for further longitudinal studies with much larger samples, over extended time-frames, in order to develop our understanding of the time-lags involved between changes mental models of competition on the one hand, and, on the other hand, changes in strategic behaviour and the material conditions of the marketplace.

The results of the required cross-lagged correlational analysis are presented in Table 5.4. A number of the correlations are found to be highly significant suggesting that the relationships between the logarithmically transformed participant source weight ratios and the exogenous variables

Table 5.4 Cross-lagged correlations (Pearson product-moment) between the logarithmically transformed ratios of the participant source weights and the various self-report measures of the participants' individual and organizational characteristics across the two time periods[†]

| Variable | Correlation with Log (dim II/dim 1 | |
	Cognition at T1, strategy etc at T2	Cognition at T2, strategy etc at T1
On the job experience/maturity[§]	N/a	−0.04
Education and training[§]	N/a	−0.13
Environmental scanning (Frequency)	0.25**	0.19*
Environmental scanning (Threat vs. opportunity)	0.34***	0.17
Strategic locus of control	−0.21*	−0.05
Strategy	0.29**	0.21*
Structure	0.23**	0.33***
Environmental variation	0.29**	0.29**
Wealth	0.24*	0.13
Markets	0.15	0.15
Adaptability	0.21*	0.08
Organizational climate	−0.09	0.19
Prospects for growth	0.13	−0.01

* P < 0.05, ** P < 0.01, *** P < 0.001 (2-tailed)
[†] N = 114–106; variation is due to missing data.
[§] These variables were measured at T1 only

incorporated in this study are indeed dynamic across time. The overall pattern of results emerging from these analyses, taken in conjunction with the findings presented in the previous sections of this chapter, indicates that these relationships are highly complex (multidirectional). A number of the relationships which emerged at T1, but subsequently failed to materialize at T2, have re-emerged in the analyses investigating the links between the transformed source weight ratios at T1 and the various exogenous variables at T2. Several of these relationships have also re-emerged in the analyses investigating the links between the exogenous variables at T1 and the transformed source weight ratios at T2. The correlations with the strategy, structural sophistiction and environmental variation scales are particularly noteworthy in this respect. The pattern of results obtained suggests that these particular relationships are probably reciprocal over time. Several other relationships, however, seem to be uni-directional, running from cognition at T1 to strategic behaviour at T2. Particularly noteworthy here are the correlations with environmental scanning behaviours and, to a much lesser extent, strategic locus of control, wealth and adaptability.

Taken as a whole, the findings of this chapter suggest a self-perpetuating cycle may have been operating in the residential estate agency industry over the period of the study, in which the relatively strategically proactive organizations were differentially attending to the quality dimension relative to the market power dimension. Conversely, the strategically less proactive organizations were attending to the market power dimension at the relative expense of quality.

However, once again, it must be emphasized that the presentation of these results should not be construed as an attempt to formally test an underlying causal model. Nevertheless, at a descriptive level, these results have proven highly informative. A number of relationships have been detected empirically between the logarithmically transformed source weight ratios and various self-report measures designed to tap the research participants' individual and organizational characteristic strategic behaviours. To the extent that these self-report measures are reliable and valid indicators of the variables and constructs they have been designed to represent, the findings have added empirical substance to one of the most fundamental, yet largely untested, claims of the competitive enactment notion and related conceptions, namely, that competitor cognition and strategic behaviour are related, in a dynamic interplay.

Summary and conclusions

This chapter has examined empirically, the proposition that competitor cognition and strategic behaviour are inextricably intertwined with the material conditions of the marketplace. The findings presented have generally supported this fundamental, though largely untested, proposition derived from Porac et al.'s (1989) embryonic notion of competitive enactment.

The group space configuration derived in connection with the three-way scaling analysis reported above suggests that during the late 1980s estate agency businesses located in the north east Midlands area of the UK enacted their competitive strategies within a two-dimensional arena, bounded by considerations of market power and quality. An examination of this configuration revealed that the successful firms were generally perceived to enjoy greater power in the marketplace and to be offering a superior quality of service in comparison to their less successful counterparts. A series of correlational analyses revealed a number of theoretically meaningful relationships between the source weight ratios (logarithmically transformed to correct for positive skew), reflecting individual differences in the saliences of the group space dimensions, and several of the exogenous variables incorporated in the study that might have been expected to have a bearing on competitor cognition. However, when viewed against the objective market conditions that prevailed at the time the data associated with this analysis was collected, this image of competitive space is clearly an over simplification, fundamentally out of step with the performance realities of the organizations that were being held up as role models. As we saw in Chapter 3, many of these organizations were in deep financial distress during this period.

Taken as a whole, the findings presented in this chapter provide strong evidence, albeit using self-report measures, for the validity the CAQ – in conjunction with three-way scaling – as a method for investigating actors' mental models of competitive industry structures. In this way, the present investigation has added to the small but growing number of studies (e.g. Bowman & Johnson, 1992; Calori et al., 1994; McNamara et al., 2002, 2003; Osborne et al., 2001) answering calls to establish the nature and extent of relationships between actors' mental models of competitor definition and key intra- and inter-organizational processes and outcomes (Ginsberg, 1994; Hodgkinson, 1997a), thereby validating the basic notion of competitive enactment.

6
Homogeneity and Diversity

The previous chapter was concerned with the first of the three substantive issues that the present study was designed to investigate, namely, the extent to which actors' 'private' mental models of competitive space are meaningfully correlated with a range of exogenous variables that might be expected to have a bearing on competitor cognition. As we have seen, a number of the correlations observed between the exogenous variables incorporated in the study (reflecting key differences in the background characteristics of the participants and (perceived) aspects of their organizations' strategy, structure/processes and context) and the logarithmically transformed participant source weight ratios associated with the three-way scaling analysis (reflecting variations in the relative salience of the quality and market power dimensions of the group space configuration in accommodating their personal competitor assessments) were found to to be substantial, thereby adding empirical weight to the claims of social constructionist theortists (e.g. Porac et al., 1989, 1995; Porac & Thomas, 1990) that competitor cognition and choice are inextricably intertwined with the material conditions of the marketplace.

In this chapter we turn to consider the second of our substantive concerns, namely, the extent to which mental models of competitive space within an established industry sector are homogeneous or vary systematically as a function of actors' objective positions within the marketplace. The basic notion of competitive enactment developed by Porac et al. (1989) and related conceptions, such as the cognitive life cycle notion advanced by Levenhagen et al. (1993), imply that as market domains evolve from their earliest stages to fully institutionalized competitive structures, individuals' mental representations of competitor definition become highly unified over time. To the extent that this basic proposition is valid, we would expect to be able to find evidence of such belief convergence across a range of well-established industry sectors. Unfortunately, however, as discussed in Chapter 2, previous studies of competitor cognition have failed to demonstrate such convergence, due to a variety of methodological shortcomings, which the present study was designed to overcome.

As we have seen, previous researchers have tended to either assumed away the importance of potentially significant intra- and inter-organizational variations in actors' mental models and hence not searched for individual or subgroup differences (e.g. Porac et al., 1987, 1989, 1995; Porac & Thomas, 1994), or have adopted idiographic elicitation techniques (e.g. Calori et al., 1992, 1994; Daniels et al., 1994, 2002; Hodgkinson & Johnson, 1994; Johnson et al., 1998), which tend to accentuate surface-level differences in cognition at the expense of fundamental, underlying commonalities (Hodgkinson, 1997a, 2002). The primary advantage of basic three-way scaling techniques, as demonstrated in the previous chapter, lies in their ability to model competitor cognition in such a way that both commonalities (represented by the group space configuration) and subjective differences (captured by variations in the participant source weights) are revealed, thereby combining the strengths of idiographic and nomothetic procedures, while overcoming some of their characteristic limitations.

I concluded the previous chapter by suggesting that during the late 1980s, residential estate agents within the geographical area encompassed by this study enacted their competitive strategies within a common two-dimensional competitive space, with marked variations in the degree to which particular individuals attended to one dimension or the other. The fact that a number of meaningful correlations emerged at the individual-level of analysis, linking the participant source weights to a range of exogenous variables, greatly strengthened this conclusion. It is possible, however, that in the process of deriving the group space configuration that formed the underlying basis of this analysis that a number of salient differences in actors' revealed mental representations of competitive space have been inadvertently masked. One of the limitations associated with the use of profile proximities matrices (i.e. proximities matrices derived from bipolar ratings) in three-way scaling exercises is that on occasion certain dimensions may get 'washed out'. In particular this is likely to occur in studies involving large samples, where a given dimension is associated with a relatively small number of individuals (Kruskal & Wish, 1978).

As argued in Chapter 2, there are compelling theoretical reasons that point to the need for a more through investigation of the extent to which and in what ways the structural complexity of actors' representations of competitor definition systematically vary within and between organizations in the same industrial sector. Notwithstanding the methodological criticisms I have levelled against the growing number of studies that have sought to identify such variation the fact remains that the findings of these studies, which have revealed marked differences at both the individual- and subgroup-levels of analysis, are entirely commensurate with a strong line of theoretical reasoning that asserts the primacy of intra- and inter-organizational differences in cognition in a variety of non-trivial processes associated with strategy formulation and implementation, thereby opening up to question the validity of the fundamental assumption of industry-level homgeniety that has underpinned the development of competitive enactment and related notions.

In order to rule out the possibility that the aggregation procedure adopted to derive the group space configuration reported in the previous chapter has resulted in the masking of salient subgroup variations in structural complexity (and hence stem the potential criticism that the group space configuration tentatively taken to represent the industry mental model was an inadequate representation of the dimensional structure of the sample as a whole) separate subgroup analyses are required, in which multiple group space configurations are derived and systematically compared. As we have seen, two factors in particular that might influence the structural characteristics of actors' mental models of competitive space are the type of job a given individual performs and organizational membership. To the extent that the group spaces derived for separate subgroups comprising individuals drawn from different organizations and/or functional backgrounds were found to differ substantially this would greatly strengthen the claims of those researchers who have argued for the central importance of organizational structures and processes as determinants of cognitive homogeneity or heterogeneity (e.g. Hodgkinson & Johnson, 1994; Starbuck, 1976; Weick, 1979). Conversely, to the extent that these group space configurations were found to be highly similar, this would support the claims of those theorists who have asserted the primacy of social processes within the extra-organizational environment (e.g. Huff, 1982; Lant & Baum, 1995; Peteraf & Shanley, 1997; Phillips, 1994; Porac et al., 1989; Spender, 1989).

We shall begin our search for evidence of cognitive diversity by considering the group space configurations of a number of organizational subgroups. Following this we shall go on to consider the group space configurations of various functional subgroups.

Inter-organizational subgroup comparisons

In order to explore the extent of structural diversity and homogeneity in the group space configurations emerging across different types of organization involved in the study the T1 sample was divided into nine independent subgroups, as follows. Six of the subgroups were formed straightforwardly on an organization-by-organization basis, drawn from the larger local independents, regional operators and national chains. (Fortunately the six organizations in question provided generous access to relatively large numbers of individuals: 'North East Midlands Estates': N = 19; 'Brian Warner Ltd': N = 13; 'Bolton Holdings': N = 19; 'Harrison and Black': N = 17; 'Stansfield,

Gordon and Lewis': N = 20; 'Paul Schofield': N = 39).[1] The three additional subgroups were formed by sub-dividing the remainder of the sample on the basis of whether a particular individual belonged to a relatively high (N = 33 individuals from 12 firms), medium (N = 20 individuals from 19 firms) or low (N = 26 individuals from 19 firms) performing organization.[2]

A separate MDS configuration was derived for each of the nine subgroups in turn, by adopting the procedure outlined in the previous chapter for generating the group space based on the full sample. A separate set of profile proximity matrices (i.e. construct source proximity matrices) was computed for each of the nine subgroups (i.e. one matrix per construct/ attribute, aggregated across the various individual subgroup members). As in the previous run based on the full sample, analyses were performed from six down to two dimensions. Taking into account both the diagnostic criteria and substantive interpretability of the output associated with each of the nine subgroups, with the notable exception of one particular organization, 'North East Midlands Estates' (to be discussed shortly), a two-dimensional solution was strongly indicated in each case.

Comparison of the dimension weights

As reported in Appendix 2, the general pattern of dimension weights emerging from eight of the organizational subgroup analyses bears a striking resemblance to the findings presented in Table 5.1 of the previous chapter. The market power and quality dimensions which emerged in the previous analysis of the complete T1 dataset, have re-emerged in all but one case (for details of the exception see Table 6.2, in the next section).

Clearly this is a very strong indication that the process of aggregating the data at the industry-level in order to derive the results reported in the previous chapter, has not unduly distorted the dimensional complexity of the participating organizations' mental models of competitive space, with the possible exception of one particular case. Taken as a whole, these organizational-level findings are entirely consistent with what would have been expected on the basis of the body of theory outlined in Chapter 2. They indicate that at the time of intial data collection within the UK residential estate agency industry there were high levels of belief similarity across rival

---

[1] These names are aliases, adopted in order to protect the true identity of the organizations concerned, so as to safeguard anonymity agreements.

[2] This was determined on the basis of the overall relative performance evaluations, derived from the independent panel of experts (reported in Chapter 4). While less than ideal, in some respects, this strategy of aggregating across firms, on the basis of organizational performance, was adopted in order to ensure adequate sample sizes for conducting reliable subgroup analyses. In many cases, access in these smaller organizations was unavoidably restricted to a single participant. Faced with the alternative of not performing any subgroup analyses on the data gathered from these firms this strategy was seen as a reasonable compromise.

firms, thus providing empirical substance for the competitive enactment notion and related conceptions.

The results of these analyses strengthen greatly our interpretation of the findings discussed in the previous chapter. The two-dimensional structure derived from the full T1 sample, which was taken tentatively to represent 'the industry mental model', has been replicated in all but one case, suggesting that the majority of organizations in this industry, at least within the geographical region encompassed by this study, had indeed come to share highly similar beliefs about the nature of competition. Market power and quality were seen as the key ingredients for competitive success within a widely held two-dimensional space in which the various players enacted their strategies.

North East Midlands Estates: An exception to the norm?

Turning to consider the case of North East Midlands Estates, it is clear that the dimensional structure associated with this particular organization is somewhat different to the structures derived for the other organizational subgroups. As Table 6.1 shows, the two-dimensional solution associated with this particular subgroup results in a considerable reduction in the variance accounted for in the input proximities matrices upon which the analysis is based, in comparison to the three-dimensional solution (72.4 versus 81.4 percent – a net loss of 9 percent). Further increases in the dimensionality of the solution, however, yield only negligible increments in the explained variance. (As many as six dimensions, results in a net increase of a mere further 0.26 in the R square value, i.e. a marginal increase of 2.6 percent of the explained variance in comparison with the results for the three-dimensional solution.) Furthermore, the resulting pattern of dimension weights associated with the two-dimensional solution does not make sense conceptually. For these reasons the three-dimensional solution was chosen as the preferred solution for interpretation in this particular case. The dimension weights associated with this analysis are presented in Table 6.2.

The first dimension seems to reflect the differing marketing strategies (high versus low profile) of competitors, as indicated by relatively high

Table 6.1 Changes in stress and RSQ values with decreasing dimensionality for North East Midlands Estates (N = 19)

Number of dimensions	Stress	RSQ
6	0.133	0.840
5	0.154	0.836
4	0.172	0.832
3	0.209	0.814
2	0.255	0.724

Table 6.2 Dimension weights for the ratings of the attributes aggregated across the participants from North East Midlands Estates at T1 (N = 19)

Attribute	Dimension		
	1	2	3
Service to vendors	0.04	0.93	0.10
Quality of staff	0.05	0.94	0.04
Service to purchasers	0.12	0.91	0.08
Training of staff	0.45	0.61	0.47
Operating practices	0.14	0.92	0.07
Quality of advertising	0.68	0.57	0.20
Profitability	0.67	0.66	0.08
Location of business premises	0.64	0.62	0.16
Size of branch network	0.66	0.22	0.57
Range of services	0.40	0.60	0.46
Geographical coverage	0.47	0.03	0.73
Scale of charges	0.37	0.07	0.61
Degree of personal attention	0.00	0.90	0.11
Market share	0.75	0.51	0.19
Marketing profile	0.79	0.44	0.24
Degree of local knowledge	0.46	0.79	0.02
Strategic influence/power	0.76	0.49	0.27
Amount of advertising	0.74	0.56	0.18
Financial resources	0.59	0.33	0.63
Links with financial services companies	0.28	0.58	0.48
Typical range of properties for sale	0.75	0.43	0.23

source weights for the 'marketing profile' (0.79), 'strategic influence/power' (0.76), 'market share' (0.75), 'typical range of properties on sale' (0.75), 'amount of advertising' (0.74) and 'quality of advertising' (0.68) attributes. The second dimension, in contrast, appears to reflect general quality, as indicated by relatively high source weights for the 'service to vendors' (0.93), 'quality of staff' (0.94), 'service to purchasers' (0.91), 'operating practices' (0.92), 'degree of personal attention' (0.90) and 'degree of local knowledge' (0.79) attributes. Finally, the third dimension, seems to reflect differences in the financial stability/scale of competitors (large and expensive versus smaller and lower cost), as indicated by relatively high source weights for the 'geographical coverage' (0.73), 'financial resources' (0.63), and 'scale of charges' (0.61) attributes.

The results of the MDS analysis for this particular organization reveal a relatively complex structure in comparison to the other configurations considered thus far. In contrast to the other subgroups, it seems that this organization perceived the market in terms of a more highly differentiated competitive space in which the attributes are organized within a three-dimensional configuration (see Figure 6.1).

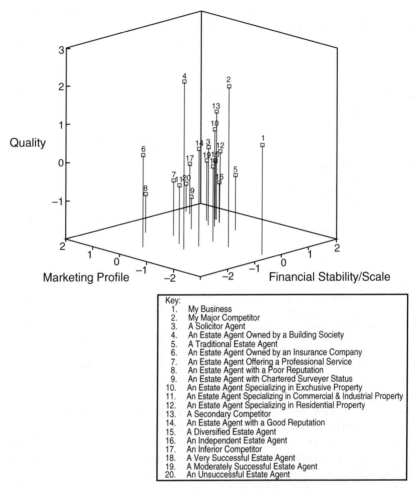

Key:
1. My Business
2. My Major Competitor
3. A Solicitor Agent
4. An Estate Agent Owned by a Building Society
5. A Traditional Estate Agent
6. An Estate Agent Owned by an Insurance Company
7. An Estate Agent Offering a Professional Service
8. An Estate Agent with a Poor Reputation
9. An Estate Agent with Chartered Surveyer Status
10. An Estate Agent Specializing in Exclusive Property
11. An Estate Agent Specializing in Commercial & Industrial Property
12. An Estate Agent Specializing in Residential Property
13. A Secondary Competitor
14. An Estate Agent with a Good Reputation
15. A Diversified Estate Agent
16. An Independent Estate Agent
17. An Inferior Competitor
18. A Very Successful Estate Agent
19. A Moderately Successful Estate Agent
20. An Unsuccessful Estate Agent

Figure 6.1   The three-dimensional representation of the 20 estate agency categories for North East Midlands Estates at T1 (N = 19; Stress = 0.209; RSQ = 0.814)

It is noteworthy that in contrast to previous analyses, 'size of branch network' is seen to be associated with both the marketing strategy dimension (0.66) and the financial stability/scale dimension (0.57), whereas 'profitability' is seen to be associated with marketing strategy (0.67) and overall quality (0.66). Thus, for this particular organization there appears to have been be a shared view that the larger firms are not necessarily the most profitable.

Whereas the majority of firms in this industry during the period of the study appeared to subscribe to a view that larger organizations were generally more effective, by virtue of their greater dominance in the market place, this organization saw size as an important facet of marketing profile. However, the fact that 'size of branch network' is also grouped with the 'financial resources' and 'scale of charges' attributes, but not 'profit', suggests that there was a recognition of the greater running costs involved in servicing extensive branch networks. Size was not directly related to profit within the cognitive structure of this organization. Here, overall quality and a high profile marketing strategy were the order of the day. Larger branch networks require greater financial resources, which in turn are associated with higher fees. Presumably, within this logic, those organizations with both a higher marketing profile (which may or may not entail an extensive branch network in order to increase visibility) and offering a superior quality service, but charging optimum fees (i.e. neither too expensive, nor too cheap) were considered to be more likely to succeed in comparison to their counterparts who did not possess this combination of attributes.

In sum, it appears that this organization was engaged in a series of complex tradeoffs, sandwiched between, on one hand, the larger and more powerful national chains, and on the other hand, the smaller local firms. This is a highly vulnerable position to occupy for any length of time, with the dangers of takeover from the larger firms and the risk of failure, due to the inability to sustain high levels of local market share, being ever present threats.[3]

Comparison of the group space configurations

Thus far, we have confined our discussion of the present findings to a consideration of the optimum dimensionality and interpretation of the dimension weights associated with the three-way scaling solutions derived for the various organizational subgroups. We turn now to consider the actual group space configurations (stimulus plots) associated with these subgroup analyses.

While the general pattern emerging from the dimension weights associated with these analyses suggests there were very high levels of belief similarity among rival firms in the residential estate agency industry concerning the overall underlying dimensionality of the competitive space in which their competive strategies were being enacted, we must also consider the possibility of variation in terms of the positioning of the competitor definition categories across the various organizational subgroup. Such a finding would imply that although organizations were in basic agreement regarding the fundamental bases of competition in this industry, there was

---

[3] This interpretation is reinforced by the fact that the organization ceased trading, soon after the completion of my fieldwork.

a lack of consensus regarding the competitive positioning of particular types of firm. In other words this would signify that rival firms differed in terms of the internal organization of their category structures within a shared mental model of competitive space. Such a finding would cast doubt on the claims of a number of theorists and researchers over the years that strategic groups, traditionally detected through the use of secondary financial data, are also enduring cognitive phenomena (e.g. Bogner & Thomas, 1993; Dandrove et al., 1998; Lant & Baum, 1995; Peteraf & Shanley, 1997; Porac & Thomas, 1990; Reger & Huff, 1993).

However, as observed by Coxon (1982), considerable caution must be exercised in attempting to make comparisons of multiple MDS configurations. In particular, researchers should strongly resist the temptation to engage in simple visual comparisons. This is because it is the *relative distances* between the various stimuli within a given configuration that contains the vital information regarding cognition, rather than the actual location of particular stimulus points. All too often, seemingly different cognitive structures, even of varying dimensionalities, turn out to be highly similar when this factor is taken into account. Clearly, researchers are fundamentally limited in terms of the extent to which this geometric information can be processed accurately using simple visual techniques of comparison, particularly, as here, in cases involving numerous stimuli and configurations (cf. Daniels et al., 1994, 1995, 2002; Daniels & Johnson, 2002; Hodgkinson, 2001a, 2002). Fortunately, however, there is a procedure available which has been designed to enable researchers to compare multiple MDS configurations geometrically.

The PINDIS model

The PINDIS (Procrustean INdividual DIfferences Scaling) model and associated algorithm, developed by Borg and Lingoes (see e.g. Borg & Lingoes, 1978, 1987; Lingoes & Borg, 1976, 1978), comprises a hierarchy of interrelated techniques which perform a series of increasingly complex transformations on the input datasets (i.e. previously derived MDS configurations) in order to maximize their commonality. The goal of a PINDIS analysis is to determine the extent to which the various configurations are comparable, or, often more importantly, in what ways they systematically differ from one another.

In cases where PINDIS is used for exploratory purposes, the various configurations (X_i's) are compared to a centroid configuration (Z), which represents the cognitive structure of the average participant (or, as in the present case, average subgroup of participants). This centroid configuration is analogous, in many respects, to the group space created by ALSCAL and related basic three-way scaling procedures. Analysis commences by performing a series of 'permissible transformations' on the original configurations (i.e. transformations that preserve the relative distances within each configuration) so as to ensure that any differences observed are real rather than apparent. For example, it is frequently the case that two configurations which appear radically different on the basis of their surface characteristics (such as the relative positioning of particular stimulus points) are more or less identical, save for the fact that one of the configurations has a dimension that has been inverted and is thus a mirror image (reflection) of its counterpart. In fact, as Coxon observes:

> ...configurations can be shrunken or expanded at will (1), moved – rigidly rotated through any angle (2), and may have the origin translated to any point in the space (3) in order to get them into greater conformity with each other. The value of any index of similarity between configurations should remain unchanged whenever these operations are performed (Coxon, 1982, p. 204).

PINDIS commences by performing whichever of these transformations that preserve the relative distances are necessary in order to maximize the communality between the individual configurations (X_i's) and the centroid configuration (Z). The communality values [r^2 (X_i, Z)] resulting from this phase of the analysis (P0) acts as a benchmark against which later solutions (i.e. ones involving the use of 'inadmissible transformations') can be evaluated. PINDIS then moves through a succession of phases in which various 'inadmissible transformations' are performed, in order to maximize the communality between the (now re-scaled) individual configurations and the centroid configuration (Z).

During the first phase (P1), PINDIS performs a transformation similar to the basic three-way scaling model employed in the analyses reported in the previous chapter. The axes of the various configurations are differentially stretched or shrunk in order to maximize the correspondence between the optimally reorientated X_i's and Z. The resulting weights $w_a^{(i)}$ reflect the saliences of the dimensions in Z for the individual X_i's and the corresponding communality, r^2 (X_i, ZW_i), denotes the goodness of fit between the X_i's and Z under this particular transformation. Any substantial changes in the communalities from P0 to P1 reflect incremental differences in the psychological information obtained.

During the next phase (P2), PINDIS calculates individual optimally reoriented Z's for each individual or subgroup (Z_i), i.e. the centroid configuration is rotated to an optimal orientation for each case. However, Coxon (1982, p. 211) has warned would-be users that, of the various PINDIS procedures, this particular model is rather complex and relatively ill-understood. Moreover, there have not been any very compelling empirical examples and he cautions researchers 'to proceed with care.' Clearly, in view of these limitations, it would be most unwise to consider adopting this particular model in the present analyses.

In the next phase (P3), vector weights $v_p^{(i)}$ ($p = 1, ..., n$) are constructed for each stimulus point. During this phase, each point in X_i and Z is regarded as the terminus at the end of a vector emanating from the origin of the multi-dimensional space and the role of the vector weights is to minimize the squared distance between the termini of the vectors in Z and the corresponding termini in the X_i's. A vector weight of unity signifies that a particular point in Z occupies an identical location in X_i. Weights that depart from unity suggest that particular stimuli within the X_i's are 'scrambled' in relation to Z. (For this reason P3 is often referred to as the 'unscrambling transformation'). A positive weight in excess of unity indicates that a particular stimulus point has been shifted further towards the extreme corner of a given quadrant, whereas a negative weight indicates a shift towards the diagonally opposite quadrant. Thus a weight of –1 indicates that the stimulus co-ordinates should be multiplied by a factor of –1 in order to 'unscramble' the relevant stimulus point for a given individual or subgroup. Once again, any changes in the goodness of fit index $[r^2 (V_iZ, X_i)]$ in comparison to values obtained under the P0, P1 and P2 transformations, indicate incremental differences in the psychological information obtained. Again, as Coxon observes:

> With some justice, the P3 model has been hailed as the major innovation introduced into MDS by PINDIS. It certainly provides a powerful and subtle form of analysis of individual difference and often gives insight into the detail about the source of variation in configurations (Coxon, 1982, p. 215).

In its fourth phase (P4), PINDIS allows each individual configuration to have its own 'point of view' (idiosyncratic origin). Given that a change of origin will undoubtedly affect the relative separation of vectors, the same set of vector weights may well have markedly different effects on differently centred configurations under this transformation. Thus, within P4, it is the idiosyncratic positions of the origins that are directly comparable and form the main focus of attention. Under this transformation the vector weights are no longer directly comparable unless the idiosyncratic shift in origin is taken into account, which entails constructing a new set of vectors all emanating from the same origin. However, as Coxon (1982) observes, as in the case of P2, this particular model has been employed very infrequently and has not generally proven fruitful. It will not be adopted in the present study.[4]

---

[4] A further 'double weighted' model (P5) is also available, in which the dimension weights and vector weights are estimated simultaneously. However, as noted by Coxon (1982), this model consumes a considerable number of degrees of freedom, and like the P2 and P4 models discussed earlier, it has rarely given richer insights into research problems. Moreover, the algorithm is notoriously unstable, frequently giving sub-optimal solutions. Consequently its use is not generally recommended.

In confirmatory mode, the procedures for the various PINDIS models are very similar to those described above, except that the various configurations under investigation are compared to an *a priori* fixed configuration, specified by the researcher as a hypothesized cognitive structure. It is evident from this brief review of PINDIS, that this procedure is highly suited for addressing the substantive concerns of this chapter. To the extent that the various subgroup configurations are found to conform to the centroid configuration (Z), following the application of permissible transformations (P0), we will have uncovered yet further evidence of belief similarity at the subgroup-level. However, should the communality values associated with these analysis fail to suggest high levels of agreement, it will be possible to investigate the nature and sources of this diversity, using the various inadmissible transformations associated with the P1 and P3 models.

PINDIS analysis of the organizational subgroup configurations

In order to examine the similarities and differences between the stimulus configurations associated with the various organizational subgroups, the nine configurations derived earlier, using the ALSCAL procedure, were submitted to PINDIS – available in the MDS(X) suite of programmes (Davies & Coxon, 1983). The results of this analysis are summarized in Table 6.3, while the accompanying centroid configuration is presented in Figure 6.2. (For details of the dimension weights and accompanying stimulus configurations associated with this analysis see Figure 6.1, Table 6.2 and Appendix 2.)

Table 6.3 Communalities between the nine organizational subgroup configurations (X_i's) and Z, under the various PINDIS transformations

	Transformation		
	0	*I*	*III*
Configuration	*Z,X (I)*	*ZW(I),X(I)*	*V(I)Z,X(I)*
North East Midlands Estates	0.71	0.74	0.78
Brian Warner Ltd.	0.86	0.88	0.93
Bolton Holdings	0.87	0.88	0.90
Harrison and Black	0.89	0.91	0.94
Stansfield, Gordon and Lewis	0.85	0.86	0.90
Paul Schofield	0.83	0.84	0.92
Low performance small firms	0.76	0.78	0.88
Medium performance small firms	0.81	0.82	0.88
High performance small firms	0.97	0.97	0.98
MEAN	0.84	0.85	0.90

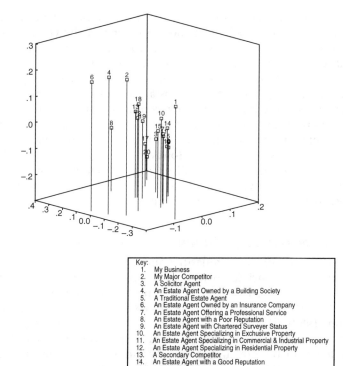

Key:
1. My Business
2. My Major Competitor
3. A Solicitor Agent
4. An Estate Agent Owned by a Building Society
5. A Traditional Estate Agent
6. An Estate Agent Owned by an Insurance Company
7. An Estate Agent Offering a Professional Service
8. An Estate Agent with a Poor Reputation
9. An Estate Agent with Chartered Surveyer Status
10. An Estate Agent Specializing in Exchusive Property
11. An Estate Agent Specializing in Commercial & Industrial Property
12. An Estate Agent Specializing in Residential Property
13. A Secondary Competitor
14. An Estate Agent with a Good Reputation
15. A Diversified Estate Agent
16. An Independent Estate Agent
17. An Inferior Competitor
18. A Very Successful Estate Agent
19. A Moderately Successful Estate Agent
20. An Unsuccessful Estate Agent

Figure 6.2 The PINDIS centroid configuration derived from the nine ALSCAL configurations for the organizational subgroups

Fitting the X_i's to this Z yields an average communality of $r^2(X_i, Z) = 0.84$, suggesting that there is considerable internal agreement between the various organizational-level configurations, which is attributable to admissible transformations. Seven of the nine subgroup configurations are especially well fitted, with communalities in excess of 0.80. As would be expected, North East Midlands Estates is the poorest fitted configuration. However, even this organization is relatively well fitted with an $r^2(X_i, Z) = 0.71$. This means that some seventy one percent of the variance in this particular configuration can be explained by the centroid configuration derived from the nine organizational subgroups, without any distortions of the relative distances amongst the points, following the application of permissible transformations. Clearly, there are very considerable similarities between each of these configurations, suggesting a high level of agreement among the participants at the organizational-level of analysis.

Turning to the 'inadmissible transformations', we see that the application of the P1 and P3 models makes very little difference to the communality values associated with the various subgroups. (The P1 model results in negligible increases of between one and three percent in the communality values associated with eight of the subgroup configurations and no increase what so ever in the case of the ninth – an average gain of one percent overall. The P3 model fairs little better with increases of between one and twelve percent over P0 – an average gain of six percent overall in comparison to P0.) In view of the relatively small incremental gains in the communality values associated with the various subgroups under P1 and P3, in comparison to the values under the P0 transformations, further investigation using these higher-order models is not warranted.[5]

The results of this analysis illustrate well the dangers of researchers relying on simple techniques of visual comparison when considering multiple revealed mental representations of competitor definition. The differences we noted earlier between the three-dimensional group space configuration derived from the North East Midlands Estates participants and the highly similar two-dimensional structures associated with the other eight organizational subgroups have turned out to be more apparent than real when submitted to the rigours of PINDIS.

The overall conclusion to be derived from these subgroup analyses is that there were very high levels of consensus indeed, at the organizational-level, regarding the bases of competition and the positioning of various types of organization within the UK residential estate agency industry, at the time of initial data collection, thus adding further empirical substance to the body of sociocognitive theory outlined in Chapter 2. We turn now to explore the extent to which these findings are replicated when we consider the mental models of competitive space associated with particular functional subgroups.

---

[5] The number of 'informative' parameters that need to be estimated under P1 and P3 to bring about the incremental gains recorded in Table 6.3 are considerable (see e.g. Borg & Groenen, 1997; Coxon, 1982; Everitt & Rabe-Hesketh, 1997; Langeheine, 1980). Under P1, for each separate configuration this corresponds to the number of dimensions of the configuration with the highest dimensionality ($r = 3$ dimensions). The number of parameters to be estimated under P3, in contrast, corresponds to the number of stimuli under consideration ($i = 20$ stimuli per configuration). Hence, the 12 percent improvement in the communality value associated with the North East Midlands Estates MDS configuration, under P3, is rather modest to say the least, considering the fact that 20 additional parameters (stimulus vectors) have been estimated, relative to P0. The average gain of six percent overall under P3 is thus a product of some 180 (i.e. 20×9) estimated parameters.

Functional subgroup comparisons

Given the extent of cognitive homogeneity observed at the organizational-level within this study, it is highly unlikely that meaningful variations will be observed across functional subgroups. Nevertheless, there is still a remote possibility that the dimensionality and structure of the competitor definition categories used to elicit the participants' mental models of competitive space in this study are influenced by the type of job an individual performs and that aggregating the data at the organizational- and industry-levels has masked this key source of variation. In order to explore this possibility, the sample was divided into seven independent subgroups on the basis of the participants' job titles at the time of data collection: area managers (N = 23), branch managers (N = 62), partners (N = 32), negotiators (N = 26), valuers (N = 19), sole principals (N = 18) and a miscellaneous subgroup (N = 26). The latter group comprised the remainder of the sample, drawn from a variety of technical and service functions, too small in number to sub-divide any further, if the resulting analyses were to be reliable.[6]

As previously, separate MDS solutions were derived for each subgroup in turn. Once again, multiple analyses were performed from six down to two dimensions in order to determine the optimum dimensionality for each subgroup. As expected, given the pattern of results reported above, in each case a two-dimensional solution was selected for further analysis on the basis of the goodness of fit criteria and the overall interpretability of the output. In all seven cases, the now highly familiar market power and quality dimensions emerged, adding even further empirical substance to Porac et al.'s (1989) competitive enactment notion and related conceptions (for details of the dimension weights and accompanying stimulus configurations associated with these subgroup analyses see Appendix 3).

In order to examine the extent of similarity between the stimulus configurations associated with these subgroup analyses, as with the organizational subgroup configurations discussed above, the data were submitted to PINDIS. The results of this analysis are summarized in Table 6.4, while the accompanying centroid configuration is presented in Figure 6.3.

To an even greater extent than in the previous analysis (of the organizational subgroup configurations), the communality values associated with the seven functional subgroup configurations under P0 are high, suggesting very strong agreement indeed between the MDS solutions following the application of permissible transformations. Fitting the X_i's to the centroid configuration (Z) under P0 yields an average communality of

---

[6] The exact composition of this particular subgroup was as follows: surveyors (N = 2), valuers and negotiators (N = 5), valuers and surveyors (N = 3), trainee managers (N = 1), personnel (N = 1), finance (N = 3), administration (N = 5) and sales managers (N = 6).

Table 6.4 Communalities between the seven functional subgroup configurations (X_i's) and Z, under the various PINDIS transformations

	Transformation		
	0	*I*	*III*
Configuration	*Z,X (I)*	*ZW(I),X(I)*	*V(I)Z,X(I)*
Area managers	0.90	0.91	0.95
Branch managers	0.95	0.95	0.97
Partners	0.92	0.92	0.95
Negotiators	0.91	0.92	0.95
Valuers	0.92	0.92	0.95
Sole principals	0.80	0.80	0.87
Miscellaneous	0.95	0.95	0.97
MEAN	0.91	0.91	0.94

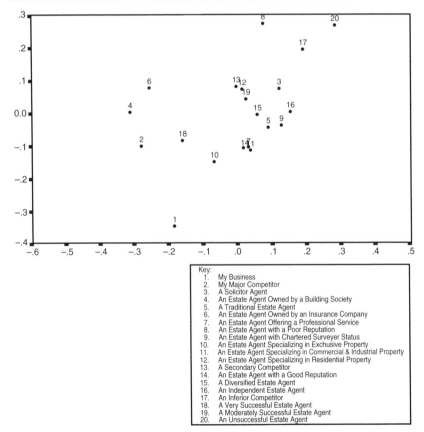

Key:
1. My Business
2. My Major Competitor
3. A Solicitor Agent
4. An Estate Agent Owned by a Building Society
5. A Traditional Estate Agent
6. An Estate Agent Owned by an Insurance Company
7. An Estate Agent Offering a Professional Service
8. An Estate Agent with a Poor Reputation
9. An Estate Agent with Chartered Surveyer Status
10. An Estate Agent Specializing in Exclusive Property
11. An Estate Agent Specializing in Commercial & Industrial Property
12. An Estate Agent Specializing in Residential Property
13. A Secondary Competitor
14. An Estate Agent with a Good Reputation
15. A Diversified Estate Agent
16. An Independent Estate Agent
17. An Inferior Competitor
18. A Very Successful Estate Agent
19. A Moderately Successful Estate Agent
20. An Unsuccessful Estate Agent

Figure 6.3 The PINDIS centroid configuration derived from the seven ALSCAL configurations for the functional subgroups

$r^2(X_iZ) = 0.91$. This means that some ninety one percent of the variance in these seven configurations can be explained by the centroid configuration, without undue distortion of the relative distances among the stimulus points.

As would be expected, given such high communality values under P0, there is nothing of any substantive significance to be gained from considering the results of the higher-order models. (The P1 model results in negligible increases of one percent in the communality values associated with two of the subgroup configurations and no increase whatsoever in the case of the other five – an average gain of zero percent overall. The P3 model fares little better, with increases of between two and seven percent over P0 – an average gain of just three percent.)

Summary and conclusions

This chapter has further investigated the claim that the two-dimensional group space configuration that emerged from the initial analysis of the T1 dataset as a whole, as reported in Chapter 5, constitutes an adequate representation from which to infer an industry-level mental model of competitor definition. The results obtained provide very strong support indeed for this assertion, fundamental to a number of the social constructionist conceptions outlined in Chapter 2.

A two-dimensional group space configuration, highly similar in form to that which was reported in the previous chapter, has emerged in all but one of 16 subgroup analyses reported in this chapter. This suggests that the configuration reported in Chapter 5 was indeed representative of the wider sample of participants. It was not unreasonable, therefore, to conclude that during the late 1980s, within the geographical locality encompassed by this study, there was a commonly perceived two-dimensional space in which the overwhelming majority of firms enacted their competitive strategies. The fact that this representation was recovered across multiple subgroups, transcending both functional and organizational boundaries, adds considerable empirical credence to the claims of sociocognitive theorists concerning the convergence of mental models of competitor definition in competitive fields that have entered the advanced stages of the cognitive life-cyce (cf. Greve, 1998; Hodgkinson, 1997a; Lant & Baum, 1995; Levenhagen et al., 1993). The findings of the PINDIS analyses reported in this chapter provide further evidence to support this line of reasoning. The fact that average communalities in excess of 80–90 percent were obtained, following permissible transformations of the various group space configurations, points overwhelmingly to the conclusion that at the time the intial fieldwork was undertaken in connection with this study there were very high levels of similarity in the dimensional and category structures of actors' mental models of competitive space.

In summary, the results reported in this chapter strongly indicate that the basic two-dimensional cognitive structure revealed through the analyses reported in Chapter 5 appears to have been highly pervasive at the time of initial data collection, transcending a number of organizational and functional boundaries. As discussed in Chapter 5, when viewed in the context of the trading figures that were reported during this period (discussed in Chapter 4), it is clear that this widely held image of competitive space was considerably out of step with the objective market conditions that prevailed at the time. These observations are entirely consistent with the cognitive inertia hypothesis, discussed in Chapter 2. As we have seen, a number of theorists and empirical researchers (e.g. Hodgkinson, 1997a; Porac & Thomas, 1990; Reger & Palmer, 1996) have argued that changes in mental models of competitor definition tend to significantly lag behind changes in the material conditions of the wider marketplace. Ultimately, however, the validity of this hypothesis can only be ascertained through the analysis of prospective, longitudinal datasets. It is to this task that we now turn in the next chapter.

7
Longitudinal Stability

The findings presented in the previous two chapters have greatly strengthened the competitive enactment notion and related conceptions, offering support for two fundamental, though previously untested, assertions. The results reported in Chapter 5 demonstrated that actors' mental models of competitive space are fundamentally intertwined with the material conditions of the marketplace. A number of substantial correlations were obtained between the logarithmically transformed source weight ratios derived from the multidimensional scaling analysis of the T1 dataset and the self-report measures of scanning behaviour, organizational structure, environmental variation, strategy and performance. We also explored these relationships over time, by calculating the cross-lagged correlations between the source weight ratios and the self-reported ratings of the research participants' individual and organizational characteristics.

In Chapter 6, we uncovered very strong evidence for a second fundamental, though previously unsubstantiated, assertion of socio-cognitive theorists of inter-organizational rivalry, namely, that within industries and markets that have entered the advanced stages of their life cycles, actors' mental models of competitive space converge to form a highly homogeneous world-view. Repeated analyses of the T1 dataset across a number of organizational and functional subgroups, failed to reveal any substantively meaningful differences in terms of the dimensional complexity of the various group space representations of competitive space or the positioning of particular types of organization within these representations.

Thus far we have been concerned primarily with the analysis and interpretation of the data from one time period. While we briefly considered the relationships between the participant source weights derived from the T2 dataset and the various self-report measures of the research participants' individual and organizational characteristics in Chapter 5, the focus of those analyses was on an exploration of the extent to which there were meaningful relationships over time between actors' revealed mental models of competitive space and the various exogenous variables incorporated in the study. As such, they did not address the issue of focal concern in the present chapter, namely, the question of the extent to which actors' mental models of competitive space are stable or change over time. As observed in Chapter 2, with one or two notable exceptions (Gronhaug & Falkenberg, 1989; Osborne et al., 2001; Reger & Palmer, 1996) almost all of the previous studies of competitor cognition have been cross-sectional in nature, this issue having largely been neglected. While the general reluctance of scholars to employ longitudinal research designs is understandable, for the reasons which we noted earlier, this field of inquiry has now reached a critical stage in its development where such studies have become an unavoidable necessity, if we are to test the rapidly developing body of socio-cognitive theory concerning the evolution of competitive structures in industries and markets to its limits.

Should it transpire that mental models of competitive space are found to be stable in the face of significant down-turns in the market, from one time period to another, this would be very powerful evidence indeed for another fundamental, though once again previously unsubstantiated, assertion of competitive enactment theory and related notions. Such a finding would demonstrate that mental models of competitive space play a key role in perpetuating the conditions of market decline, through cognitive inertia.

We turn now to consider the evidence gathered in the present study pertaining to this issue. We shall begin by considering patterns of change and stability amongst the various self-report measures of the research participants' individual and organizational characteristics across the two time periods. This will enable us to gain insights into the local market conditions that prevailed during the periods when the research participants' mental models were assessed. Having considered these findings, we will then go on to compare the participants' mental models of competitive space over time. As in Chapter 5, for the purposes of this particular exercise, we shall confine our attention to a consideration of the individual- and industry-levels of analysis.

Longitudinal comparison of market conditions and strategic behaviours

In order to assess the extent to which local market conditions and the strategic behaviours of the individual participants and their organizations remained stable or changed during the period of the study, matched-pairs *t*-tests were computed for each variable in turn, together with test-retest correlation coefficients. The former procedure informs us of the extent to which the mean levels of each variable have changed or remained stable from one time period to another, whereas the latter provides an indication of the extent of stability and change in individual scores over time. A situation in which a particular variable was characterized by a significant *t*-value, but a low and non-significant test-retest correlation, would imply that the overall direction of the change from T1–T2 which produced the significant *t*-value was not a typical pattern for the sample as a whole. Rather, this would indicate considerable diversity among individuals, with some scores increasing over time, others decreasing, the remainder being largely unchanged.

The means and standard deviations for the various self-report measures of strategic behaviour and local market conditions at T1 and T2, together with the *t*-values and the test-retest stability coefficients are presented in Table 7.1. The results clearly indicate that there have been very few changes over time amongst the variables, with moderately large and highly significant stability coefficients and non-significant *t*-values in all but three cases. The notable exceptions are the organizational climate, prospects for future growth in the immediate year ahead, and market buoyancy scales. The mean values for these three variables differ significantly from T1–T2, indicating that some changes have occurred within the period of the study. In the case of the market buoyancy scale, the *t*-value is very significant indeed, indicating that there has undoubtedly been a decline in the market between T1 and T2. Clearly this trend is very marked, as evidenced by the relatively large *t*-value and the moderately large, but nevertheless highly significant, stability coefficient associated with this particular variable.

As shown in Table 7.1, the means for responses to the six-point market buoyancy scale were 3.09 (SD = 0.85) at T1, and 2.33 (SD = 0.78) at T2, respectively. These data indicate a shift from a general perception that the local property market was 'moderately depressed' at T1 to a perception that the market was 'depressed' at T2. The result of the matched pairs *t*-test was highly significant (t = 8.43, df = 113, $P < 0.001$), indicating that there has undoubtedly been a decline in the market between T1 and T2. The test-retest correlation, though rather moderate in size, was also found to be highly significant (r = 0.32, df = 112, $P < 0.001$), providing a further indication that this trend is very marked.

These findings bear out our earlier discussion concerning the history of this industry. As we have seen, the period immediately leading up to the initial wave of data collection was characterized by a marked boom in the property market across the country as a whole. For a number of years following this period, however, estate agents endured a major long-term recession. Responses to the market buoyancy scale at T1 indicate that this recession was just beginning to emerge during the initial period of data collection. By the time of the second wave of data collection, the recession was well and truly developed, as evidenced by the highly significant decrease in scores on this scale at T2.

Before considering the meaning of the significant *t*-values associated with the organizational climate and prospects for future growth scales,

Table 7.1 Means, standard deviations, t-values and stability coefficients for the various self-report measures of market conditions and strategic behaviour across the two time periods[†]

Variable	T1		T2		t-value	Test-retest stability
	Mean	SD	Mean	SD		
Environmental scanning (Frequency)	4.23	0.74	4.25	0.70	−0.37	0.68***
Environmental scanning (Threat vs. opportunity)	5.08	1.01	5.18	1.00	−1.04	0.54***
Strategic locus of control	2.56	0.45	2.55	0.47	0.30	0.51***
Strategy	4.14	1.17	4.03	1.12	1.47	0.76***
Organizational structure	3.90	1.00	3.86	0.92	0.57	0.62***
Environmental variation	4.21	0.77	4.14	0.72	1.13	0.65***
Wealth	4.41	1.34	4.18	1.28	1.68	0.44***
Markets	4.38	1.12	4.43	1.05	−0.38	0.43***
Adaptability	4.85	1.06	4.90	1.00	−0.48	0.42***
Organizational climate	5.64	1.07	5.38	1.10	2.03*	0.24*
Prospects for future growth	4.84	0.88	4.61	0.96	2.02*	0.07
Market buoyancy	3.09	0.85	2.33	0.78	8.43***	0.32***

* P < 0.05, ** P < 0.01, *** P < 0.001
[†] N = 114–108; variation is due to missing data.

once again we must bear in mind the note of caution issued earlier, regarding situations in which multiple statistical tests have been performed on common datasets. As noted in Chapter 4, for every twenty statistical tests performed on a given sample, we would expect to obtain at least one significant result on the basis of chance alone, taking the conventional five percent cut-off level as the criterion. It is particularly important that we bear this point in mind at this juncture on account of the fact that the *t*-values associated with these variables barely reach significance at the five percent level. Given the fact that as many as twelve *t*-tests have been performed on the present dataset, there is a strong possibility that either or both of these significant results has occurred due to chance factors.

Bearing this caution in mind, it is clear that there have been slight declines in the average levels of organizational climate and prospects for future growth across the sample between T1 and T2. However, the stability coefficients for these particular variables are rather low, suggesting that there are also considerable deviations from this general trend within the sample. In the latter case, this variation within the sample is particularly pronounced, as evidenced by a stability coefficient of virtually zero ($r = 0.07$). This result implies that there is no clear discernible pattern, a number of individuals probably having severely underestimated their prospects for growth at T1 and having experienced a pleasant surprise in the interim period, others having overestimated their prospects for growth at T1 and having been shocked by the extent of the subsequent down-turn in the market in the interim period, and still others having experienced no change on this particular variable.

We should also bear in mind that the sample of non-returners was found to differ significantly (at the one percent level) from the returners in relation to this particular variable, as reported in Chapter 4. The mean value for the non-returners was found to be significantly higher than the mean value for the returners, suggesting that the sample at T2 is biased, with an under-representation of those individuals who had a tendency towards an optimistic outlook regarding future growth during the earlier period.

Nevertheless, the overall pattern emerging from these analyses is highly informative. The results strongly suggest that, on the whole, there have been no discernible changes in the strategic behaviours of the research participants and their organizations, accompanying the obvious decline in the property market which occurred during the intervening period between the two data collection points. Having established that the participants perceived a significant decline in the state of the property market property from T1–T2, but the perceived strategic behaviours of estate agents were generally stable across time, it now remains to be seen to what extent the research participants' mental models of competitive space changed or remained stable during the same period.

Longitudinal analyses of mental models of competitive space

Longitudinal comparison of the participant source weight ratios

In order to establish the extent of stability and change in actors' 'private' mental models of competitive space, the logarithmically transformed ratios of the source weights associated with each of the individual participants were compared over time. As discussed in Chapter 5, these ratios (which were derived from the two-dimensional group space reported in Figure 5.1), represent the relative salience of each dimension (i.e. market power and quality) for each individual. (Recall that the greater the magnitude of this variable in the direction of the positive pole, the greater the salience of the quality dimension relative to the market power dimension; conversely, the greater the magnitude of this variable in the direction of the negative pole, the greater the salience of the market power dimension relative to the quality dimension.)

The mean values of the logarithmically transformed ratios of the source weights (i.e. the geometric means of the ratios) were -0.18 (SD = 0.25) at T1, and -0.19 (SD = 0.26) at T2, respectively. These results clearly indicate that there has been no meaningful change whatsoever in the mean source weight ratios over time. This finding was confirmed by the results of a matched-pairs t-test which yielded a non-significant difference ($t = 0.17$, df = 113, $P > 0.05$). Conversely, the test-retest correlation was found to be highly significant (r = 0.57, df = 112, $P < 0.001$), suggesting considerable stability in the relative saliencies of the market power and quality dimensions, from T1–T2, despite a considerable down-turn in the market.

While the previous analyses have indicated considerable stability in the relative saliencies of the dimension weights associated with the individual research participants across the time periods covered by this study, there is a strong possibility that the research participants who dropped out of the study after the first phase differed significantly in their initial cognitions from those who subsequently returned at T2. If this should turn out to be the case, we would have to re-consider the meaning of the findings reported above. Such a finding would render the results of our longitudinal analysis inconclusive. The apparently high levels of stability we have observed would be potentially confounded due to bias resulting from sample attrition. In order to explore the extent to which sample attrition poses a threat to the validity of the findings, the mean logarithmically transformed source weight ratios associated with the returners and non-returners derived at T1 were compared using an unrelated t-test. The means were -0.18 (SD = 0.25) and -0.16 (SD = 0.23) for the returners and non-returners, respectively. Fortunately, the results of the *t*-test performed on these data confirmed that this negligible difference is not statistically significant ($t = 0.68$, df = 204, $P > 0.05$).[1]

Comparison of the group space configurations

The previous analyses demonstrated that there are high levels of stability of competitor cognition in this industry, as assessed by the logarithmically transformed source weight ratios. The relative saliencies of the market power and quality dimensions did not differ from T1–T2 and the test-retest correlation was found to be highly significant. Moreover, the fact that there are no discernible differences between the T2 returners and non-returners in terms of the source weight ratios derived at T1, indicates that the longitudinal stability we have observed is not confounded by bias due to sample attrition.

Clearly, to the extent that the group space from which the source weight ratios have been derived is stable from one time period to another, the results of these analyses are informative. Unfortunately, however, this particular method of assessing cognitive stability does not take account of the possibility that meaningful changes may have occurred in terms of the dimensional structure of the industry-level mental model from T1–T2 (cf. Reger & Palmer, 1996). Such changes would imply that rival firms within the estate agency industry were actively attempting to adjust the bases on which they compete with one another, in response to the significant down-turn in the property market which occurred during this period. Clearly this would call into question fundamentally the role of industry-level mental models in market decline.

---

[1] As noted in Chapter 5, strictly speaking, formal hypothesis testing involving the use of source weights from three-way scaling analyses is inappropriate, due to the fact that the weights lack true independence, being conditional upon the group space configuration from which they have been derived. Nevertheless, when used for descriptive purposes, as a broad indication of the magnitude of the correlations among and differences between the means of the source weights over time, along similar lines to the use of the significance tests reported in Chapter 5 in respect of the correlations between the source weights and the various exogenous variables incorporated in the study, the findings are revealing, showing that the overall pattern of source weights is highly similar over both time periods, with no discernible differences between those who dropped out of the study at the end of T1 and those who completed the CAQ on both occasions. The findings are entirely commensurate with the cognitive inertia hypothesis discussed in Chapter 2. The magnitude of the test-retest (T1–T2) correlation between the logarithmically transformed source weight ratios is very substantial indeed, as revealed by the highly significant accompanying *P*-value, while the non-significant t-values mean that there is no evidence to reject the null hypotheses in respect of cognitive change and sample bias due to attrition, thus greatly strengthening the confidence that can be placed in my interpretation of the findings, as outlined above.

Given the relatively short timeframe surrounding this study, if the dimensional structure of the industry-level mental model was found to vary concomitantly with the changes in market conditions experienced over the two data collection periods, this would imply that competitor cognition is little more than a covariate. If, on the other hand, the highly pervasive two-dimensional cognitive structure we obtained repeatedly at T1 was to be replicated at T2, this would constitute powerful evidence for the assertion that changes in industry-level mental models of competitive space lag behind changes in market conditions. In other words, this finding would offer strong empirical support for the cognitive inertia hypothesis advanced in Chapter 2. That is, industry-level mental models of competitive space and associated 'recipes' (Grinyer & Spender, 1979a, 1979b; Huff, 1982; Spender, 1989) may perpetuate the conditions of industry decline, by causing organizations to continue competing on the bases of strategies which have become outmoded by the changed demands of the marketplace (cf. Bogner & Barr, 2000; Murphy, Mezias & Chen, 2001; Sutcliffe, 2001).

In order to explore the extent to which the basic two-dimensional industry-level mental model observed repeatedly at T1 was replicable over time, separate MDS configurations were derived for the returners using the competitor analysis questionnaire data from both time periods (i.e. separate configurations were derived for T1 and T2). In addition, a third configuration was derived for the non-returners (using the T1 dataset), in order to compare the extent to which the group-level mental model associated with this particular subgroup differed from the group-level mental model associated with the returners assessed at T1. Once again, any substantial differences between the configurations associated with the returners and non-returners – assessed at T1 – would alert us to the strong possibility that the T2 dataset was unduly biased, due to sample attrition.

As in previous runs, analyses were performed from six down to two dimensions, in order to ascertain the optimum dimensionality for each subgroup in turn. In each case a two-dimensional solution was selected on the basis of the goodness of fit criteria and a consideration of the interpretability of the output. Once again, the general patterning of the dimension weights associated with these analyses seems to reflect market power and quality, suggesting that there are no substantive differences between the returners and non-returners in terms of the structural characteristics of their mental models at T1, and that the industry-level cognitive structure is highly stable over time. (For details of the stimulus co-ordinates and dimension weights associated with these analyses see Appendix 4.)

In order to assess the extent of the similarity between these cognitive structures, the various stimulus configurations were submitted to PINDIS. This analysis was performed in confirmatory mode, with the configuration derived from the competitor analysis questionnaire data associated with the returners assessed at T1 input as the fixed hypothesis configuration (Z).

Thus the goal of this analysis was to ascertain the degree of fit between this particular configuration and the configurations associated with the same group of participants assessed at T2 and the non-returners assessed at T1. To the extent that the T2 configuration departs from Z under P0, as evidenced by a relatively low communality value relating that particular configuration to the reference configuration (i.e. Z), the industry-level cognitive structure has changed from T1–T2. To the extent that the T1 non-returners' configuration departs from Z under P0, this will signify that there are systematic differences in the cognitive structures of the returners and non-returners at T1. If such differences should turn to out to be substantial, again as evidenced by a relatively low communality value relating that configuration to the reference configuration (Z), for the reasons which we noted above, this would imply that any changes observed across the two time periods are potentially confounded by bias arising from sample attrition. The results of this analysis are summarized in Table 7.2. Fitting the X_i's to the reference configuration, Z, yields an average communality of $r^2(X_i, Z) = 0.96$, indicating that there is virtually perfect internal agreement under the P0 transformations between the configurations associated with the non-returners assessed at T1 and the returners assessed at T2 in relation to the configuration associated with the returners assessed at T1. The results reveal that some 95 percent of the variance in the configuration associated with the non-returners assessed at T1 can be explained by the configuration associated with the returners assessed at T1 without unduly distorting the relative distances amongst the data points. An even greater proportion of the variance (98 percent) associated with the returners' configuration assessed at T1 can be accounted for by the reference configuration under P0.

The overwhelming conclusion to be drawn from this analysis is that the two-dimensional cognitive structure we have observed on numerous occasions throughout this study is highly stable over time and that there are no discernible differences in terms of the cognitive structures associated with those research participants who dropped out of the study at the end of the

Table 7.2 Communalities between the group space configurations for the non-returners assessed at T1 and the returners assessed at T2 (X_i's) with the returners assessed at T1 (Z), under the various PINDIS transformations

Configuration	Transformation		
	0	*I*	*III*
	Z,X (I)	ZW(I),X(I)	V(I)Z,X(I)
Non-returners assessed at T1	0.95	0.95	0.95
Returners assessed at T2	0.98	0.98	1.00
Mean	0.96	0.96	0.98

first phase and those who subsequently returned completed questionnaires for a second time. The results clearly indicate that the highly significant down-turn in the property market from T1–T2 has had no material impact on the way in which estate agents generally construe their competitive worlds.

Summary and conclusions

In this chapter we have explored empirically the extent to which mental models of competitive space are stable or change over time. With very few exceptions, previous studies of competitor cognition have neglected to address this fundamentally important issue, due to an understandable reluctance of scholars to employ research designs which necessitate data collection at more than one point in time. The few studies that have previously addressed the focal concerns of this chapter, have done so using inadequate research designs and associated research methods, as discussed in Chapter 2.

The present findings demonstrate powerfully the benefits to be gained from *prospective* longitudinal studies, using relatively sophisticated methods of data collection and analysis. As we have seen, the results clearly indicated that despite a considerable down-turn in the housing market from T1–T2, neither the strategic behaviours of the research participants and their organizations nor their mental models of competitive space have changed to any meaningful extent. On the contrary, we observed minimal changes in terms of the various self-report measures of organizational strategy, structure, environmental variation, strategic locus of control, environmental scanning behaviour and organizational performance. The changes observed were found to be significant for only two organizational performance variables, namely, organizational climate and prospects for future growth in the immediate year ahead. The differences associated with these particular variables were found to be barely significant at the five percent level when analyzed using the matched pairs *t*-test, suggesting they are of little practical consequence. In short, the overall pattern emerging from the longitudinal analyses of the various measures of strategic behaviours, strongly indicated that, in general, within the duration of time encompassed by this study, estate agents had not changed their strategies in response to the highly significant down-turn in the property market experienced from T1–T2. This is not to say that we would have failed to observe such changes had the study been conducted over a longer time-frame.

As we saw in Chapter 3, a number of significant changes occurred in this industry in the years immediately following the fieldwork associated with this study, not least of which was the significant down-sizing of many operations in response to the continuing recession in the housing market. Subsequently, the UK housing market as a whole has enjoyed a substantial period of unprecedented buoyancy and growth. However, the analysis of the self-reported strategic behaviours and the revealed mental models of the research participants presented in this chapter indicated stability within the time period encompassed by the study. Actors' mental models of competitive space were found to remain highly stable over time, both at the level of the individual research participant and at the more general level of the industry as a whole, despite significant changes in market buoyancy from T1–T2. Clearly these findings provide a convincing demonstration of the deleterious role played by mental models of competitor definition in the evolution of the competitive behaviour of groups of firms (see also Gronhaug & Falkenberg, 1989; Porac & Thomas, 1990; Reger & Palmer, 1996).

The findings reported in this chapter add empirical substance to the claim that the reason markets and industries mature and eventually fall into terminal decline is that changes in mental models of competitor definition generally lag too far behind changes in the material conditions of the marketplace. Over time, entire industries may become impervious to the fact that their competitive strategies are outmoded in relation to the demands of the environment. This negative cycle is only broken when somehow particular organizational actors manage to stand back and distance themselves from the highly pervasive industry-level world view that has come to prevail, or new competitors, not constrained by this mode of thinking, enter the arena and create new recipes for competitive success (cf. Bogner & Barr, 2000; Lant & Phelps, 1999; Levenhagen et al., 1993; Zajac & Bazerman, 1991).

8
Conclusions and Implications

As we have noted at several junctures, in a number of respects the socio-cognitive analysis of competitor definition is still at an embryonic stage of development. Despite the tremendous growth in the advancement of concepts in an effort to account in social constructionist terms for the emergence and evolution of competitive structures in industries and markets, there have been only limited inroads made in terms of the accumulation of high quality empirical data upon which to develop and test substantive theory in this area. Clearly, the time has now come to move beyond the small-scale, inductive studies that served the field so well in its early years, if the theoretical notions that have emerged from this body of work are to subjected to adequate empirical scrutiny. The research reported in this book constitutes an early response to this basic challenge, being one of the first relatively large scale, multi-level longitudinal empirical studies within this rapidly growing field of inquiry.

As we have seen, much of the theorizing that has occurred over past 10–15 years (e.g. Lant & Baum, 1995; Lant & Phelps, 1999; Levenhagen et al., 1993; Peteraf & Shanley, 1997; Porac et al., 1987; Porac & Thomas, 1990; Reger & Huff, 1993) has developed in a cummulative fashion, drawing inter alia on the insights of cognitive categorization theory (Rosch et al., 1976; Rosch, 1978), social identity theory (Ashforth & Mael, 1989; Tajfel & Turner, 1979, 1986), social learning theory (Bandura, 1986; Wood & Bandura, 1989) and schema theory (Bartlett, 1932) from the psychological sciences and sociologically informed notions from the writings of Berger and Luckmann (1967), institutional theory (DiMaggio & Powell, 1983; Meyer & Rowan, 1977), situated learning theory (Wenger, 1998) and population ecology theory (Tuma & Hannan, 1984), in an attempt to develop an integrated social constructionist explanation of business rivalry, one that is fully commensurate with the theory of strategic groups and related conceptions (Caves & Porter, 1977; Hunt, 1972; Porter, 1980) grounded ultimately in the structure → conduct → performance paradigm of industrial economics (Bain, 1956; Mason, 1957). One notion in particular that has proven to be foundational throughout the development of this body of work is the notion of competitive enactment, first introduced by Porac and his colleagues in their study of the Scottish knitwear sector (Porac et al., 1989), drawing in turn on the seminal work of Weick (1969, 1979). The present study was designed in order to explore three unresolved empirical issues arising from the competitive enactment notion that remain as pressing today as they were during the late 1980s-early 1990s, at the time of data collection, namely:

1. The extent to which measurable features of actors' mental models of competitor definition correlate with measurable strategic behaviours and measurable features of the organization and its environment;
2. The extent to which and in what ways actors within a given industry hold similar or diverse mental models of competitor definition;
3. The extent to which these mental models remain stable or change over time.

The UK residential estate agency industry, an industry characterized by high rates of environmental change over relatively short timescales and fundamental inter-organizational dependencies, represents an ideal laboratory in which to explore these issues. As we saw in Chapter 3, the estate agency industry was beset with a number of seemingly intractable difficulties in the period leading up to and during in the fieldwork. The findings of the present investigation provide insights into the ways in which these problems impacted on estate agents' collective mental model of competitor definition, and in turn how this cognitive structure came to shape, and subsequently dominate, competition throughout the industry during the late 1980s and early 1990s.

In keeping with the predictions derived from the work of Porac and his colleagues, this study has revealed that within the geographical area and time period encompassed by the fieldwork, there is very clear evidence that there are indeed detectable empirical linkages between actors' mental models and a number of exogenous variables of theoretical interest, reflecting key differences in the background characteristics of the participants, and their individual and organizational strategic behaviours and organizational performance. Also in keeping with the predictions of this embryonic theory, actors' mental models were found to be highly convergent, with virtually no meaningful differences at the organizational- and functional subgroup-level of analysis in terms of the number and nature of the dimensions characterizing the participants' judgements of competitor definition categories. Furthermore, participants' mental models were found to remain highly stable in the face of significant changes in market conditions, again entirely in keeping with the predictions of extant theory. In this final chapter, we shall consider the wider implications of this work for the advancement of socio-cognitive theories of competitor definition, the development of methodological approaches for the elicitation and comparative analysis of actors' representations of competitor definition, and the practice of strategic management.

Implications for theory

This study has uncovered a two-dimensional model of competitive space which seems to have been widely shared throughout the UK estate agency industry. With the notable exception of one organizational subgroup, repeated multidimensional scaling analyses using the SPSS ALSCAL routine have revealed a highly similar two-dimensional representation that transcends the various organizational and functional subgroups investigated. The PINDIS analyses provided additional evidence that the competitive space maps of the various subgroups are highly similar to one another. The fact that such high communality values were obtained for each of the subgroups, following permissible transformations (under P0), indicates that there was a strong consensus throughout the industry concerning the competitive positioning of various types of firm.

Despite the inclusion of a relatively large number of attributes within the competitor analysis questionnaire, time-and-again the multidimensional scaling analyses revealed a highly undifferentiated cognitive structure, which encapsulated the bases of competition within a two-dimensional space. These findings further enrich our understanding of the ways in which actors' represent reality when thinking about competitors, revealing the bases of competition in this industry in general to be highly simplified. It seems that not only do individuals attend to a limited subset of the myriad of potential competitors, they also reduce the potential complexity of competitive space to a small number of dimensions, as evidenced by the various subgroup analyses of the competitor analysis questionnaire data (cf. Clark & Montgomery, 1999; de Chernatony et al., 1993; Gripsrud & Gronhaug, 1985; Hodgkinson & Johnson, 1994; Odorici & Lomi, 2001; P. Johnson et al., 1998; Porac et al., 1987, 1989, 1995; Porac & Thomas, 1994; Reger & Huff, 1993). The findings strongly imply that the two-dimensional image of competitive space widely held among the research participants severely constrained innovation throughout the industry. The results reveal that the entrance into estate agency of the major national chains led each of the various players, smaller local and larger regional/national firms alike, to focus primarily on the strategies of the latter. Multiple analyses of the competitor analysis questionnaire data revealed time and again a similar two-dimensional structure in which the national and regional chains are typically regarded as highly successful, in contrast with the smaller, local operators.

Various supplementary analyses of the biographical, attitudinal and organizational characteristics questionnaire data add credence to this interpretation of the findings. As we have seen, a number of significant correlations were obtained between organizational size and performance, on one hand, and, on the other hand, the various self-reported measures of strategy, structure, environmental variation, organizational performance, environmental scanning and strategic locus of control. These findings provide a convincing demonstration of the existence and negative impact of strongly held collective mental models of competitor definition within the estate agency sector on strategy and performance. The overall picture emerging from the correlational analyses of these exogenous variables variously reported in Chapters 4 and 5 is one of an industry in which the larger national, semi-national and stronger regional firms were generally the shapers of innovative competitive strategies, with the smaller, locally based firms at the mercy of what they considered to be largely uncontrollable environmental forces.

Moreover, the analyses of the longitudinal data revealed that despite highly significant differences from T1–T2 in relation to self-reported perceptions of overall levels of market activity, with a general down-turn in market conditions being widely experienced, virtually no significant differences occurred in relation to any other variable measured in the study. These results provide an even stronger indication that, at the time of the fieldwork, strategic innovation in the UK residential estate agency industry had largely stagnated. Companies were deadlocked into strategies that were no longer appropriate to the general market conditions in which they were competing.

Competitive enactment and related conceptions

The results of the present investigation bear out the observations of Porac and his associates in their study of the Scottish knitwear industry (Porac et al., 1989). As in the Scottish knitwear study, the present results clearly indicate that during the late 1980s–early 1990s within the estate agency industry there was a shared set of beliefs about how firms compete in the marketplace, which was so widespread that it came to over-ride any differences which may previously have existed between various organizational and functional subgroups. As in the case of the Scottish knitwear study, the present findings provide a powerful illustration of the basic features of competitive enactment (Porac et al., 1989; Porac & Thomas, 1990).

According to Weick (1969, 1979) organizations actively construe their environments through processes of collective sensemaking. However, in time these social constructions of reality come to shape the behaviour of organizations as if they were true environmental forces. As we saw in Chapter 2, extending this argument to the problem of competitor definition, Porac and his colleagues have suggested that competitive structures within industries and markets are developed through the emergence of group-level mental models which transcend organizational boundaries:

> These shared beliefs establish the identity of individual firms and help to create a stable transactional network in which the actions of rivals are at least somewhat predictable (Porac et al., 1989: 400).

According to Porac et al., belief similarity develops over time because organization members from rival firms continually confront similar technical/material problems with a finite number of solutions. Belief similarity results from interpreting the same environmental cues and solving the same problems. The present findings give strong empirical substance to these arguments. The continual uncertainty within the estate agency industry created the need for competing firms to gather information about their relative strengths and weaknesses. This information was represented within the minds of organization members in the form of a mental model. However, these mental models did not develop in social isolation. Rather, the various transactions between individuals from rival firms led to the creation of socially shared beliefs, which in turn came to define the competitive arena and inform the strategic choices of particular organizations.

As we observed in Chapter 3, within the estate agency industry there are very high levels of interdependency both within and between rival firms. Organization members continually cross organizational and functional boundaries in the performance of their various tasks. Direct and indirect transactions occur between partners, valuers, negotiators, surveyors and the other individuals occupying key boundary spanning roles within and between rival firms, on a frequent basis. During the course of these transactions formal and informal communications take place, communications which permit the sharing of information about market conditions and activities. It is this mutual exchange of information that resulted in an externalizing of individual mental models in a publicly observable form. The net result of these regular direct and indirect contacts within this close-knit transactional network is that organization members from rival firms came to develop highly unified perceptions of how to compete and the competitive positioning of the various types of firm within the industry.

The high levels of belief similarity observed in this study are also entirely commensurate with other social constructionist notions that have been advanced more recently by theorists in an attempt to further enrich our understanding of the development of stable competitive structures, not least the notions of mimetic adoption and normative isomorphism from the realms of institutional theory (Daniels et al., 2002; Greve, 1998; Lant & Baum, 1995; Spencer et al., 2003). Arguably, one reason for the unusually high levels of homogeneity in the group space configurations derived from the three-way scaling analyses of the competitor analysis questionnaire data associated with the various organizational and functional subgroups is because the extensive interactions among valuers, surveyors and negotiators across rival firms that necessarily occur within this industry led to a convergence of mental models through mutually reinforcing processes of normative isomorphism and mimetic adoption, along similar lines to those observed by Greve (1998) and Lant and Baum (1995) in their respective studies of competition among Manhattan hotels and the spread of new radio formats among commercial radio stations. The present findings are also entirely compatible with the social learning theory concepts of relational modelling and vicarious learning, as employed by Peteraf and Shanley (1997) in their theory of strategic group formation.

Industry recipes and cognitive inertia

As in the Scottish knitwear study of Porac et al. (1989, 1995), the present results clearly indicate that within the UK residential estate agency industry (during the late 1980s–early 1990s) a generic recipe (Huff, 1982; Grinyer & Spender, 1979a, 1979b; Spender, 1989) developed, which in turn came to define a limited number of strategic possibilities for individual firms. Mutually enacted perceptions of competitive space provided the basic weaponry with which battles in the marketplace were to be fought. As in the knitwear study, the present findings illustrate how a firmly established mental model of competitive space can limit the strategic options of individual firms, as cognition and choice become inextricably intertwined with the material conditions of the marketplace. The findings in general indicate that firms within this industry attempted to differentiate themselves on the basis of two broad dimensions, namely, market power and general quality of service. As we have seen, more radical strategic innovations, such as differentiating on the basis of price and/or the types of properties sold, perhaps underpinned by elaborate marketing arrangements were not considered feasible by the vast majority of estate agents.

The notion of industry recipes has enjoyed popular credence among strategic management scholars over the years, as a means of explaining the emergence and diffusion of competitive strategies (see e.g. Bogner & Barr, 2000; Grinyer & Spender, 1979a, 1979b; Huff, 1982; Huff & Huff with Barr, 2000; Porac et al., 2002; Porac & Thomas, 2002; Spender, 1989; Whitley, 1992). However, the concept is not without its critics (e.g. Baden-Fuller & Stopford, 1992; Phillips, 1994; Slater, 1984; Stopford & Baden-Fuller, 1990). In particular, one of the dangers associated with this term is the tautological implication that firms must necessarily imitate or adapt the strategies of other successful firms within an industry in order to prosper. As noted by Baden-Fuller and Stopford (1992), the inevitable consequence of this process is that eventually all industries will reach a stage of stagnation and ultimate decline, as industry-level cognition becomes inextricably intertwined with the material conditions of past successes, thus filtering out the objective reality of changing circumstances and giving rise to outmoded practices (see also Zajac & Bazerman, 1991). The present findings illustrate empirically the reality of these dangers. The collective outlook of the smaller, less powerful organizations studied was generally one of defeatism, as revealed through the analyses of the questionnaire responses. As will be discussed later, these observations have considerable implications for the practice of strategic management, pointing to the need for the adoption of tools, techniques and processes that promote the questioning of actors' underlying assumptions, with a view to attaining the requisite variety in mental models to avoid the potential pitfalls of cognitive bias and cognitive inertia (cf. Bogner & Barr, 2000).

Mental models of competitive space, strategy and performance

In Chapters 5 and 7, I drew attention to a number of limitations associated with the analysis of individual differences in cognition using three-way scaling procedures. To reiterate, the fact that the source weights reflecting differences in the salience of the group space dimensions among participants are conditionally dependent, by virtue of having been estimated from a common group space configuration, places a number of restrictions on the conclusions that can be derived from the findings. Particular caution is required when subjecting such weights to tests of statistical inference because any changes to the group space configuration can have quite dramatic effects on the outcome and commentators are generally agreed that significance testing, if employed at all, should be undertaken for descriptive purposes only (see e.g. Coxon, 1982). With this caveat firmly in mind, the T1 analyses of the individual participant source weights associated with the industry-level ALSCAL solution provided further illuminating insights into the negative, self-defeating cycle of decline which seems to have imprisoned the smaller firms during the period encompassed by this study. These analyses revealed significant correlations (indicating that the relationships are sizeable) between the relative saliences of the dimensions for individual organization members and a number of measures of organizational structure and strategy. The results clearly indicated that those organizations pursuing relatively long-term, proactive, innovative strategies attached greater weight to the quality dimension relative to the market power dimension, in contrast with their less proactive/innovative counterparts. As we have seen, these firms were generally the larger and more powerful organizations, with considerable assets at their disposal. It is highly significant, therefore, that these organizations attached greater weight to the quality dimension relative to the market power dimension.

My findings provide us with further insights into the processes of competitive enactment. The results reveal that while rival firms shared a common awareness of the competitive weapons available within the residential industry, individuals within particular firms were differentially attending to the two dimensions, their relative salience depending on the actor's social location within the competitive arena. The findings point overwhelmingly to the conclusion that cognition, strategic choice and the material conditions of the market place had become inextricably intertwined with one another in a self-perpetuating cycle. These results provide an indication of the processes by which successful firms within this industry were able to sustain their competitive advantage by giving a relatively greater emphasis to quality. By definition, these organizations enjoyed much greater power in the marketplace, by virtue of their extensive branch networks, high profile advertising (e.g. peak time radio and television advertisements) and so on. During the period within which the field work associated with this study was undertaken, the larger/successful firms had considerable slack resources at their disposal, which they were able to direct towards improving the overall quality of their service by investing in comprehensive staff development programmes, superior quality sale details, high gloss colour brochures and so on. In short, the results suggest that the 'successful' organizations were able to project a superior image in the marketplace by virtue of their advantageous material capabilities, which in turn further enhanced their access to resources (for corroborating evidence see Chapter 3).

In contrast, in the case of the smaller, local operators, the entrance of the national chains forced these organizations to be primarily concerned with basic day-to-day survival, rather than longer-term ventures. As noted earlier, these organizations seemed to be engaged in a negative, self-defeating cycle, in which short-term performance pressures focused the attention of organization members to the market power dimension at the expense of quality. In the longer-term, however, this selective cognition may well only have served to perpetuate yet more declines in the market power available to these organizations, as the larger firms sought to introduce further innovations in quality, which in turn may have attracted an even greater share of the limited vendors and purchasers available, in what was a dwindling market.

Wider theoretical implications

The findings of the present study stand in marked contrast to those of a number of other cognitive studies of competitive positioning strategy, which have suggested that there may be considerable individual and subgroup differences in mental models of competitive space within industries and markets (e.g. Calori et al., 1992, 1994; Daniels et al., 1994, 2002; Hodgkinson & Johnson, 1994; P. Johnson et al., 1998; Reger, 1990a). While these other studies have found very low levels of agreement between research participants concerning the basic structure and content of mental models of competitor definition, a finding which has been attributed to the impact of such factors as functional responsibility, career history and individual- and organizational-level belief systems (see Chapter 2), the present study, in contrast, has found almost no evidence of such variation. On the contrary, this study has revealed very high levels of consensus across organizational and functional subgroups, regarding both the dimensional structure of competitive space and the positioning of particular types of organization. How then shall we account for these discrepant findings?

The broader theoretical contribution to be discerned from this programme of research is concerned with the processes by which industries and markets fall into general decline. The overwhelming pattern emerging from the present findings, as noted earlier, suggests that as industries enter the advanced stages of their life cycles actors' mental models of competitive space converge to form a highly homogeneous mindset, which in turn leads to the development of industry-wide norms regarding the bases of competition, dysfunctional norms which stifle innovation and change (cf. Baden-Fuller & Stopford, 1992; Bogner & Barr, 2000; DiMaggio & Powell, 1983; Greve, 1998; Lant & Baum, 1995; Levenhagen et al., 1993; Meyer & Rowan, 1977; Porac et al., 2002; Reger & Palmer, 1996). The implications are that once a relatively small number of highly successful firms have established themselves in the marketplace, there is a danger that over time the strategies pursued by these players come to dominate the thinking of organizations in general, throughout the entire industry. In other words, the strategic options of rival firms within such industries are eventually confined within the narrowly defined boundaries of accepted custom and practice. The consequence of this process for any given industry sector, if followed through to its concluding stages, is long-term stagnation and, ultimately, terminal decline.

This theoretical interpretation of the present findings does not preclude the possibility of recovery from decline. Nor is it incompatible with the predictions of those researchers cited above, whose studies have yielded substantial differences in competitor cognition at both individual- and subgroup-levels of analysis.

Regarding the first point, as Baden-Fuller and Stopford (1992) observe in the context of their study of mature businesses, there are innumerable creative measures which can and indeed should be taken by companies in declining markets in order to achieve turn-around, even in the most hostile of conditions. Indeed, the present findings demonstrate powerfully the value of cognitive analysis, as a means whereby companies can identify industry-wide blind-spots of competition, in order to provide an informative basis upon which new strategies can be developed. In this sense, the approach to competitive space mapping adopted in this study provides a powerful addition to the general stock of environmental analysis techniques (cf. Lenz & Engledow, 1986), an issue to which I shall return in due course, when considering the implications of this study for strategic management practitioners. At this stage, it is sufficient to note that the multiple analyses of the competitor analysis questionnaire data have revealed the potential efficacy of my approach to cognitive modelling as a basis for identifying the limitations of existing strategies, while, at the same time, providing strategists with illuminating insights that could inform the development of new strategic choices.

Regarding the second point, it is highly noteworthy that the organizations studied by previous researchers where the outcomes have indicated variation in perceptions of the bases of competition and competitive positioning have almost invariably been ones experiencing major upheavals at the time of data collection. Reger's (1990a) study, for example, was conducted in the Chicago banking market, following a number of recent changes to the rules regulating business practices. Similarly, in Hodgkinson and Johnson's (1994) study, which focussed on competition in the UK grocery retail industry, the vast majority of participants were drawn from an organization going through a period of major organizational and strategic change. Calori et al.'s (1992, 1994) study focussed on competition in European countries during the period in the run up to the development of the single market. In hindsight, each of these studies was conducted at a time when participants were, in all probability, still in the process of coming to terms with major new developments. Had the data been collected at later points in time, these observed differences may well have been less apparent. This discussion serves to highlight the dangers of researchers utilizing cross-sectional research designs in this field of inquiry, an issue discussed further in the next section.

Methodological implications

This study has illustrated the benefits of a number of methodological innovations, which, while by no means new within the broader spectrum of strategic management research in general, are certainly novel in the context of cognitive studies of competitive positioning strategy. Future researchers interested in advancing the progress of knowledge accumulation in this field beyond its present levels would be well advised to consider the methodological lessons learned from the present study before embarking on further inquiries. Four features in particular of the present study are worthy of discussion.

Research design and analysis

In contrast to many of the previous studies in this field of inquiry, which have tended to employ cross-sectional designs, the present study adopted a two-wave panel design in order to observe the extent to which mental models of competitive space changed or remained stable over time. Longitudinal research designs undoubtedly place considerable additional burdens on the researcher, both in terms of data collection and analysis. However, this study has demonstrated that there are a number of benefits to be gained from such approaches, benefits which greatly exceed the associated drawbacks.

My findings suggest that once established, mental models of competitive space remain highly stable. The longitudinal analyses revealed stability both in terms of the dimensional structure and the positioning of the various types of firms within the competitive space maps. Furthermore, the source weights associated with the individual participants' private competitive space maps were also found to remain stable over time. The research design adopted in the present study has thus greatly strengthened the confidence that can be placed in the contribution of the findings to the theory of competitive enactment. As we have seen, the fact that the industry-level mental model of competitive space was found to remain stable in the face of a significant down-turn in the market, provides compelling evidence for this social constructionist explanation of how industries ultimately fall into decline, or, alternatively, how new entrants, not bound by the market norms, come to establish new niches and overturn previous market leaders (cf. Levenhagen et al., 1993; Porac & Thomas, 1990; Reger & Palmer, 1996). Without the necessary longitudinal evidence, this interpretation of my findings would have to have been moderated, to the extent that it would not be possible to have concluded with any degree of certainty whether the (cross-sectional) findings observed would have persisted in the event of further down-turns in the market, and hence substantiated competitive enactment theory, or whether the high levels of consensus concerning the bases of competition and the competitive positioning of various types of firm observed might have dissipated, as firms sought to identify new strategies for competitive success.

Contextual embeddedness

Although it is the case that research into competitor cognition is still in its infancy, as noted in Chapter 2, far too many studies have accumulated in recent years in which cognitive structures have been explored in isolation, i.e. without due attention given to the background characteristics of the individual research participants and their work organizations. However, these factors may well have a profound bearing upon the way in which particular actors and subgroups come to construe their competitive worlds. As observed in Chapter 2, without such additional information, assessed via reliable and valid indicators, we are not in a position to evaluate adequately the contribution of mental models of competitive space to wider organizational life (see also Ginsberg, 1994).

The present study illustrates some of the many benefits to be gained from incorporating a range of theoretically important exogenous biographical and attitudinal variables in studies of managerial and organizational cognition in general and competitor cognition in particular. The addition of the various self-report measures of previous work experience, education, training and development, strategic locus of control, environmental scanning behaviour and organizational structure, environmental variation, strategy and performance enabled us to gain a much richer picture of the estate agency industry than would have been possible using cognitive modelling procedures *per se*. The incorporation of these exogenous variables provided the means by which we were able to contextualize the various subgroups' revealed mental models of competitor definition. As we have seen, the additional information gained from the supplementary biographical, attitudinal and organizational characteristics instruments, enabled us to go considerably further than previous studies of competitor cognition, inasmuch as we were able to derive comprehensive profiles of the characteristic differences and similarities of the various subgroups whose mental models of competitive space were investigated. This additional data greatly enriched our understanding of the industry, by revealing some key insights into the principal differences between the national chains and the smaller local and regional operators. In turn, these findings led to a more detailed understanding of the processes of competitive enactment, by enabling me to relate particular structural features of the research participants' representations of competitive space to a variety of objective and subjective indicators of individual and organizational behaviour, strategy and performance.

While previous studies have undoubtedly provided many illuminating insights with regard to the development of methodological techniques for revealing actors' mental models of competitor definition, and suggested some fruitful lines of inquiry for the development of theory, on the whole these studies have failed to locate these mental models in their wider context. The present programmme of research has begun to remedy this situation. The incorporation of the various exogenous variables into the study enabled me to begin the task of systematically exploring the empirical relationships between mental models of competitive space on one hand and on the other hand various characteristics of the participants (e.g. education and training, strategic locus of control beliefs, scanning behaviours) and their organizations (various aspects of organizational structure, strategy-making behaviour, environmental variation, and performance).

Despite the fact that a relatively large number of exogenous variables was incorporated in the present study, it must be emphasized that the research reported in this book has been but an embryonic attempt to broaden this field of inquiry. Further studies along these lines, extended into other industry contexts, are badly needed. In the absence of such exogenous information about the research participants and their organizations, it is difficult to see how additional studies of competitor cognition will advance our theoretical understanding of strategic management beyond present levels (see also Ginsberg, 1994).

Sampling characteristics

The third methodological feature of the present study which has enhanced the quality of the data obtained in comparison to previous studies in this field concerns the characteristics of the sample of research participants, both in terms of its relatively large numerical size *and* in terms of its scope. These design features have greatly increased the extent to which we can meaningfully explore subgroup differences in competitor cognition and generalize our findings to the wider estate agency industry as a whole.

Size

Previous studies have tended to use relatively small samples, both in terms of the numbers of individual participants and the numbers of participating organizations, making comparative analyses and generalization very difficult. As noted in Chapter 2, with the notable exception of Bowman and Johnson's (1992) work, typical studies involving the comparison of multiple subgroups in this field have employed between 22 and 33 participants from a considerably smaller number of organizations, making legitimate subgroup comparisons, using appropriate statistical techniques, difficult if not impossible to accomplish (see e.g. Calori et al., 1992, 1994; Daniels et al., 1994, 2002; Hodgkinson & Johnson, 1994; P. Johnson et al., 1998). The present sample, comprising 206 participants from 58 firms at T1, and 114 participants from 41 firms at T2, renders this study one of the largest comparative investigations into competitor cognition undertaken to date, within the confines of a single industrial sector.

Given the present sample sizes, considerably more confidence can be placed in the findings, particularly when seeking to derive meaningful conclusions at the industry-level of analysis. The relatively large number of individual participants and participating organizations enabled a more reliable comparison of actors' representations of competitive space across various organizational and functional subgroups than has been possible hitherto. (Often the smallest cell sizes in the present study, greatly exceeded the total sample sizes reported in previously published studies.) Additional studies using even larger samples, enabling meaningful comparisons within and between various industries, are now needed, in order to further enrich our understanding of the impact of task and institutional influences on actors' representations of competitor definition (cf. Daniels et al., 2002; Daniels & Johnson, 2002; Hodgkinson, 2002).

Scope

Turning to the scope of the present sample, it is noteworthy that the overwhelming majority of previous studies of competitor cognition have tended to focus almost exclusively on senior and middle level managers. Implicit within this body of work is the assumption that only the views of senior and middle managers matter, that somehow it is their beliefs that come to shape the bases of competition and the views of other organization members are of little or no consequence. As observed in Chapter 2, at best, the dominance of the upper echelons tradition within the strategy process literature (Finkelstein & Hambrick, 1996; Hambrick & Mason, 1984) has led many researchers of competitor cognition, particularly North American ones, to assume that business strategies emanate from the most senior levels of the organization and that the role of staff within the lower reaches is merely to implement their dictates (see e.g. Peteraf & Shanley, 1997). The present study, in contrast, was predicated on a rather different assumption, namely, that strategy development and the competitive positioning of organizations is the business of every organization member, irrespective of seniority (cf. Floyd & Lane, 2000; Pettigrew & Whipp, 1991). As far as the present author is aware, this is the only study, to date, to have extended the cognitive analysis of competitor definition in work organizations beyond managerial populations (cf. Huff, 1997). The fact that no major differences were observed between the various managerial and non-managerial subgroups investigated, adds further support to competitive enactment theory and the associated life cycle conception of industry and market decline (Levenhagen et al., 1993; Porac & Thomas, 1990).

However, in order that competitive enactment theory can be further refined, future studies should explore in greater depth, using even larger samples, the extent to which managerial and non-managerial subgroups share common or distinctive perceptions of competitive space. Although the present study addressed this issue in part, the sample size was too small to carry out detailed analyses at the intra-organizational level. Given larger samples, drawn from a variety of industry contexts (of varying maturity levels), it should be possible to engage in a detailed comparative analysis both within and between organizations and across sectors. Such large-scale research is undoubtedly necessary, if we are to fully evaluate and extend competitive enactment theory. Clearly, to the extent that this theory is correct, we would expect to find considerably less homogeneity and longitudinal stability in cognition in industries at earlier stages of development, in comparison with those in the more advanced stages, irrespective of whether the life-cycle notion is conceptualized in social constructionist terms (cf. Levenhagen et al., 1993) or in the more conventional sense, as widely adopted in the fields of marketing and strategic management more generally (see e.g. Easton et al., 1993).

Advances in cognitive modelling

The present study has also enabled the development and validation of an alternative approach for the assessment of actors' mental models of competitive business environments. As in Walton's (1986) and Reger's (1990a) studies of competitor cognition in the USA financial services industry, the spatial metaphor has been found to be particularly apposite in the present programme of research. While these earlier studies demonstrated the power of spatial analytical techniques such as multidimensional scaling and principal components analysis for representing individual- and group-level mental models of competitive space, the present study has introduced a number of refinements which have been found to enrich our understanding of cognition, strategic behaviour and market decline.

As noted in Chapter 2, the majority of previous studies of competitor cognition have suffered from a number of methodological drawbacks at the knowledge elicitation phase and/or the data analysis phase, which have rendered problematic the comparison of mental models of competitive space across differing subgroups of participants. Previous studies have tended to adopt either nomothetic knowledge elicitation procedures, such as standardized questionnaires (e.g. Dess & Davis, 1984) or between-participants taxonomic interviews (e.g. Porac et al., 1987), predicated on the assumption that there are high levels of consensus within industries and markets but which prevent the researcher from exploring differential cognition, or idiographic procedures, such as individually based repertory-grid techniques (Daniels et al., 1994, 2002; Reger, 1990a, 1990b) or relatively open ended interviews (Calori et al., 1992, 1994), which run the risk of accentuating surface-level differences in cognition at the expense of deeper-level homogeneity. In short, previous researchers have either assumed away the importance of differential cognition or adopted knowledge elicitation and/or data analysis techniques that render the resulting mental models of individuals and/or subgroups, thus revealed, methodologically non-comparable (Hodgkinson, 1997a, 2002).

Advances in knowledge elicitation

The present study sought to overcome these limitations through the use of an adaptive questionnaire, in which the participants were required to draw up their own list of competitors in response to a series of standardized categories. These competitors, together with the participant's own organization, were then systematically evaluated on the basis of a series of standardized attributes. However, both the categories used to elicit the competitors and the standardized list of attributes presented to the research participants for evaluation were elicited through interviews with knowledgeable experts drawn from within the focal industry, together with an analysis of relevant trade publications and advertising literature, rather than researcher imposed. In this way, the present study has sought to capitalize on the major strengths of both idiographic and nomothetic knowledge elicitation procedures, while minimizing some of their respective associated weaknesses. The net result of adopting this hybrid approach to repertory grid has been that the study has yielded data from a research task which is meaningful to the individual research participants but also enables the researcher to make direct comparisons at a number of different levels of analysis, without having to impose arbitrary coding procedures on the resulting outputs (cf. Calori et al., 1992, 1994; Daniels et al., 1994, 2002; Reger, 1990a; Spencer et al., 2003).

Advances in data analysis

The present research has also illustrated the incremental benefits to be gained from adopting three-way scaling procedures/WMDS, in comparison with conventional two-way techniques, in studies of competitor cognition. As we have seen, previous studies have used procedures which are capable of representing either the cognitive structures of individual research participants or the shared cognitive structures of particular groups of participants (e.g. at the level of the industry or organization), but not both. The three-way multidimensional scaling procedure adopted in the present study, in contrast, enabled us to explore systematically the extent to which the individual research participants' 'private mental models' of competitive space deviated from the industry-level group space representation. The logarithmically transformed ratios of the participant weights associated with this analysis provided an appropriate index of differential cognition which we were able to relate systematically to the various exogenous self-report measures of the participants' background characteristics, environmental scanning behaviour, strategic locus of control, and organizational structure, environmental variation, strategy and peformance. In this way, we were able to develop a comprehensive picture of the principal characteristic similarities and differences between the various types of estate agent investigated in the study and in turn explore the relationships between these characteristics and variations in the weightings attached to the dimensions underpinning the group space representation. As observed above, these supplementary analyses have enriched considerably our understanding of competitive enactment theory.

The comparison of the group space representations associated with the various organizational and functional subgroups of participants and the longitudinal comparison of the groups spaces derived from the data associated with the complete samples at T1 and T2 was greatly aided by the use of Borg and Lingoes's (1978, 1987) PINDIS procedure. As observed in Chapters 6 and 7, the application of this technique provided strong evidence of cognitive homogeneity and stability, in keeping with predictions derived from the notions of competitive enactment and cognitive inertia (Porac et al., 1989, 1995; Porac & Thomas, 1990; Reger & Palmer, 1996). In Chapter 6 we noted that one of the principal dangers associated with spatial techniques for the modelling of cognition is the temptation to make rather naive visual comparisons between the resulting outputs associated with differing subgroups, on the basis of their surface-level characteristics. The findings of the PINDIS analyses reported in this book bear strong testimony to the fact that such basic comparisons should be avoided at all costs. These findings stand in marked contrast with those of a number of studies reported by Daniels et al. (1994, 1995, 2002), in which participants were required to compare a number of cognitive maps elicited by means of an idiographic variant of the repertory grid procedure (their own maps, maps generated at random for control purposes and the maps of fellow participants), using abstract rating scales designed to assess the overall degree of similarity/dissimilarity among the maps. As I have argued elsewhere (Hodgkinson, 2001a, 2002), and as strongly borne out by the present work, such abstract assessments more than likely yield highly misleading results. As we have seen, revealed mental representations which at first can appear to be structurally diverse, on the basis of their varying dimensionalities and/or apparently significant variations in the relative positioning of particular stimuli, can turn out to be highly convergent, when submitted to the rigours of PINDIS.

Implications for practice

In this section I consider the implications of my study for the practice of strategic management, focussing primarily on the potential role of tools, techniques and processes of intervention as a basis for minimizing the principal dangers highlighted by my findings. To the extent that the above arguments concerning the idea that industry and market decline results from cognitive myopia and cognitive inertia are valid, this study has important normative and prescriptive implications, namely, that strategists should periodically engage in processes of reflection and dialogue, in order to challenge their otherwise taken for granted beliefs and assumptions regarding the strategic imperatives confronting their organizations, with a view to broadening their perceptions. The aim of such an exercise is to attain the requisite variety in mental models necessary in order to identify potential blind spots in competitor awareness (Zajac & Bazerman, 1991), and thus, anticipate the future, thereby developing a strategically responsive organization, identifying viable bases upon which to build effective strategies for competitive success, and mediating the potentially deleterious impact of cognition on action (cf. Baden-Fuller & Stopford, 1992; Bogner & Barr, 2000; Bowman & Johnson, 1992; Huff, 1990; Mitroff, 1988; Morecroft, 1994; Senge, 1990). Fortunately, there are a number of tools, techniques and processes that might help strategic management practitioners and policy makers to accomplish this goal.

Survey feedback for fostering organizational development

Survey feedback is one of the oldest and most popular and effective methods of organizational development (OD) intervention (Bowers, 1973; Lussier, 1990). A rather obvious step that organizations could take in order to minimize the likelihood of falling prey to the effects of cognitive myopia and cognitive inertia discussed above would be to periodically survey all key staff within the company, in order to re-assess the mental models of competitor definition implicitly underpinning their activities. The results of this exercise could then be fed-back to the participants in the form of a 'strategy process workshop', in which they would be encouraged to actively explore ways of creatively enhancing their organization's competitive positioning strategy.

Bowman and Johnson (1992) reported some preliminary attempts to facilitate the strategic thinking of top management teams using a form of survey feedback. They employed a modified version of the questionnaire devised by Dess and Davis (1984) in order to investigate the extent to which senior management teams were able locate their organizations within one of Porter's (1980) generic strategies. The participants' responses to the questionnaire were computer analyzed in order to derive a two-dimensional representation, in which particular individuals were positioned in relation to the various strategic possibilities within Porter's framework. The results were fed-back to the workshop participants in order to provide a basis of intervention in strategy debates among senior management teams. While in the longer term it is desirable that such interventions should be subjected to rigourous scrutiny before making claims about their effectiveness, Bowman and Johnson's experience provides us with sufficient preliminary evidence to suggest that a more general survey feedback approach to understanding bases of competition and competitive positioning may well prove to be fruitful as an OD intervention technique for fostering strategic debate and organizational renewal.

In sum, what I am suggesting is that the idea of cognitive analysis as a means of galvanizing strategic debate amongst senior management teams should be extended to the lower reaches of the organization, in an effort to identify potential blindspots in competitor definition and stimulate the development of new strategies for competitive success. The approach to cognitive analysis developed in the present programme of research could be applied on a periodic basis across multiple levels, in order to generate individual, group and organizational representations of competitor definition as a basis for stimulating 'break away thinking' (cf. Baden-Fuller & Stopford, 1992; Mitroff, 1988).

Scenario planning for fostering competitive foresight

In recent years scenario planning techniques have increasingly been advocated as a basis for overcoming the potentially deleterious consequences of cognitive myopia and inertia of the sort identified in this study (see e.g. Fahay & Randall, 1998; Goodwin & Wright, 2001; van der Heijden, 1996; van der Heijden et al., 2002; Wright & Goodwin, 1999). The aim of these techniques is to reveal potential weaknesses in organizations' current strategies by closely examining the extent to which the strategy is sufficiently robust to withstand various major changes that might plausibly occur at some future point in time. Scenario techniques assist with this endeavour through a process akin to the use of wind tunnels in the fields aerospace and automotive engineering (van der Heijden, 1996). Various 'plausible futures' are identified, which, were they to unfold, might pose a major threat to the organization. The objective is to ensure that the extant strategy is able to withstand this buffeting process, much as an engineer might examine airframe structures for potential damage following a period of exposure to severe turbulence under laboratory conditions. In the event that the strategy is found wanting, the scenario team reconsiders its options. Hence, in this context, the strategic options are analogous to aeroplane designs and the scenarios are analogous to wind tunnel conditions. An appropriately crafted strategy should perform well – or least be sufficiently robust – to withstand the 'environmental stressors' embedded in the various scenarios. In this way, the salience of potential threats to the organization is heightened, since the nature(s) of the future is/are put into sharp focus by the process of critical reflection that scenario planning techniques foster.[1]

---

[1] Applications of scenario-based interventions for facilitating strategic conversations about competitive positioning strategy have been illustrated at some length in the volume edited by Fahay and Randall (1998). However, as observed by Hodgkinson (2001a) and Hodgkinson and Sparrow (2002), in the final analysis scenario planning techniques and related procedures are ultimately practioner-derived methods with very little supporting evidence, other than basic anecdotal evidence, for their efficacy (though for a notable exception in this respect see Schoemaker, 1993). As noted by Mintzberg (1994), accounts of the use of scenarios in the (limited) extant literature have been restricted to "success stories," such as Pierre Wack's highly acclaimed account of scenario planning in the Royal Dutch/Shell organization (Wack, 1985a, 1985b), which enabled the company to anticipate the dramatic shift in the world market for petroleum that occurred in 1973. For a variety of reasons, as illustrated in the case study recently reported by Hodgkinson and Wright (2002), participants may be unwilling, or unable, to confront the future in the manner that scenario techniques require. It is not always be possible to identify viable alternatives to the present course of action, even in situations where major strategic change is clearly warranted. Work presently underway within the ESRC/EPSRC (UK) Advanced Institute of Management Research (AIM) (Hodgkinson, 2004) is seeking to identify more precisely the boundary conditions within which scenario planning and related techniques of intervention for stimulating strategic thought, such as causal mapping, are more or less effective and the mechanisms underpinning their effectiveness (see also Hodgkinson et al., 1999, 2002, 2004; Hodgkinson & Maule, 2002; Maule & Hodgkinson, 2002). In the meantime, the fact remains that faced with cognitive myopia and inertia on the scale revealed in the study reported in this book, policy makers and strategic management practitioners must continue to experiment with such techniques in an attempt to minimize the concomitant dangers of stagnation and decline, which, left unchecked, pose a potentially terminal threat not only to individual firms but entire populations of firms, as discussed by Porac and Thomas (1990).

There are a variety of approaches in the literature that may be grouped under the umbrella of 'scenario planning'. However, they each share in common a number of discernible key features which render the technique in general potentially useful as a means for overcoming the dangers of myopia and inertia discussed above and in previous chapters. Specifically, scenario planning techniques are both systematic yet highly flexible in nature and highly participative, involving extensive data gathering and reflection both at an individual and collective level. Rather than attempting to predict the future, scenario planning techniques involve the use of speculation and human judgement in an effort to gain fresh insights and 'bound' future uncertainties, forcing strategists to explicitly confront the changing world and consider its implications for the current strategy. In contrast with traditional strategic planning techniques, which seek to forecast the future in probabilistic terms, in an attempt to plan for a predetermined future, scenario planning techniques seek to develop a series of stylized portraits of the future, capturing what may or may not happen, thereby providing a basis for the development of a strategy for dealing with the various contingencies so identified. In this way, uncertainty is directly incorporating into the analysis (van der Heijden, 1994). For all of the above reasons, scenario planning techniques are potentially an ideal basis for redressing the principal cognitive dangers highlighted in this book.

Comparison with strategic groups analysis

As noted in Chapter 2, by far the most dominant approach to environmental analysis for understanding bases of competition and competitive positioning in industries and markets within the strategic management literature over the years has been the strategic groups approach, in which the analyst attempts to model competitive structures using a range of 'objective' indicators (typically secondary accounting and financial data) which are thought to differentiate the strategies being pursued by various players (see e.g. McGee & Thomas, 1986). However, as we have seen, the concept of strategic groups has come under increasingly critical scrutiny, not least because of the danger that the analyst may happen to select a subset of variables which particular companies who operate within the focal industry or market would not regard as important, while omitting to consider the variables which are actually driving competition and strategy development (see also Barney & Hoskisson, 1990; Birnbaum-More & Weiss, 1990; Calori et al., 1992; Hatten & Hatten, 1987; Hodgkinson & Johnson, 1994; Pettigrew & Whipp, 1991; Porac et al., 1989; Porac & Thomas, 1990; Reger, 1990a; Reger & Huff, 1993; Thomas & Venkatraman, 1988). The present study has added to a growing number of socio-cognitive investigations seeking to address concerns with the strategic groups approach to environmental analysis (e.g. Calori et al., 1992, 1994; Daniels et al., 1994; Dess & Davis, 1984; Fombrun & Zajac, 1987; Porac et al., 1987, 1989, 1995; Reger, 1990a; Reger & Huff, 1993). Far from conflicting with conventional approaches to competitive analysis, however, the approach developed through this study provides a complementary method for gaining insights into bases of competition in industries and markets.

As discussed above, the present study has demonstrated repeatedly that there are very strong commonalities of perception, widely held throughout the industry, regarding the bases of competition, thus providing additional support for claims that competitive structures may have an ontological status grounded in the cognitions of strategic decision makers (e.g. Bogner & Thomas, 1993; Osborne et al., 2001; Porac et al., 1989; Reger & Huff, 1993). However, the fact that the competitor analysis questionnaire was both designed and completed by knowledgeable actors, meant that the potentially serious problems of haphazard variable selection and the seemingly arbitrary choice of particular firms for strategic analysis – associated with conventional studies of competitive structures – were avoided (cf. Calori et al., 1992, 1994; Daniels et al., 2002; Daniels & Johnson, 2002; Reger, 1990a; Thomas & Venkatraman, 1988).

Strategic locus of control

Before concluding this discussion of the practical implications emanating from this study it is useful to briefly consider the implications for practice arising from the development and validation of the Strategic Locus of Control Scale, reported in Chapter 4 and Appendix 1. Unfortunately, the strategic locus of control scale turned out to be only moderately useful in relation to the substantive concerns of this study. Relatively weak correlations were observed between strategic locus of control and the logarithmically transformed source weight ratios associated with the three-way scaling analysis reported in Chapter 5. Nevertheless, the fact that substantial correlations were observed between this variable and a number of indicators of strategic behaviour and organizational performance, both at the individual- and organizational-levels of analysis (as reported in Chapter 4) suggests that the strategic locus of control scale may be useful as a diagnostic tool in the development of individuals and organizations, and as an aid for the selection of staff into the corporate strategy function. These findings suggest that strategic control expectancies are partly dispositional and partly a reflection of past and present organizational circumstances. In other words, responses to the strategic locus of control scale result from an interaction between the individual and his or her meaningful environment (cf. Boone & De Brabander, 1993; Rotter, 1990, p. 491). Consequently, individuals within particular organizations may vary in terms of their strategic locus of control beliefs. On the other hand, in organizations where there is very little variation at the individual-level, the collective generalized expectancies of organization members about the transformational capacities of strategic management principles, techniques and processes may have a marked impact on the organization's capabilities for action.

As I have argued in Hodgkinson (1993b), certain organizations may be characterized by varying climates or cultures of internal and external strategic control expectancies, sustained through processes of attraction, selection and attrition (Schneider, 1987) and the transformation of these climates/cultures might play a vital role in periods of organizational turnaround and major strategic and organizational change. If this is indeed the case, the use of the strategic locus of control scale as a diagnostic tool, could prove useful as an aid for OD practitioners seeking to facilitate such change. However, whether or not it is uniformly desirable for organizations to appoint individuals with extreme internal scores into positions involving a key role in strategy development is an open question that requires further investigation.

Limitations

As discussed earlier, a number of methodological innovations were incorporated in the present study, the purpose of which was to enhance the quality of the resulting data. While these innovations have clearly increased the degree of confidence that can be placed in the overall conclusions derived from the resulting dataset, as with any large scale field study it was inevitable that some compromises and tradeoffs had to be made in respect of the research design, sampling process and methods employed, in order for the work to proceed.

First, while every effort was made to obtain as large a sample of organizations and individual participants as possible, in an effort to overcome the limitations of the smaller-scale investigations that have sought to make inferences about industry-level mental models of competitor definition (e.g. Lant & Baum, 1995; Porac et al., 1987, 1989) and compare actors' revealed mental models of competitor definition across organizational and functional subgroups of analysis (e.g. Daniels et al., 1994, 2002; Hodgkinson & Johnson, 1994; P. Johnson et al., 1998), the fact remains that like these other studies, the present work was based on a convenience sample, albeit one which was better positioned, given its enhanced scale and scope, to address both of these substantive concerns. Although it is highly unlikely that the sample was unrepresentative of the particular geographical locality from which it was drawn, the north east Midlands region of England, the extent to which the findings are truly representative of the UK residential estate agency industry as a whole remains uncertain, given that the study was restricted to this one regional area. As observed in Chapter 4, this particular region was by no means the worst affected by the (then) recession in the housing market and it would have been desirable to have extended the fieldwork into other areas of the UK, particularly those areas most badly affected, namely, East Anglia, London and the south east of England, before attempting to derive firm conclusions relating to the industry in general.

A second limitation concerns the timeframe encompassed by the study. Twelve–eighteen months was a relatively short period in which to observe the effects of industry change on actors' representations of competitor definition. While no evidence emerged from this investigation to suggest significant cognitive change, a rather different pattern of findings might have emerged had the study been conducted over a longer time frame. Within the period encompassed by the present study, the mean level of the participants' perceptions of the local property market conditions shifted only from 'moderately depressed' at T1 to 'depressed' at T2. While highly significant statistically, this change may have been of insufficient magnitude to be of cognitive significance. It could be that mental models of competitor definitions are updated most significantly when there is a fundamental qualitative change in market conditions (for example from 'moderately buoyant' to 'moderately depressed'), but not for a quantitatively equal shift with no qualitative change, as observed presently. Nevertheless, the present results are consistent with Reger and Palmer's (1996) findings (based on data gathered over a nine year time frame) and previous theorizing in this area (Huff, Huff & Thomas, 1992; Porac & Thomas, 1990), adding further empirical substance to the claim that within volatile business environments, changes in mental models of competitive space significantly lag behind changes in the material conditions of the marketplace.

Implications for future research

As in any newly developing field, this study probably raises as many questions as it answers. As predicted on the basis of competitive enactment theory, little variation was observed in the dimensionality of the participants' mental models of competitive space from one organizational and functional subgroup to another, actors' cognitions were found to be stable over time (despite significant changes in market conditions) and substantial correlations were observed between the logarithmically transformed source weight ratios (reflecting individual differences in the relative salience of the dimensions of competitive space) on one hand and on the other hand a number of self-reported measures of strategic behaviour and organizational performance. While these findings strengthen the empirical support for some of the basic elements of competitive enactment theory, providing a firmer evidence base than previous studies for the existence of industry-level mental models of competitor definition and useful insights concerning the deleterious role that such mental models might potentially play in the decline of industries and markets, a more extensive database is ultimately required if we are to refine our understanding of the processes of market decline and rejuvenation.

The present research now needs to be extended into other industries, with varying time intervals between data collection periods, in order to increase the generalizability of the findings and further our knowledge of the effects of cognitive inertia over longer periods, under qualitatively differing market conditions. Future studies should also extend the range of exogenous variables incorporated, in an attempt to better understand the interplay between individual, task, organizational and wider institutional influences on actors' private and collective representations of competitor definition. At this stage in the development of the cognitive analysis of competitive structures in industries and markets, it is only by substantially increasing the empirical knowledge base concerning the antecedents and consequences of competitor cognition that we will be in a position to significantly advance beyond present levels the body of theory that has emerged thus far and subject the testable hypotheses emanating from that body of theory to appropriate scrutiny.

At the time of data collection, the UK residential estate agency industry was an industry which in Levenhagen et al.'s (1993) terms had entered the advanced stages of the cognitive life-cycle of market domains. As observed in Chapter 3, the high levels of both intra- and inter-organizational interdependency that characterized this industry (and still do so to the present day), plus the fact that it was passing through turbulent times, rendered it an ideal context in which to address all three of the substantive research questions identified at the outset. However, it is also apparent that this is a relatively simple industry, in which only limited cognitive demands are placed upon particular individuals, functional subgroups and wider organizations. Had the present study been undertaken in an industry characterized by greater complexity, a rather different set of outcomes to those reported here might well have been observed. If the rapidly developing body of socio-cognitive theory centred on the notion of competitive enactment is to be tested to its limits, further studies are now needed, which attempt to replicate the present findings in the context of other, more complex industries that have also entered the later stages of their cognitive life-cycles.

Further studies are also now needed to investigate changing patterns of cognition and the differential impact of mental models of competitor definition on strategy and performance, as organizations and industries pass through the various stages of the cognitive life-cycle. Alternatively, though somewhat less satisfactory, researchers could explore these issues using cross-sectional designs, in which organizations and industries at varying stages within the cognitive life cycle were compared systematically on a case-by-case basis (cf. Easton et al., 1993). If the interpretation placed on the findings emerging from the present study is correct, we would expect to find that the results reported in this book are replicated in the context of other industries which have entered the advanced stages of the cognitive life-cycle. In the case of newly emergent industries, however, a rather different scenario would be predicted. Here, we would expect to find considerable variations in cognition with little evidence of longitudinal stability.

In sum, the time has now come for researchers to further advance the field by conducting more large-scale, multi-method, multi-level, longitudinal field studies, in which patterns of competitor cognition are identified and monitored systematically over varying time-periods and organizational and industry contexts. This implies the need for collaboration amongst multi-disciplinary teams of researchers, rather than the more typical pattern of isolated cells of workers from disparate institutions competing for scarce funds and methodological and theoretical supremacy. This up-scaling of resources is vital, if we are to be able to tease out with much greater rigour than has been possible hitherto the role of mental models of competitor definition in the evolution business strategies and the long-term decline and rejuvenation of individual businesses, industries and markets. Clearly, the research councils and other sponsoring bodies, together with the various learned societies with a vested interest in fostering excellence in management research, have a potentially significant role to play in this respect.

Given the numerous variables at the individual-, organizational- and industry-levels that might mediate and/or moderate the relationships between competitor cognition, strategic behaviour and organizational performance, such studies will require very large sample sizes indeed, both in terms of the number of individual research participants and the number of participating organizations. Only then will we be able to disentangle the multitude of cause and effect relationships that potentially influence and are influenced by actors' mental representations of competition. However, if this highly ambitious research agenda is to be realized, we will have to engage in much greater levels of inter-disciplinary collaboration than has been the case hitherto. We must also search for methodological procedures of greater sophistication than those adopted in the present study and previous work, if we are to attempt to model such cause-effect relationships with a sufficient degree of precision.

One possibility that has the potential to reduce the amount of effort required in terms of data collection in the field in order to investigate the sorts of complex, multi-level effects envisaged here entails the use of formal mathematical modelling and simulation techniques. Recently, D. R. Johnson and Hoopes (2003) have reported the findings of a study which sought to model competitive processes in such a way that the apparent conflict between field studies showing low levels of intra-organizational belief similarity (e.g. Daniels et al., 1994; Hodgkinson & Johnson, 1994; P. Johnson et al., 1998) might be reconciled with those suggesting common views across organizations (e.g. Lant & Baum, 1995; Porac et al., 1989, Reger & Huff, 1993). Using techniques developed in complexity science and economics, they developed a simulation model in which fundamental constraints in the economic environment were interwoven with bounded rationality in such a way that variations in managerial beliefs, firm-level strategies and intra-industry performance could be accommodated within a unified explanation. In the final analysis, however, while this type of approach, using computer generated, artificial data, can prove helpful in developing new lines of theoretical reasoning and has the potential to eliminate some of the less promising lines of empirical inquiry, as the results of the present study demonstrate, the fields of managerial and organizational cognition and strategic management have now reached a point where there can be no substitute for the gathering of high quality, multi-level, longitudinal datasets involving human actors.

Conclusion

The embryonic theory of competitive enactment advanced by Porac and his colleagues during the late 1980s and early 1990s (Porac et al., 1989; Porac & Thomas, 1990) has turned out to be foundational in the development of the wider body of socio-cognitive theory that has permeated the literature on inter-organizational rivalry during the 15-year period that has now elapsed since this notion first appeared in the literature. However, as we have seen, high quality datasets of the sort that are ultimately required in order to ascertain the validity of this fundamental notion have, for the most part, not been forthcoming. Much of the research directed towards the study of competitor cognition over the ensuing years has continued to be primarily small scale, cross-sectional and inductive in nature, with only limited attempts to ascertain the validity of the key theoretical building blocks that are central to the advancement of our understanding of the evolution of competitive structures in industries and markets. In consequence, theory development is now running well ahead of supporting evidence. To the extent that the empirical study reported in this book has helped to remedy this situation, it has accomplished its primary objective.

Appendix 1   Development and Validation of the Strategic Locus of Control Scale

This appendix describes in greater detail the development of the Strategic Locus of Control Scale and presents further evidence concerning its reliability and construct validity. The scale was created from an initial item pool comprising a total of 36 questions derived from a conceptual analysis of the locus of control construct as it relates to the strategic management field.

The questions comprising the initial item pool were balanced in terms of the extent to which they were intended to reflect locus of control beliefs about the strategic management of organizations in general and the strategic management of participants' own particular firms. The rationale for this design of the item pool follows directly from an analysis of Rotter's (1966) original conception of the construct. The I-E Scale contains several items of a personal nature (e.g. 'I have often found that what is going to happen will happen'; 'When I make plans, I am almost certain that I can make them work'.) Other items within the scale, however, are of a more general nature (e.g. 'Most students don't realize the extent to which their grades are influenced by accidental happenings'; 'In the long run the people are responsible for bad government on a national as well as on a local level'.) Given that the aim was to develop a domain-specific scale reflecting, as closely as possible, the underlying rationale of the original concept of locus of control as conceived by Rotter, it was deemed appropriate to develop a set of items that were balanced, in terms of their content, between statements relating to Strategic Locus of Control beliefs about organizations in general and belief statements pertaining to the participant's own particular organization. The items were also balanced with respect to the number of internally and externally worded items. Participants were required to indicate the extent to which they agree with statements on a five-point Likert Scale ranging from 1 ('strongly disagree'), through 3 ('unsure') to 5 ('strongly agree'). As explained in Chapter 4, internally worded items were reverse-scored in order to render the scoring system compatible with the Rotter I-E and Work Locus of Control scales.

Four criteria were employed in order to select items for inclusion in the the final scale, namely, acceptable item-total correlations, lack of correlation with social desirability, and that the scale should be balanced with respect to the number of general and specific items on one hand, and, on the other hand, internally and externally worded items, thus following the rationale adopted in the design of the initial item pool, as discussed above. As noted in Chapter 4, a sixteen-item scale emerged from the application of these criteria.

Method

Participants

The initial empirical work undertaken in connection with the development and validation of this scale was carried out in the late spring of 1989, prior to the commencement of the fieldwork associated with the main study. A total of 100 personnel, mainly owner-managers of local small businesses in the Sheffield area, of whom 94 returned usable questionnaires, took part in the research, on an unpaid voluntary basis.

Research instruments

Strategic locus of control

The complete pool of 36 items pertaining to the concept of strategic locus of control was administered to the above sample, with a view to devising a final scale with a reduced number of items, following a reliability and validity analysis of the full set.

General I-E and work locus of control

General I-E and Work Locus of Control were assessed using the Rotter I-E scale (Rotter, 1966) and Spector's (1988) Work Locus of Control scales, respectively. These measures were incorporated in this phase of the study in order to assess the convergent validity of the Strategic Locus of Control Scale. It was predicted that the Strategic, Work and Rotter I-E locus of control scales would all be positively intercorrelated with one another, but that the Strategic Locus of Control Scale would be more strongly related to the Work Locus of Control Scale than to the Rotter scale.

Social desirability

Social desirability was assessed using the Crowne and Marlowe (1964) social desirability scale. Following Spector (1982, 1988), it was predicted that the Marlowe-Crowne social desirability scale would correlate negatively with the Rotter I-E scale, but not with the Work Locus of Control Scale. As explained previously, items selected for inclusion in the final version of the Strategic Locus of Control Scale, were chosen in part on the basis that they did not correlate significantly with responses to this social desirability scale.

Procedure

Each participant was approached on a face-to-face basis by the researcher, who explained that the purpose of the study was to develop a high quality questionnaire for inclusion in a wider investigation. The participants were asked to complete the instruments for personal collection by the researcher within a week-to-ten days. In view of the obvious degree of conceptual overlap between the various locus of control scales, the order in which the various instruments were presented was randomized, so as to minimize the possibility of order effects.

Results and discussion

The means, standard deviations, and reliability coefficients, together with the scale inter-correlations are presented in Table A1.1. The corrected item-total correlations for the Strategic Locus of Control Scale associated with the present sample (Sample 1), together with the corrected item-total correlations associated with the sample of participants employed in the main study at T1 (Sample 2), are shown in Table A1.2.

Table A1.1 Means, standard deviations, reliability coefficients and scale inter-correlations for the various scales

Scale	N	Mean	SD	Alpha	Scale inter-correlations		
					1.	2.	3.
1. Strategic locus of control†	94	2.68	0.53	0.82			
2. Work locus of control†	93	2.69	0.69	0.83	0.43**		
3. General I–E	91	11.65	4.31	–	0.34**	0.42**	
4. Social desirability	93	14.37	5.00	–	0.08	–0.15	–0.26*

* P < 0.01, ** P < 0.001, (1-tailed).
† The scores for these scales were computed by averaging across the items for each respondent.

Table A1.2 Corrected item-total correlations for the Strategic Locus of Control Scale (continued overleaf)

Item*	Corrected item-total Correlations **	
	Sample 1 (N = 94)	Sample 2 (N = 208)
1 There is very little my company can do in order to change the 'rules of competition' in our industry.	0.63	0.52
2 Many of the problems experienced by businesses can be avoided through careful planning and analysis.	0.34	0.35
3 To a great extent the competitive environment in which my company operates is shaped by forces beyond its control.	0.43	0.41
4 Becoming a successful company is a matter of creating opportunities, luck has little or nothing to do with it.	0.26	0.27
5 There is little point in the majority of companies taking an active interest in the wider concerns of their industry because only the larger more powerful companies have any real influence.	0.46	0.29
6 It is not always wise to make strategic plans far ahead because many things may turn out to be a matter of good or bad fortune anyhow.	0.51	0.36
7 My company can pretty much accomplish whatever it sets out to achieve.	0.45	0.27
8 Most companies can have an influence in shaping the structure of the market.	0.22	0.42
9 As regards competing in the marketplace, most companies are the victims of forces they cannot control.	0.42	0.53

Table A1.2   Corrected item-total correlations for the Strategic Locus of Control Scale – *continued*

	Corrected item-total Correlations **	
*Item**	*Sample 1 (N = 94)*	*Sample 2 (N = 208)*
10 There is little point in engaging in detailed strategic analyses and planning because often events occur that my company cannot control.	0.49	0.38
11 Usually companies fail because they have not taken advantage of their opportunities.	0.42	0.36
12 My company is able to influence the basis upon which it competes with other firms.	0.42	0.36
13 Businesses who rarely experience strategic problems are just plain lucky.	0.42	0.15
14 There is a direct connection between the interest you take in your competitors' businesses and the success of your own company.	0.35	0.30
15 My company has a direct role in shaping the environment in which it competes.	0.34	0.45
16 Market opportunities in my industry are largely pre-determined by factors beyond my company's control.	0.53	0.48

* Items 2, 4, 7, 8, 11, 12, 14 & 15 are reversed scored.
** This is the correlation between each item's score and the scale scores, computed from the other items in the set.

Both the Strategic Locus of Control Scale and the Work Locus of Control Scale were found to have good reliabilities, with alpha coefficients of 0.82 and 0.83, respectively. The data indicate that the Strategic Locus of Control Scale demonstrates acceptable convergent validity with respect to the Rotter I-E and Work locus of control scales. As expected, the Strategic Locus of Control Scale shows significant positive correlations with the Rotter and Work Locus of control scales and a very low and non-significant correlation with the Marlowe-Crowne social desirability scale. In contrast, the Rotter I-E scale correlated significantly with the Marlowe-Crowne scale ($r = -0.26$, df = 89, $P < 0.01$), thus suggesting that the previous studies which have investigated locus of control and organizational strategy, as outlined in Chapter 4, may well be confounded by a lack of control for social desirability response set. Given the overall pattern of these results, together with the findings reported in Chapter 4, it would appear that the Strategic Locus of Control Scale is sufficiently reliable and valid for use in future strategic management studies.

Appendix 2   MDS Solutions for the Various Organizational Subgroups

The following tables report the basic two-dimensional MDS solutions associated with the various organizational subgroups, as discussed in Chapter 6. The stimulus co-ordinates are presented, followed by the dimension weights, for each subgroup in turn (see also Figure 6.1 and Table 6.2 in Chapter 6).

Table A2.1(a)   Stimulus coordinates associated with the two-dimensional MDS representation of participants' aggregated perceptions of competitors in Brian Warner Ltd (N = 13; stress = 0.291; RSQ = 0.674)

	Dimension	
Stimulus	*1*	*2*
My Business	1.73	2.72
My Major Competitor	1.74	0.54
A Solicitor Agent	– 0.94	– 0.52
An Estate Agent Owned by a Building Society	0.86	– 0.31
A Traditional Estate Agent	– 0.90	– 0.12
An Agent Owned by an Insurance Company	1.37	– 0.71
An Agent Offering a Professional Service	– 0.41	0.99
An Agent with a Poor Reputation	– 1.12	– 1.42
An Agent with Chartered Surveyor Status	– 1.14	– 0.12
An Agent Specializing in Exclusive Property	0.21	0.84
An Agent Specializing in Commercial/Industrial Property	0.56	0.02
An Agent Specializing in Residential Property	0.49	– 0.47
A Secondary Competitor	0.62	– 0.36
An Agent with a Good Reputation	0.24	0.76
A Diversified Estate Agent	– 0.55	0.19
An Independent Estate Agent	– 0.84	– 0.19
An Inferior Competitor	– 1.17	– 1.59
A Very Successful Estate Agent	0.60	1.32
A Moderately Successful Estate Agent	0.39	– 0.03
An Unsuccessful Estate Agent	– 1.74	– 1.55

Table A2.1(b)   Dimension weights for Brian Warner Ltd (N = 13)

	Dimension	
Attribute	1	2
Service to vendors	0.35	0.84
Quality of staff	0.32	0.82
Service to purchasers	0.33	0.78
Training of staff	0.45	0.75
Operating practices	0.32	0.85
Quality of advertising	0.67	0.49
Profitability	0.42	0.76
Location of business premises	0.53	0.53
Size of branch network	0.81	0.14
Range of services	0.46	0.57
Geographical coverage	0.78	0.11
Scale of charges	0.71	0.21
Degree of personal attention	0.24	0.83
Market share	0.72	0.46
Marketing profile	0.78	0.30
Degree of local knowledge	0.41	0.53
Strategy influence/power	0.63	0.58
Amount of advertising	0.74	0.23
Financial resources	0.87	0.00
Links with financial services companies	0.66	0.13
Typical range of properties on sale	0.70	0.43

Table A2.2(a)   Stimulus coordinates associated with the two-dimensional MDS representation of participants' aggregated perceptions of competitors in Bolton Holdings (N = 19; stress = 0.286; RSQ = 0.682)

	Dimension	
Stimulus	1	2
My Business	1.80	2.08
My Major Competitor	1.14	1.60
A Solicitor Agent	−0.29	−1.11
An Estate Agent Owned by a Building Society	0.45	1.44
A Traditional Estate Agent	−0.33	−1.22
An Agent Owned by an Insurance Company	−0.56	1.74
An Agent Offering a Professional Service	0.21	−0.51
An Agent with a Poor Reputation	−2.03	−0.75
An Agent with Chartered Surveyor Status	0.53	−0.61
An Agent Specializing in Exclusive Property	1.03	0.18
An Agent Specializing in Commercial/Industrial Property	0.99	−0.62
An Agent Specializing in Residential Property	−0.14	0.58
A Secondary Competitor	−0.69	0.03
An Agent with a Good Reputation	0.83	0.06
A Diversified Estate Agent	0.06	−0.07
An Independent Estate Agent	0.06	−1.08
An Inferior Competitor	−1.26	−0.62
A Very Successful Estate Agent	0.79	0.14
A Moderately Successful Estate Agent	−0.28	0.08
An Unsuccessful Estate Agent	−2.23	−1.34

Table A2.2(b)   Dimension weights for Bolton Holdings (N = 19)

	Dimension	
Attribute	*1*	*2*
Service to vendors	0.08	0.86
Quality of staff	0.01	0.94
Service to purchasers	0.14	0.84
Training of staff	0.55	0.66
Operating practices	0.14	0.85
Quality of advertising	0.27	0.79
Profitability	0.16	0.81
Location of business premises	0.35	0.69
Size of branch network	0.92	0.01
Range of services	0.61	0.45
Geographical coverage	0.90	0.14
Scale of charges	0.32	0.59
Degree of personal attention	0.09	0.88
Market share	0.67	0.40
Marketing profile	0.73	0.40
Degree of local knowledge	0.23	0.62
Strategy influence/power	0.75	0.45
Amount of advertising	0.58	0.55
Financial resources	0.77	0.24
Links with financial services companies	0.77	0.22
Typical range of properties on sale	0.51	0.54

Table A2.3(a)   Stimulus coordinates associated with the two-dimensional MDS representation of participants' aggregated perceptions of competitors in Harrison and Black (N = 17; stress = 0.288; RSQ = 0.683)

	Dimension	
Stimulus	*1*	*2*
My Business	2.72	0.80
My Major Competitor	0.91	1.54
A Solicitor Agent	−0.40	−0.89
An Estate Agent Owned by a Building Society	0.70	2.06
A Traditional Estate Agent	0.12	−0.92
An Agent Owned by an Insurance Company	−0.54	1.87
An Agent Offering a Professional Service	0.34	−0.88
An Agent with a Poor Reputation	−1.53	0.64
An Agent with Chartered Surveyor Status	−0.24	−1.19
An Agent Specializing in Exclusive Property	1.24	0.19
An Agent Specializing in Commercial/Industrial Property	0.89	0.02
An Agent Specializing in Residential Property	−0.99	−0.69
A Secondary Competitor	−0.85	0.23
An Agent with a Good Reputation	0.29	−0.52
A Diversified Estate Agent	−0.06	−0.79
An Independent Estate Agent	−0.15	−0.53
An Inferior Competitor	−0.92	−0.68
A Very Successful Estate Agent	0.61	1.08
A Moderately Successful Estate Agent	−0.47	−0.07
An Unsuccessful Estate Agent	−1.65	−1.29

Table A2.3(b)   Dimension weights for Harrison and Black (N = 17)

Attribute	Dimension	
	1	2
Service to vendors	0.10	0.90
Quality of staff	0.11	0.92
Service to purchasers	0.24	0.88
Training of staff	0.46	0.74
Operating practices	0.04	0.87
Quality of advertising	0.41	0.69
Profitability	0.33	0.69
Location of business premises	0.45	0.69
Size of branch network	0.89	0.16
Range of services	0.54	0.29
Geographical coverage	0.87	0.00
Scale of charges	0.48	0.27
Degree of personal attention	0.04	0.91
Market share	0.46	0.64
Marketing profile	0.77	0.35
Degree of local knowledge	0.35	0.71
Strategy influence/power	0.59	0.56
Amount of advertising	0.69	0.45
Financial resources	0.87	0.00
Links with financial services companies	0.86	0.05
Typical range of properties on sale	0.49	0.53

Table A2.4(a)   Stimulus coordinates associated with the two-dimensional MDS representation of participants' aggregated perceptions of competitors in Stansfield, Gordon and Lewis (N = 20; stress = 0.285; RSQ = 0.629)

Stimulus	Dimension	
	1	2
My Business	−1.86	−1.20
My Major Competitor	−1.78	−1.03
A Solicitor Agent	0.76	1.31
An Estate Agent Owned by a Building Society	−1.24	−0.21
A Traditional Estate Agent	0.94	−0.52
An Agent Owned by an Insurance Company	−1.67	0.81
An Agent Offering a Professional Service	0.55	−1.03
An Agent with a Poor Reputation	1.68	1.44
An Agent with Chartered Surveyor Status	0.76	−0.51
An Agent Specializing in Exclusive Property	0.06	−1.15
An Agent Specializing in Commercial/Industrial Property	0.82	−0.74
An Agent Specializing in Residential Property	−0.21	0.73
A Secondary Competitor	−0.68	0.58
An Agent with a Good Reputation	0.08	−1.07
A Diversified Estate Agent	−0.11	−0.20
An Independent Estate Agent	1.11	0.61
An Inferior Competitor	1.08	1.20
A Very Successful Estate Agent	−0.70	−1.31
A Moderately Successful Estate Agent	−0.05	0.32
An Unsuccessful Estate Agent	1.46	1.97

Table A2.4(b) Dimension weights for Stansfield, Gordon and Lewis (N = 20)

	Dimension	
Attribute	*1*	*2*
Service to vendors	0.35	0.81
Quality of staff	0.26	0.86
Service to purchasers	0.40	0.76
Training of staff	0.64	0.42
Operating practices	0.25	0.85
Quality of advertising	0.45	0.55
Profitability	0.12	0.81
Location of business premises	0.60	0.33
Size of branch network	0.89	0.02
Range of services	0.66	0.38
Geographical coverage	0.86	0.09
Scale of charges	0.30	0.47
Degree of personal attention	0.24	0.73
Market share	0.75	0.22
Marketing profile	0.76	0.21
Degree of local knowledge	0.37	0.51
Strategy influence/power	0.81	0.28
Amount of advertising	0.42	0.35
Financial resources	0.89	0.11
Links with financial services companies	0.88	0.00
Typical range of properties on sale	0.65	0.39

Table A2.5(a) Stimulus coordinates associated with the two-dimensional MDS representation of participants' aggregated perceptions of competitors in Paul Schofield (N = 39; stress = 0.236; RSQ = 0.830)

	Dimension	
Stimulus	*1*	*2*
My Business	3.29	1.26
My Major Competitor	0.99	1.99
A Solicitor Agent	−0.33	−0.93
An Estate Agent Owned by a Building Society	0.66	1.64
A Traditional Estate Agent	−0.17	−0.35
An Agent Owned by an Insurance Company	0.51	1.25
An Agent Offering a Professional Service	0.43	0.45
An Agent with a Poor Reputation	−1.19	−0.21
An Agent with Chartered Surveyor Status	−0.35	−0.51
An Agent Specializing in Exclusive Property	0.92	0.54
An Agent Specializing in Commercial/Industrial Property	−0.05	−0.59
An Agent Specializing in Residential Property	−0.46	−0.26
A Secondary Competitor	−0.23	0.35
An Agent with a Good Reputation	0.34	0.13
A Diversified Estate Agent	−0.51	−0.73
An Independent Estate Agent	−0.76	−1.25
An Inferior Competitor	−1.23	−1.51
A Very Successful Estate Agent	0.01	0.82
A Moderately Successful Estate Agent	−0.54	−0.45
An Unsuccessful Estate Agent	−1.33	−1.62

Table A2.5(b)　Dimension weights for Paul Schofield (N = 39)

Attribute	Dimension 1	Dimension 2
Service to vendors	0.96	0.00
Quality of staff	0.95	0.01
Service to purchasers	0.95	0.00
Training of staff	0.94	0.10
Operating practices	0.97	0.04
Quality of advertising	0.68	0.62
Profitability	0.23	0.82
Location of business premises	0.29	0.74
Size of branch network	0.40	0.80
Range of services	0.69	0.65
Geographical coverage	0.69	0.54
Scale of charges	0.83	0.41
Degree of personal attention	0.94	0.00
Market share	0.14	0.89
Marketing profile	0.65	0.64
Degree of local knowledge	0.70	0.47
Strategy influence/power	0.48	0.80
Amount of advertising	0.24	0.90
Financial resources	0.51	0.75
Links with financial services companies	0.49	0.74
Typical range of properties on sale	0.32	0.80

Table A2.6(a)　Stimulus coordinates associated with the two-dimensional MDS representation of participants' aggregated perceptions of competitors from the low performance firms (N = 26 individuals from N = 19 organizations; stress = 0.307; RSQ =0.666)

Stimulus	Dimension 1	Dimension 2
My Business	0.88	−1.96
My Major Competitor	−1.15	−1.09
A Solicitor Agent	0.37	−0.06
An Estate Agent Owned by a Building Society	−1.97	0.09
A Traditional Estate Agent	−0.08	−0.39
An Agent Owned by an Insurance Company	−1.79	0.21
An Agent Offering a Professional Service	−0.62	−0.76
An Agent with a Poor Reputation	−0.12	2.16
An Agent with Chartered Surveyor Status	0.75	−0.60
An Agent Specializing in Exclusive Property	−0.47	−0.15
An Agent Specializing in Commercial/Industrial Property	0.68	−0.64
An Agent Specializing in Residential Property	0.14	0.70
A Secondary Competitor	0.39	−0.06
An Agent with a Good Reputation	0.53	−0.72
A Diversified Estate Agent	−0.39	−0.04
An Independent Estate Agent	0.88	−0.10
An Inferior Competitor	1.12	1.68
A Very Successful Estate Agent	−1.32	−0.44
A Moderately Successful Estate Agent	0.01	0.01
An Unsuccessful Estate Agent	2.16	2.17

Table A2.6(b)   Dimension weights for the low performance firms (N = 26 individuals from N = 19 organizations)

	Dimension	
Attribute	*1*	*2*
Service to vendors	0.07	0.95
Quality of staff	0.04	0.90
Service to purchasers	0.09	0.94
Training of staff	0.30	0.83
Operating practices	0.13	0.92
Quality of advertising	0.50	0.63
Profitability	0.44	0.70
Location of business premises	0.51	0.47
Size of branch network	0.79	0.06
Range of services	0.55	0.52
Geographical coverage	0.79	0.03
Scale of charges	0.55	0.37
Degree of personal attention	0.22	0.84
Market share	0.76	0.20
Marketing profile	0.84	0.06
Degree of local knowledge	0.17	0.71
Strategy influence/power	0.80	0.15
Amount of advertising	0.71	0.20
Financial resources	0.85	0.11
Links with financial services companies	0.81	0.04
Typical range of properties on sale	0.58	0.30

Table A2.7(a)   Stimulus coordinates associated with the two-dimensional MDS representation of participants' aggregated perceptions of competitors from the medium performance firms (N = 20 individuals from N = 19 organizations; stress = 0.301; RSQ = 0.597)

	Dimension	
Stimulus	*1*	*2*
My Business	– 0.41	1.85
My Major Competitor	1.58	– 0.10
A Solicitor Agent	– 1.02	– 0.90
An Estate Agent Owned by a Building Society	1.96	0.04
A Traditional Estate Agent	– 0.61	0.01
An Agent Owned by an Insurance Company	1.65	– 0.18
An Agent Offering a Professional Service	0.11	1.13
An Agent with a Poor Reputation	– 0.54	– 2.02
An Agent with Chartered Surveyor Status	– 0.87	0.12
An Agent Specializing in Exclusive Property	– 0.14	1.07
An Agent Specializing in Commercial/Industrial Property	– 0.34	1.04
An Agent Specializing in Residential Property	0.60	– 0.38
A Secondary Competitor	– 0.33	– 0.88
An Agent with a Good Reputation	0.47	1.51
A Diversified Estate Agent	– 0.16	0.48
An Independent Estate Agent	– 0.72	0.33
An Inferior Competitor	– 1.25	–1.27
A Very Successful Estate Agent	1.46	0.13
A Moderately Successful Estate Agent	0.33	– 0.30
An Unsuccessful Estate Agent	– 1.76	– 1.69

Table A2.7(b)   Dimension weights for the medium performance firms (N = 20 individuals from N = 19 organizations)

	Dimension	
Attribute	*1*	*2*
Service to vendors	0.11	0.88
Quality of staff	0.22	0.76
Service to purchasers	0.28	0.73
Training of staff	0.57	0.49
Operating practices	0.14	0.83
Quality of advertising	0.50	0.45
Profitability	0.44	0.47
Location of business premises	0.53	0.48
Size of branch network	0.89	0.03
Range of services	0.49	0.48
Geographical coverage	0.80	0.15
Scale of charges	0.48	0.41
Degree of personal attention	0.14	0.79
Market share	0.80	0.16
Marketing profile	0.83	0.16
Degree of local knowledge	0.44	0.45
Strategy influence/power	0.84	0.15
Amount of advertising	0.79	0.17
Financial resources	0.84	0.15
Links with financial services companies	0.73	0.20
Typical range of properties on sale	0.65	0.28

Table A2.8(a)   Stimulus coordinates associated with the two-dimensional MDS representation of participants' aggregated perceptions of competitors from the high performance firms (N = 33 individuals from N = 12 organizations; stress = 0.250; RSQ = 745)

	Dimension	
Stimulus	*1*	*2*
My Business	1.08	2.10
My Major Competitor	1.77	0.82
A Solicitor Agent	−0.76	−0.84
An Estate Agent Owned by a Building Society	1.95	0.28
A Traditional Estate Agent	−0.82	0.35
An Agent Owned by an Insurance Company	1.86	−0.61
An Agent Offering a Professional Service	−0.66	0.62
An Agent with a Poor Reputation	−0.05	−1.73
An Agent with Chartered Surveyor Status	−0.92	0.30
An Agent Specializing in Exclusive Property	0.29	1.07
An Agent Specializing in Commercial/Industrial Property	−0.28	0.98
An Agent Specializing in Residential Property	−0.12	−0.61
A Secondary Competitor	0.18	−0.75
An Agent with a Good Reputation	−0.37	0.65
A Diversified Estate Agent	−0.53	0.24
An Independent Estate Agent	−0.93	−0.23
An Inferior Competitor	−1.02	−1.21
A Very Successful Estate Agent	0.95	0.93
A Moderately Successful Estate Agent	−0.05	−0.31
An Unsuccessful Estate Agent	−1.56	−2.04

Table A2.8(b)   Dimension weights for the high performance firms (N = 33 individuals from N = 12 organizations)

Attribute	Dimension	
	1	2
Service to vendors	0.13	0.93
Quality of staff	0.10	0.95
Service to purchasers	0.25	0.91
Training of staff	0.54	0.70
Operating practices	0.08	0.94
Quality of advertising	0.51	0.66
Profitability	0.29	0.79
Location of business premises	0.47	0.63
Size of branch network	0.92	0.02
Range of services	0.54	0.61
Geographical coverage	0.88	0.00
Scale of charges	0.48	0.41
Degree of personal attention	0.18	0.88
Market share	0.66	0.44
Marketing profile	0.91	0.13
Degree of local knowledge	0.33	0.67
Strategy influence/power	0.82	0.36
Amount of advertising	0.82	0.24
Financial resources	0.87	0.10
Links with financial services companies	0.90	0.02
Typical range of properties on sale	0.64	0.48

Appendix 3   MDS Solutions for the Various Functional Subgroups

The following tables report the basic two-dimensional MDS solutions associated with the various functional subgroups, as discussed in Chapter 6. As in the previous appendix, the stimulus coordinates are presented, followed by the dimension weights, for each subgroup in turn.

Table A3.1(a)   Stimulus coordinates associated with the two-dimensional MDS representation of the area managers' aggregated perceptions of competitors (N = 23; stress = 0.262; RSQ = 0.696)

	Dimension	
Stimulus	*1*	*2*
My Business	– 1.63	– 1.94
My Major Competitor	– 1.74	– 0.82
A Solicitor Agent	0.82	1.20
An Estate Agent Owned by a Building Society	– 1.57	– 0.11
A Traditional Estate Agent	0.56	– 0.25
An Agent Owned by an Insurance Company	– 1.49	0.84
An Agent Offering a Professional Service	0.68	– 0.77
An Agent with a Poor Reputation	0.95	1.76
An Agent with Chartered Surveyor Status	0.94	– 0.52
An Agent Specializing in Exclusive Property	– 0.25	– 1.19
An Agent Specializing in Commercial/Industrial Property	0.57	– 1.06
An Agent Specializing in Residential Property	– 0.01	0.75
A Secondary Competitor	0.54	0.61
An Agent with a Good Reputation	– 0.17	– 0.78
A Diversified Estate Agent	– 0.58	0.15
An Independent Estate Agent	0.97	0.08
An Inferior Competitor	1.05	1.24
A Very Successful Estate Agent	– 1.11	– 0.99
A Moderately Successful Estate Agent	0.02	0.12
An Unsuccessful Estate Agent	1.45	1.66

Table A3.1(b)   Dimension weights for the area managers (N = 23)

Attribute	Dimension	
	1	2
Service to vendors	0.29	0.83
Quality of staff	0.28	0.86
Service to purchasers	0.36	0.80
Training of staff	0.71	0.48
Operating practices	0.26	0.87
Quality of advertising	0.65	0.51
Profitability	0.25	0.80
Location of business premises	0.67	0.41
Size of branch network	0.90	0.01
Range of services	0.63	0.49
Geographical coverage	0.82	0.12
Scale of charges	0.45	0.48
Degree of personal attention	0.15	0.77
Market share	0.77	0.24
Marketing profile	0.87	0.12
Degree of local knowledge	0.41	0.55
Strategy influence/power	0.81	0.34
Amount of advertising	0.77	0.21
Financial resources	0.87	0.10
Links with financial services companies	0.89	0.08
Typical range of properties on sale	0.76	0.34

Table A3.2(a)   Stimulus coordinates associated with the two-dimensional MDS representation of the branch managers' aggregated perceptions of competitors (N = 62; stress = 0.242; RSQ = 0.799)

Stimulus	Dimension	
	1	2
My Business	– 1.98	– 2.53
My Major Competitor	– 1.92	– 0.79
A Solicitor Agent	0.78	0.54
An Estate Agent Owned by a Building Society	– 1.57	– 0.20
A Traditional Estate Agent	0.80	– 0.05
An Agent Owned by an Insurance Company	– 1.46	0.55
An Agent Offering a Professional Service	0.08	– 0.77
An Agent with a Poor Reputation	0.38	1.63
An Agent with Chartered Surveyor Status	0.82	– 0.19
An Agent Specializing in Exclusive Property	– 0.10	– 1.00
An Agent Specializing in Commercial/Industrial Property	0.31	– 0.58
An Agent Specializing in Residential Propertya	– 0.07	0.39
A Secondary Competitor	– 0.27	0.30
An Agent with a Good Reputation	0.16	– 0.77
A Diversified Estate Agent	0.51	0.08
An Independent Estate Agent	1.04	0.48
An Inferior Competitor	1.12	1.39
A Very Successful Estate Agent	– 0.57	– 0.76
A Moderately Successful Estate Agent	0.38	0.28
An Unsuccessful Estate Agent	1.55	2.01

Table A3.2(b)   Dimension weights for the branch managers (N = 62)

	Dimension	
Attribute	*1*	*2*
Service to vendors	0.18	0.93
Quality of staff	0.23	0.91
Service to purchasers	0.21	0.90
Training of staff	0.65	0.65
Operating practices	0.25	0.90
Quality of advertising	0.44	0.73
Profitability	0.34	0.78
Location of business premises	0.71	0.47
Size of branch network	0.94	0.00
Range of services	0.76	0.41
Geographical coverage	0.93	0.00
Scale of charges	0.68	0.43
Degree of personal attention	0.31	0.87
Market share	0.86	0.06
Marketing profile	0.93	0.06
Degree of local knowledge	0.51	0.63
Strategy influence/power	0.92	0.17
Amount of advertising	0.85	0.14
Financial resources	0.94	0.04
Links with financial services companies	0.91	0.07
Typical range of properties on sale	0.76	0.31

Table A3.3(a)   Stimulus coordinates associated with the two-dimensional MDS representation of the partners' aggregated perceptions of competitors (N = 32; stress = 0.289; RSQ = 0.669)

	Dimension	
Stimulus	*1*	*2*
My Business	0.04	− 1.97
My Major Competitor	− 1.52	− 1.05
A Solicitor Agent	0.68	0.66
An Estate Agent Owned by a Building Society	− 2.11	0.03
A Traditional Estate Agent	0.81	− 0.10
An Agent Owned by an Insurance Company	− 1.90	0.43
An Agent Offering a Professional Service	0.30	− 0.44
An Agent with a Poor Reputation	− 0.15	2.02
An Agent with Chartered Surveyor Status	0.75	− 0.23
An Agent Specializing in Exclusive Property	− 0.53	− 0.97
An Agent Specializing in Commercial/Industrial Property	− 0.26	− 1.17
An Agent Specializing in Residential Property	− 0.38	0.44
A Secondary Competitor	− 0.06	0.41
An Agent with a Good Reputation	0.54	− 0.74
A Diversified Estate Agent	0.94	− 0.11
An Independent Estate Agent	0.67	0.04
An Inferior Competitor	0.97	1.55
A Very Successful Estate Agent	− 1.00	− 0.97
A Moderately Successful Estate Agent	0.28	0.30
An Unsuccessful Estate Agent	1.92	1.85

Table A3.3(b)   Dimension weights for the partners (N = 32)

Attribute	Dimension	
	1	2
Service to vendors	0.08	0.91
Quality of staff	0.05	0.90
Service to purchasers	0.16	0.87
Training of staff	0.44	0.75
Operating practices	0.09	0.88
Quality of advertising	0.46	0.64
Profitability	0.30	0.77
Location of business premises	0.45	0.50
Size of branch network	0.88	0.00
Range of services	0.49	0.59
Geographical coverage	0.86	0.00
Scale of charges	0.47	0.44
Degree of personal attention	0.09	0.85
Market share	0.67	0.34
Marketing profile	0.80	0.22
Degree of local knowledge	0.31	0.61
Strategy influence/power	0.83	0.24
Amount of advertising	0.74	0.25
Financial resources	0.86	0.07
Links with financial services companies	0.80	0.08
Typical range of properties on sale	0.65	0.41

Table A3.4(a)   Stimulus coordinates associated with the two-dimensional MDS representation of the negotiators' aggregated perceptions of competitors (N = 26; stress = 0.251; RSQ = 0.795)

Stimulus	Dimension	
	1	2
My Business	2.84	1.54
My Major Competitor	1.00	1.60
A Solicitor Agent	− 0.25	− 0.72
An Estate Agent Owned by a Building Society	0.78	2.04
A Traditional Estate Agent	− 0.18	− 1.00
An Agent Owned by an Insurance Company	0.26	1.48
An Agent Offering a Professional Service	0.16	− 0.32
An Agent with a Poor Reputation	− 1.53	− 0.49
An Agent with Chartered Surveyor Status	− 0.31	− 0.57
An Agent Specializing in Exclusive Property	1.09	0.26
An Agent Specializing in Commercial/Industrial Property	0.08	− 0.66
An Agent Specializing in Residential Property	− 0.42	− 0.16
A Secondary Competitor	− 0.46	0.68
An Agent with a Good Reputation	0.34	− 0.06
A Diversified Estate Agent	− 0.16	− 0.60
An Independent Estate Agent	− 0.37	− 1.18
An Inferior Competitor	− 1.32	− 1.12
A Very Successful Estate Agent	0.79	0.75
A Moderately Successful Estate Agent	− 0.54	− 0.18
An Unsuccessful Estate Agent	− 1.80	− 1.40

Table A3.4(b)   Dimension weights for the negotiators (N = 26)

	Dimension	
Attribute	1	2
Service to vendors	0.93	0.08
Quality of staff	0.93	0.05
Service to purchasers	0.90	0.03
Training of staff	0.87	0.24
Operating practices	0.89	0.16
Quality of advertising	0.82	0.39
Profitability	0.53	0.67
Location of business premises	0.57	0.55
Size of branch network	0.27	0.88
Range of services	0.64	0.61
Geographical coverage	0.38	0.81
Scale of charges	0.83	0.24
Degree of personal attention	0.92	0.00
Market share	0.35	0.82
Marketing profile	0.39	0.85
Degree of local knowledge	0.76	0.28
Strategy influence/power	0.53	0.75
Amount of advertising	0.46	0.75
Financial resources	0.34	0.87
Links with financial services companies	0.25	0.83
Typical range of properties on sale	0.59	0.63

Table A3.5(a)   Stimulus coordinates associated with the two-dimensional MDS representation of the valuers' aggregated perceptions of competitors (N = 19; stress = 0.269; RSQ = 0.722)

	Dimension	
Stimulus	1	2
My Business	2.50	0.71
My Major Competitor	1.03	1.49
A Solicitor Agent	− 0.40	− 0.61
An Estate Agent Owned by a Building Society	0.88	2.30
A Traditional Estate Agent	0.40	− 0.51
An Agent Owned by an Insurance Company	0.20	1.84
An Agent Offering a Professional Service	0.58	− 0.06
An Agent with a Poor Reputation	− 1.64	0.53
An Agent with Chartered Surveyor Status	− 0.32	− 1.04
An Agent Specializing in Exclusive Property	1.02	0.17
An Agent Specializing in Commercial/Industrial Property	0.41	0.21
An Agent Specializing in Residential Property	− 0.74	− 0.71
A Secondary Competitor	− 0.86	0.34
An Agent with a Good Reputation	0.42	− 0.76
A Diversified Estate Agent	0.02	− 0.64
An Independent Estate Agent	− 0.31	− 1.09
An Inferior Competitor	− 1.27	− 0.92
A Very Successful Estate Agent	0.53	0.72
A Moderately Successful Estate Agent	− 0.60	− 0.53
An Unsuccessful Estate Agent	− 1.84	− 1.45

Table A3.5(b)   Dimension weights for the valuers (N=19)

Attribute	Dimension	
	1	2
Service to vendors	0.90	0.04
Quality of staff	0.92	0.00
Service to purchasers	0.90	0.12
Training of staff	0.82	0.32
Operating practices	0.86	0.00
Quality of advertising	0.68	0.46
Profitability	0.80	0.23
Location of business premises	0.77	0.33
Size of branch network	0.37	0.79
Range of services	0.63	0.47
Geographical coverage	0.23	0.82
Scale of charges	0.35	0.58
Degree of personal attention	0.91	0.00
Market share	0.72	0.38
Marketing profile	0.50	0.72
Degree of local knowledge	0.74	0.24
Strategy influence/power	0.71	0.48
Amount of advertising	0.61	0.64
Financial resources	0.27	0.83
Links with financial services companies	0.39	0.78
Typical range of properties on sale	0.61	0.48

Table A3.6(a)   Stimulus coordinates associated with the two-dimensional MDS representation of the sole principals' aggregated perceptions of competitors (N = 18; stress = 0.296; RSQ = 0.686)

Stimulus	Dimension	
	1	2
My Business	0.89	– 1.90
My Major Competitor	– 1.45	– 0.20
A Solicitor Agent	0.56	0.47
An Estate Agent Owned by a Building Society	– 2.05	0.12
A Traditional Estate Agent	– 0.20	– 0.83
An Agent Owned by an Insurance Company	– 1.53	0.21
An Agent Offering a Professional Service	– 0.12	– 0.91
An Agent with a Poor Reputation	0.31	2.13
An Agent with Chartered Surveyor Status	0.56	– 0.41
An Agent Specializing in Exclusive Property	– 0.81	– 0.69
An Agent Specializing in Commercial/Industrial Property	0.39	– 0.94
An Agent Specializing in Residential Property	– 0.11	0.30
A Secondary Competitor	0.80	0.46
An Agent with a Good Reputation	0.42	– 0.84
A Diversified Estate Agent	– 0.08	– 0.31
An Independent Estate Agent	0.85	– 0.20
An Inferior Competitor	1.24	1.44
A Very Successful Estate Agent	– 1.36	– 0.14
A Moderately Successful Estate Agent	– 0.29	– 0.05
An Unsuccessful Estate Agent	1.98	2.29

Table A3.6(b)   Dimension weights for the sole principals (N = 18)

Attribute	Dimension 1	2
Service to vendors	0.09	0.91
Quality of staff	0.16	0.90
Service to purchasers	0.15	0.86
Training of staff	0.56	0.56
Operating practices	0.08	0.93
Quality of advertising	0.54	0.57
Profitability	0.54	0.60
Location of business premises	0.53	0.54
Size of branch network	0.85	0.00
Range of services	0.55	0.48
Geographical coverage	0.77	0.02
Scale of charges	0.55	0.30
Degree of personal attention	0.29	0.81
Market share	0.84	0.10
Marketing profile	0.91	0.07
Degree of local knowledge	0.20	0.72
Strategy influence/power	0.89	0.00
Amount of advertising	0.87	0.11
Financial resources	0.84	0.13
Links with financial services companies	0.81	0.01
Typical range of properties on sale	0.71	0.24

Table A3.7(a)   Stimulus coordinates associated with the two-dimensional MDS representation of aggregated perceptions of competitors for the miscellaneous functional subgroup (N = 26; stress = 0.250; RSQ = 0.741)

Stimulus	Dimension 1	2
My Business	2.51	1.02
My Major Competitor	1.16	1.74
A Solicitor Agent	− 0.47	− 0.97
An Estate Agent Owned by a Building Society	0.04	1.85
A Traditional Estate Agent	0.02	− 0.71
An Agent Owned by an Insurance Company	− 0.33	1.76
An Agent Offering a Professional Service	0.80	− 0.69
An Agent with a Poor Reputation	− 1.60	− 0.35
An Agent with Chartered Surveyor Status	0.11	− 1.08
An Agent Specializing in Exclusive Property	0.97	− 0.06
An Agent Specializing in Commercial/Industrial Property	0.59	− 0.77
An Agent Specializing in Residential Property	− 0.37	0.06
A Secondary Competitor	− 0.27	0.56
An Agent with a Good Reputation	0.67	0.17
A Diversified Estate Agent	− 0.38	− 0.56
An Independent Estate Agent	− 0.01	− 0.96
An Inferior Competitor	− 1.50	− 0.95
A Very Successful Estate Agent	0.43	1.05
A Moderately Successful Estate Agent	− 0.30	0.29
An Unsuccessful Estate Agent	− 2.05	− 1.39

Table A3.7(b)   Dimension weights for the miscellaneous functional subgroup
(N = 26)

	Dimension	
Attribute	*1*	*2*
Service to vendors	0.90	0.12
Quality of staff	0.90	0.13
Service to purchasers	0.88	0.22
Training of staff	0.79	0.44
Operating practices	0.90	0.18
Quality of advertising	0.74	0.43
Profitability	0.59	0.43
Location of business premises	0.71	0.40
Size of branch network	0.21	0.89
Range of services	0.58	0.62
Geographical coverage	0.17	0.88
Scale of charges	0.49	0.52
Degree of personal attention	0.84	0.18
Market share	0.48	0.74
Marketing profile	0.45	0.76
Degree of local knowledge	0.76	0.32
Strategy influence/power	0.52	0.69
Amount of advertising	0.34	0.80
Financial resources	0.16	0.83
Links with financial services companies	0.21	0.87
Typical range of properties on sale	0.40	0.69

Appendix 4   MDS Solutions for the Longitudinal Comparisons

The following tables report the basic two-dimensional MDS solutions associated with the various longitudinal comparisons discussed in Chapter 7. As in Appendices 2 and 3, the stimulus coordinates are presented, followed by the dimension weights, for each subgroup in turn.

Table A4.1(a)   Stimulus coordinates associated with the two-dimensional MDS representation of the T2 returners' aggregated perceptions of competitors assessed at T1 (N = 114; stress = 0.220; RSQ = 0.827)

	Dimension	
Stimulus	*1*	*2*
My Business	1.52	2.30
My Major Competitor	1.77	0.98
A Solicitor Agent	− 0.76	− 0.63
An Estate Agent Owned by a Building Society	1.88	0.26
A Traditional Estate Agent	− 0.75	0.08
An Agent Owned by an Insurance Company	1.74	− 0.37
An Agent Offering a Professional Service	− 0.53	0.54
An Agent with a Poor Reputation	− 0.63	− 1.80
An Agent with Chartered Surveyor Status	− 0.80	0.08
An Agent Specializing in Exclusive Property	0.29	1.01
An Agent Specializing in Commercial/Industrial Property	− 0.41	0.74
An Agent Specializing in Residential Property	0.10	− 0.36
A Secondary Competitor	− 0.03	− 0.57
An Agent with a Good Reputation	− 0.17	0.73
A Diversified Estate Agent	− 0.36	0.10
An Independent Estate Agent	− 0.90	− 0.24
An Inferior Competitor	− 0.95	− 1.46
A Very Successful Estate Agent	0.81	0.84
A Moderately Successful Estate Agent	− 0.15	− 0.19
An Unsuccessful Estate Agent	− 1.65	− 2.03

Table A4.1(b)   Dimension weights for the T2 returners assessed at T1 (N = 114)

| | Dimension | |
Attribute	1	2
Service to vendors	0.11	0.96
Quality of staff	0.10	0.96
Service to purchasers	0.17	0.94
Training of staff	0.55	0.74
Operating practices	0.14	0.94
Quality of advertising	0.50	0.75
Profitability	0.29	0.85
Location of business premises	0.51	0.70
Size of branch network	0.94	0.00
Range of services	0.73	0.51
Geographical coverage	0.92	0.00
Scale of charges	0.52	0.60
Degree of personal attention	0.10	0.93
Market share	0.81	0.30
Marketing profile	0.94	0.17
Degree of local knowledge	0.31	0.76
Strategy influence/power	0.89	0.30
Amount of advertising	0.88	0.27
Financial resources	0.92	0.14
Links with financial services companies	0.94	0.07
Typical range of properties on sale	0.70	0.44

Table A4.2(a)   Stimulus coordinates associated with the two-dimensional MDS representation of the non-returners' aggregated perceptions of competitors assessed at T1 (N = 92; stress = 0.228; RSQ = 0.818)

| | Dimension | |
Stimulus	1	2
My Business	− 1.50	− 2.76
My Major Competitor	− 1.75	− 0.80
A Solicitor Agent	0.73	0.40
An Estate Agent Owned by a Building Society	− 1.90	− 0.11
A Traditional Estate Agent	0.56	− 0.28
An Agent Owned by an Insurance Company	− 1.53	0.39
An Agent Offering a Professional Service	− 0.16	− 0.70
An Agent with a Poor Reputation	0.24	1.80
An Agent with Chartered Surveyor Status	0.79	− 0.13
An Agent Specializing in Exclusive Property	− 0.30	− 0.90
An Agent Specializing in Commercial/Industrial Property	0.42	− 0.64
An Agent Specializing in Residential Property	0.41	0.45
A Secondary Competitor	− 0.05	0.13
An Agent with a Good Reputation	0.15	− 0.61
A Diversified Estate Agent	0.64	0.16
An Independent Estate Agent	0.98	0.36
An Inferior Competitor	1.26	1.31
A Very Successful Estate Agent	− 0.97	− 0.45
A Moderately Successful Estate Agent	0.34	0.48
An Unsuccessful Estate Agent	1.64	1.87

Table A4.2(b)   Dimension weights for the non-returners assessed at T1 (N = 92)

	Dimension	
Attribute	1	2
Service to vendors	0.14	0.94
Quality of staff	0.18	0.93
Service to purchasers	0.25	0.91
Training of staff	0.54	0.77
Operating practices	0.16	0.95
Quality of advertising	0.64	0.59
Profitability	0.61	0.60
Location of business premises	0.71	0.52
Size of branch network	0.94	0.00
Range of services	0.70	0.51
Geographical coverage	0.92	0.01
Scale of charges	0.72	0.42
Degree of personal attention	0.23	0.91
Market share	0.85	0.24
Marketing profile	0.93	0.14
Degree of local knowledge	0.52	0.67
Strategy influence/power	0.87	0.28
Amount of advertising	0.88	0.17
Financial resources	0.93	0.03
Links with financial services companies	0.86	0.19
Typical range of properties on sale	0.80	0.27

Table A4.3(a)   Stimulus coordinates associated with the two-dimensional MDS representation of the returners' aggregated perceptions of competitors assessed at T2 (N = 114; stress = 0.224; RSQ = 0.810)

	Dimension	
Stimulus	1	2
My Business	− 1.51	− 1.91
My Major Competitor	− 1.76	− 1.01
A Solicitor Agent	0.89	0.59
An Estate Agent Owned by a Building Society	− 1.80	− 0.25
A Traditional Estate Agent	0.86	− 0.16
An Agent Owned by an Insurance Company	− 1.49	0.50
An Agent Offering a Professional Service	0.22	− 0.65
An Agent with a Poor Reputation	0.92	1.74
An Agent with Chartered Surveyor Status	0.96	− 0.15
An Agent Specializing in Exclusive Property	− 0.07	− 1.04
An Agent Specializing in Commercial/Industrial Property	0.31	− 0.88
An Agent Specializing in Residential Property	− 0.15	0.29
A Secondary Competitor	0.02	0.51
An Agent with a Good Reputation	− 0.04	− 0.94
A Diversified Estate Agent	0.22	0.08
An Independent Estate Agent	0.99	0.36
An Inferior Competitor	1.07	1.34
A Very Successful Estate Agent	− 1.03	− 0.93
A Moderately Successful Estate Agent	− 0.17	0.22
An Unsuccessful Estate Agent	1.57	2.28

Table A4.3(b)   Dimension weights for the returners at assessed T2 (N = 114)

	Dimension	
Attribute	*1*	*2*
Service to vendors	0.24	0.91
Quality of staff	0.15	0.93
Service to purchasers	0.25	0.89
Training of staff	0.69	0.60
Operating practices	0.23	0.91
Quality of advertising	0.56	0.71
Profitability	0.16	0.87
Location of business premises	0.60	0.67
Size of branch network	0.92	0.00
Range of services	0.62	0.63
Geographical coverage	0.92	0.00
Scale of charges	0.44	0.69
Degree of personal attention	0.27	0.88
Market share	0.79	0.30
Marketing profile	0.92	0.14
Degree of local knowledge	0.34	0.75
Strategy influence/power	0.87	0.24
Amount of advertising	0.86	0.21
Financial resources	0.92	0.14
Links with financial services companies	0.91	0.05
Typical range of properties on sale	0.62	0.58

References

Abrahamson, E. and Fombrun, C. J. (1994). Macrocultures: determinants and consequences. *Academy of Management Review*, **19**, 728–755.

Adler, S. and Weiss, H. M. (1988). Recent developments in the study of personality and organizational behavior. In C. L. Cooper and I. T. Robertson (eds), *International Review of Industrial and Organizational Psychology – Volume 3* (pp. 307–330). Chichester: Wiley

Arabie, P., Carroll, J. D. and DeSarbo, W. S. (1987). *Three-Way Scaling and Clustering*. Sage University Paper Series on Quantitative Applications in the Social Sciences, 07–065. London: Sage.

Araujo, L. (1998). Knowing and learning as networking. *Management Learning*, **29**, 317–336.

Ashforth, B. and Mael, F. (1989). Social identity theory and the organization. *Academy of Management Review*, **14**, 20–39.

Athanassopoulos, A. D. (2003). Strategic groups, frontier benchmarking and performance differences: Evidence from the UK retail grocery industry. *Journal of Management Studies*, **40**, 921–953.

Baden-Fuller, C. and Stopford, J. M. (1992). *Rejuvenating the Mature Business*. London: Routledge.

Bain, J. S. (1956). *Barriers to New Competition*. Cambridge, MA: Harvard University Press.

Balogun, J., Huff, A. S. and Johnson, G. (2003). Three responses to the methodological challenges of studying strategizing. *Journal of Management Studies*, **40** (Special Issue), 197–224.

Bandura, A. (1986). *Social Foundations of Thought and Action*. Englewood Cliffs, NJ: Prentice-Hall.

Barnes, J. H. (1984). Cognitive biases and their impact on strategic planning. *Strategic Management Journal*, **5**, 129–137.

Barney, J. B. and Hoskisson, R. E. (1990). Strategic groups: Untested assertions and research proposals. *Managerial and Decision Economics*, **11**, 187–198.

Barr, P. S. (1998). Adapting to unfamiliar environmental events: a look at the evolution of interpretation and its role in strategic change. *Organization Science*, **9**, 644–669.

Barr, P. S. and Huff, A. S. (1997). Seeing isn't believing: Understanding diversity in the timing of strategic response. *Journal of Management Studies*, **34**, 337–370.

Barr, P. S., Stimpert, J. L. and Huff, A. S. (1992). Cognitive change, strategic action, and organizational renewal. *Strategic Management Journal*, **13**, 15–36.

Bartlett, F. C. (1932). *Remembering: A Study in Experimental and Social Psychology*. Cambridge: Cambridge University Press.

Bartunek, J. M. (1984). Changing interpretive schemes: The example of a religious order. *Administrative Science Quarterly*, **29**, 355–372.

Berger, P. L. and Luckmann, T. (1967). *The Social Construction of Reality*. Harmondsworth: Penguin.

Birnbaum-More, P. H. and Weiss, A. R. (1990). Discovering the basis of competition in 12 industries: Computerized content analysis of interview data from the US and Europe. In Huff, A. S. (ed.), *Mapping Strategic Thought* (pp. 53–69). Chichester: Wiley.

Bogner, W. C. and Barr, P. S. (2000). Making sense in hypercompetitive environments. A cognitive explanation for the persistence of high velocity competition. *Organization Science*, 11, 212–226.

Bogner, W. C. and Thomas, H. (1993). The role of competitive groups in strategy formulation: A dynamic integration of two competing models. *Journal of Management Studies*, 30, 51–67.

Bogner, W. C., Thomas, H. and McGee, J. (1996). A longitudinal study of the competitive positions and entry paths of European firms in the US pharmaceutical industry. *Strategic Management Journal*, 17, 85–107.

Boone, C. (1988). The influence of the locus of control of top managers on company strategy, structure and performance. In P. V. Abeele (ed.), *Psychology in Micro and Macro Economics: Proceedings of the 13th Annual Colloquium of the International Association for Research in Economic Psychology*, 1.

Boone, C. and De Brabander, B. (1993). Generalized versus specific locus of control expectancies of chief executive officers. *Strategic Management Journal*, 14, 619–625.

Borg, I. and Groenen, P. (1997). *Modern Multidimensional scaling: Theory and Applications*. New York: Springer.

Borg, I. and Lingoes, J. C. (1978). What weights should weights have in individual differences scaling? *Quality & Quantity*, 12, 223–237.

Borg, I. and Lingoes, J. C. (1987). *Multidimensional Similarity Structure Analysis*. New York: Springer.

Borgatti, S. P., Everett, M. G. and Freeman, L. C. (1992). *UCINET IV Version 1.0.* Columbia: Analytic Technologies.

Bouchet, J. L. (1976). Diversification: Composition of the top management team and performance of the firm. Paper presented at the EGOS conference on the sociology of the business enterprise, Oxford, December.

Bower, J. L. (1972). *Managing the Resource Allocation Process: A Study of Corporate Planning and Investment*. Homewood, Illinois: Irwin.

Bowers, D. (1973). OD techniques and their results in 23 organizations: The Michigan ICL study. *Journal of Applied Behavioral Science*, 9, 21–43.

Bowman, C. and Ambrosini, V. (1997a). Perceptions of strategic priorities, consensus and firm performance. *Journal of Management Studies*, 34, 241–258.

Bowman, C. and Ambrosini, V. (1997b). Using single respondents in strategy research. *British Journal of Management*, 8, 119–131.

Bowman, C. and Johnson, G. (1992). 'Surfacing competitive strategies'. *European Management Journal*, 10, 210–219.

Broadbent, D. E. (1958). *Perception and Communication*. London: Pergamon.

Bryk, A. S. and Raudenbush, S. W. (1992). *Hierarchical Linear Models: Applications and Data Analysis Methods*. Newbury Park, CA: Sage.

Calori, R., Johnson, G. and Sarnin, P. (1992). French and British top managers' understanding of the structure and dynamics of their industries: A cognitive analysis and comparison. *British Journal of Management*, 3, 61–78.

Calori, R., Johnson, G. and Sarnin, P. (1994). CEOs' cognitive maps and the scope of the organization. *Strategic Management Journal*, 15, 437–457.

Cannon-Bowers, J. A. and Salas, E. (1998). *Making Decisions Under Stress: Implications for Individual and Team Training*. Washington, DC: American Psychological Association.

Carroll, J. D. and Chang, J. J. (1970). Analyses of individual differences in multidimensional scaling via an N-way generalization of 'Eckart-Young' decomposition. *Psychometrika*, 35, 283–319.

Caves, R. E. and Porter, M. E. (1977). From entry barriers to mobility barriers: Conjectural decisions and contrived deterrence to new competition. *Quarterly Journal of Economics*, **91**, 421–434.

Centre for Business Research (1986). *A Market Analysis of Estate Agency in England and Wales*. Manchester: Centre for Business Research, Manchester Business School.

Chattopadhyay, P., Glick, W. H., Miller, C. C. and Huber, G. P. (1999). Determinants of executive beliefs: comparing functional conditioning and social influence. *Strategic Management Journal*, **20**, 763–789.

Clark, B. H. and Montgomery, D. B. (1999). Managerial identification of competitors. *Journal of Marketing*, **63**, 67–83.

Cohen, J. and Cohen, P. (1983). Applied Multiple Regression/Correlation Analysis for the Behavioral Sciences (Second Edition). Hillsdale, NJ: Erlbaum.

Cool, K. O. and Dierickx, I. (1993). Rivalry, strategic groups and firm profitability. *Strategic Management Journal*, **14**, 47–59.

Cool, K. O. and Schendel, D. E. (1987). Strategic group formation and performance: The case of the US pharmaceutical industry, 1963–1982. *Management Science*, **33**, 1102–1124.

Cool, K. O. and Schendel, D. E. (1988). Performance differences among strategic group members. *Strategic Management Journal*, **9**, 207–223.

Coxon, A. P. M. (1982). *The User's Guide to Multidimensional Scaling*. London: Heinemann.

Coxon, A. P. M. and Jones, C. L. (1978). *The Images of Occupational Prestige: A Study in Social Cognition*. London: Macmillan.

Coxon, A. P. M. and Jones, C. L. (1979). *Measurement and Meanings: Techniques and Methods of Studying Occupational Cognition*. London: Macmillan.

Coxon, A. P. M. and Jones, C. L. (1980). Multidimensional scaling: Exploration to confirmation. *Quality and Quantity*, **14**, 31–73.

Craik, K. (1943). *The Nature of Explanation*. Cambridge: Cambridge University Press.

Cronbach, L. J. (1951). Coefficient alpha and the internal structure of tests. *Psychometrika*, **16**, 297–334.

Cronbach, L. J. and Gleser, G. C. (1953). Assessing the similarity between profiles. *Psychological Bulletin*, **50**, 456–473.

Crowne, D. P. and Marlowe, D. (1964). *The Approval Motive: Studies in Evaluative Dependence*. New York: Wiley.

Cyert, R. M. and March, J. G. (1963). *A Behavioral Theory of the Firm*. Englewood Cliffs N. J.: Prentice-Hall.

D'Avini, R. A. (1994). *Hypercompetition: Managing the Dynamics of Strategic Manoeuvring*. New York: Free Press.

Daft, R. L. and Weick, K. E. (1984). Toward a model of organizations as interpretation systems. *Academy of Management Review*, **9**, 284–295.

Dandrove, D., Peteraf, M. and Shanley, M. (1998). Do Strategic Groups exist? An economic framework for analysis. *Strategic Management Journal*, **19**, 1029–1044.

Daniels, K. and Johnson. G. (2002). On Trees and Triviality Traps: Locating the Debate on the Contribution of Cognitive Mapping to Organizational Research. *Organization Studies*, **23**, 73–81.

Daniels, K., de Chernatony, L. and Johnson, G. (1995). Validating a method for mapping managers' mental models of competitive industry structures. *Human Relations*, **48**, 975–991

Daniels, K., Johnson, G. and de Chernatony, L. (1994). Differences in managerial cognitions of competition. *British Journal of Management*, **5**, S21–S29.

Daniels, K., Johnson, G. and de Chernatony, L. (2002). Task and institutional influences on managers' mental models of competition. *Organization Studies*, **23**, 31–62.

Das, T. K. and Teng, B.-S. (1999). Cognitive biases and strategic decision processes. *Journal of Management Studies*, **36**, 757–778.

Davies, P. M. and Coxon, A. P. M. (1983). *MDS(X) User Manual*. Edinburgh: University of Edinburgh Program Library Unit.

Davis, J. (1983). Does authority generalize? Locus of control perceptions in Anglo-American and Mexican-American adolescents. *Political Psychology*, **4**, 101–120.

de Chernatony, L., Daniels, K. and Johnson, G. (1993). A cognitive perspective on managers' perceptions of competition. *Journal of Marketing Management*, **9**, 373–381.

Dearborn, D. C. and Simon, H. A. (1958). Selective perception: A note on the departmental identification of executives. *Sociometry*, **21**, 140–144.

Dess, G. G. and Davis, P. S. (1984). Porter's (1980) generic strategies as determinants of strategic group membership and organizational performance. *Academy of Management Journal*, **27**, 467–488.

Dess, G. G. and Robinson, R. B. (1984). Measuring organizational performance in the absence of objective measures: The case of the privately-held firm and conglomerate business unit. *Strategic Management Journal*, **5**, 265–273.

Dietrich, M. and Holmes, P. (1990). The market structure of the estate agents industry in the 1980s: An empirical investigation. *Applied Economics*, **22**, 629–638.

Dietrich, M. and Holmes, P. (1991). Financial institutions and the estate agents industry in the 1980s. *The Services Industries Journal*, **11**, 481–490.

DiMaggio, P. J. and Powell, W. W. (1983). The iron cage revisited: Institutional isomorphism and collective rationality in organizational fields. *American Sociological Review*, **48**, 147–160.

Dunn, W. N. and Ginsberg, A. (1986). A sociocognitive network approach to organizational analysis. *Human Relations*, **40**, 955–976.

Dutton, J. E. and Dukerich, J. M. (1991). Keeping an eye on the mirror: image and identity in organizational adaptation. *Academy of Management Journal*, **34**, 517–554.

Dutton, J. E. and Jackson, S. E. (1987). Categorizing strategic issues: links to organizational action. *Academy of Management Review*, **12**, 76–90.

Dutton, J., Walton, E. J. and Abrahamson, E. (1989). Important dimensions of strategic issues: Separating the wheat from the chaff. *Journal of Management Studies*, **26**, 379–396.

Easton, G., Burrell, G., Rothschild, R. and Shearman, C. (1993). *Managers and Competition*. Oxford: Blackwell.

Eden (ed.) (1992). On the nature of cognitive maps. *Journal of Management Studies*, **29** (Special Issue), 261–389.

Eden, C. and Ackermann, F. (1998). *Making Strategy: The Journey of Strategic Management*. London: Sage.

Eden, C., Jones, S. and Sims, D. (1979). *Thinking in Organizations*. London: Macmillan.

Eden, C. Jones, S. and Sims, D. (1983). *Messing About in Problems*. Oxford: Pergamon.

Eden, C. and Radford, J. (1990). *Tackling Strategic Problems: The Role of Group Decision Support*. London: Sage.

Eden, C. and J.-C. Spender (eds) (1998). *Managerial and Organizational Cognition: Theory, Methods and Research*. London: Sage.

Everitt, B. S. and Rabe-Hesketh, S. (1997). *The Analysis of Proximity Data*. London: Arnold.

Fahay, L. and Randall, R. M. (eds) (1998). *Learning from the Future: Competitive Foresight Scenarios*. New York: Wiley.

Fiegenbaum, A. and Thomas, H. (1990). Strategic groups and performance: The US insurance industry, 1970–1984. *Strategic Management Journal*, **11**, 197–215.

Fiegenbaum, A. and Thomas, H. (1993). Industry and strategic group dynamics: Competitive strategy in the insurance industry, 1970–84. *Journal of Management Studies*, **30**, 69–105.

Finkelstein, S. and Hambrick, D. C. (1996). *Strategic leadership: top executives and their effects on organizations*. St. Paul, MN: West.

Fiol, C. M. (2002). Intraorganizational cognition and interpretation. In J. A. C. Baum (ed.), *The Blackwell Companion to Organizations* (pp. 119–137). Oxford: Blackwell.

Fiol, C. M. and Huff, A. S. (1992). Maps for managers. Where are we? Where do we go from Here? *Journal of Management Studies*, **29**, 267–285.

Floyd, S. W. and Lane, P. J. (2000). Strategizing throughout the organization: managing role conflict in strategic renewal. *Academy of Management Review*, **25**, 154–177.

Floyd, S. W. and Wooldridge, B. (2000). *Building Strategy from the Middle: Reconceptualizing Strategy Process*. Thousand Oaks, CA: Sage.

Fombrun, C. J. and Zajac, E. J. (1987). Structural and perceptual influences on intra-industry stratification. *Academy of Management Journal*, **30**, 33–50.

Forbes, D. P. and Milliken, F. J. (1999). Cognition and corporate governance: understanding boards of directors as strategic decision-making groups. *Academy of Management Review*, **24**, 489–505.

Forgas, J. P. (1976). The perception of social episodes: Categorical and dimensional representation in two subcultural millieus. *Journal of Personality and Social Psychology*, **34**, 199–209.

Forgas, J. P. (1978). Social episodes and social structure in an academic setting: The social environment of an intact group. *Journal of Experimental Social Psychology*, **14**, 434–448.

Forgas, J. P. (1981). Social episodes and group milieu: A study in social cognition. *British Journal of Social Psychology*, **20**, 77–87.

Forgas, J. P., Brown, L. B. and Menyhart, J. (1980). Dimensions of aggression: The perception of aggressive episodes. *British Journal of Social and Clinical Psychology*, **19**, 215–227.

Fransella, F. and Bannister, D. (1977). *A Manual for Repertory Grid Technique*. New York: Academic Press.

Fransella, F., Bell, R. and Bannister, D. (2004). *A Manual for Repertory Grid Technique* (second edition). Chichester: Wiley.

Furnham, A. (1986). Economic locus of control. *Human Relations*, **39**, 29–43.

Ginsberg, A. (1989). Construing the business portfolio: A cognitive model of diversification. *Journal of Management Studies*, **26**, 417–438.

Ginsberg, A. (1994). Minding the competition: From mapping to mastery. *Strategic Management Journal*, **15** (Winter Special Issue), 153–174.

Gioia, D. A. and Thomas, J. B. (1996). Identity, image, and issue interpretation: sensemaking during strategic change in academia. *Administrative Science Quarterly*, **41**, 370–403.

Golden, B. (1992). The past is past – or is it? The use of retrospective accounts as indicators of past strategy. *Academy of Management Journal*, **35**, 848–860.

Golden, B. R. (1997). Further remarks on retrospective accounts in organizational and strategic management research. *Academy of Management Journal*, **40**, 1243–1252.

Goldstein, H. (1995). *Multilevel Statistical Models*. London: Edward Arnold.

Goodwin, P. and Wright, G. (2001). Enhancing strategy evaluation in scenario planning: A role for decision analysis. *Journal of Management Studies*, 38, 1–16.

Grant, R. (1991). *Contemporary Strategy Analysis*. Oxford: Blackwell.

Greenley, G. (1989). *Strategic Management*. London: Prentice Hall.

Greve, H. R. (1998). Managerial cognition and the mimetic adoption of market positions: What you see is what you do. *Strategic Management Journal*, 19, 967–988.

Grinyer, P. H. and Spender, J. C. (1979a). Recipes, crises and adaptation in mature businesses. *International Studies of Management and Organization*, IX, 113–123.

Grinyer, P. H. and Spender, J. C. (1979b). *Turnaround – Managerial Recipes for Strategic Success: The Fall and Rise of the Newton Chambers Group*. London: Associated Business Press.

Gripsrud, G. and Gronhaug, K. (1985). Structure and strategy in grocery retailing: A sociometric approach. *Journal of Industrial Economics*, XXXIII, 339–347.

Gronhaug, K. and Falkenberg, J. S. (1989). Exploring strategy perceptions in changing environments. *Journal of Management Studies*, 26, 349–359.

Gunz, H. (1989). *Careers and Corporate Cultures: Managerial Mobility in Large Corporations*. Oxford: Basil Blackwell.

Gunz, H. P. and Whitley, R. D. (1985). Managerial cultures and industrial strategies in British firms. *Organization Studies*, 6, 247–273.

Hambrick, D. C. and Mason, P. (1984). Upper echelons: the organization as a reflection of its top managers. *Academy of Management Review*, 9, 193–206.

Handy, C. B. (1985). *Understanding Organisations* (3rd edition). Harmondsworth: Penguin.

Harrigan, K. R. (1980). *Strategies for Declining Industries*. Lexington Mass.: D. C. Heath.

Harrigan, K. R. (1985). An application of clustering for strategic group analysis. *Strategic Management Journal*, 6, 55–73.

Hatten, K. J. and Hatten, M. L. (1987). Strategic groups, asymmetrical mobility barriers and contestability. *Strategic Management Journal*, 8, 329–342.

Hatten, K. J., Schendel, D. E. and Cooper, A. (1978). A strategic model of the US brewing industry, 1952–1971. *Academy of Management Journal*, 21, 592–610.

Hawes, J. M. and Crittenden, W. F. (1984). A taxonomy of competitive retailing strategies. *Strategic Management Journal*, 5, 275–289.

Hedberg, B. and Jonsson, S. (1977). Strategy making as a discontinuous process. *International Studies of Management and Organization*, VII, 88–109.

Hodgkinson, G. P. (1992). Development and validation of the strategic locus of control scale. *Strategic Management Journal*, 13, 311–317.

Hodgkinson, G. P. (1993a). *Strategic Cognition in a Mature Industry: Differentiation, Consensus and Outcomes*. Unpublished PhD Thesis, University of Sheffield, UK.

Hodgkinson, G. P. (1993b). Doubts about the conceptual and empirical status of context-free and firm-specific control expectancies: a reply to Boone and De Brabander. *Strategic Management Journal*, 14, 627–631.

Hodgkinson, G. P. (1997a). The cognitive analysis of competitive structures: a review and critique. *Human Relations*, 50, 625–654.

Hodgkinson, G. P. (1997b). Cognitive inertia in a turbulent market: the case of UK residential estate agents. *Journal of Management Studies*, 34, 921–945.

Hodgkinson, G. P. (1998). Points or vectors? A comment on Irwin et al.'s 'Risk perception and victim perception: The judgment of HIV cases'. *Journal of Behavioral Decision Making*, 11, 73–78.

Hodgkinson, G. P. (2001a). The psychology of strategic management: diversity and cognition revisited. In C. L. Cooper and I. T. Robertson (eds), *International Review of Industrial and Organizational Psychology – Vol. 16* (pp. 65–119). Chichester: Wiley.

Hodgkinson, G. P. (2001b). Cognitive processes in strategic management: Some emerging trends and future directions. In N. Anderson, D. S. Ones, H. K. Sinangil and C. Viswesvaran (eds), *Handbook of Industrial, Work and Organizational Psychology: Volume 2 – Organizational Psychology* (pp. 416–440). London: Sage.

Hodgkinson, G. P. (2002). Comparing managers' mental models of competition: Why self-report measures of belief similarity won't do. *Organization Studies*, **23**, 63–72.

Hodgkinson, G. P. (2003). The interface of cognitive and industrial, work and organizational psychology. *Journal of Occupational and Organizational Psychology*, **76**, 1–25.

Hodgkinson, G. P. (2004). Toward a (pragmatic) science of strategic intervention: The case of scenario planning. Paper presented at the Annual Meeting of the Academy of Management, New Orleans, August.

Hodgkinson, G. P., Bown, N., Maule, A. J., Glaister, K. W. and Pearman, A. D. (1999). Breaking the frame: an analysis of strategic cognition and decision making under uncertainty. *Strategic Management Journal*, **20**, 977–985.

Hodgkinson, G. P. and Clarkson, G. P. (2005). What have we learned from almost thirty years of research on causal mapping? Methodological lessons and choices for the information systems and information technology communities. In V. K. Narayanan and D. J. Armstrong (eds), *Causal Mapping for Information Systems and Technology Research: Approaches, Advances and Illustrations* (pp. 46–79). Hershey, PA: Idea Group Inc.

Hodgkinson, G. P., Gunz, H., and Johnson, G. (1988). Understanding competitive strategy from a management cognition perspective: A critical evaluation and some research hypotheses. *Manchester Business School Working Paper No 168*. ISSN 0954–7401.

Hodgkinson, G. P. and Johnson, G. (1987). Exploring cognitive aspects of competitive strategy: A critical examination of theory and methodology. *Manchester Business School Working Paper No 150*. ISBN 0305 5639.

Hodgkinson, G. P. and Johnson, G. (1994). Exploring the mental models of competitive strategists: The case for a processual approach. *Journal of Management Studies*, **31**, 525–551.

Hodgkinson, G. P. and Maule, A. J. (2002). The individual in the strategy process: insights from behavioural decision research and cognitive mapping. In A. S. Huff and M. Jenkins (eds), *Mapping Strategic Knowledge* (pp. 196–219). London: Sage.

Hodgkinson, G. P., Maule, A. J. and Bown, N. J. (2004). Causal cognitive mapping in the organizational strategy field: A comparison of alternative elicitation procedures. *Organizational Research Methods*, **7**, 3–26.

Hodgkinson, G. P., Maule, A. J., Bown, N. J., Pearman, A. D. and Glaister, K. W. (2002). Further reflections on the elimination of framing bias in strategic decision making. *Strategic Management Journal*, **23**, 1069–1076.

Hodgkinson, G. P., Padmore, J. and Tomes, A. E. (1991). Mapping consumers' cognitive structures: A comparison of similarity trees with multidimensional scaling and cluster analysis. *European Journal of Marketing*, **25(7)**, 41–60.

Hodgkinson, G. P. and Sparrow, P. R. (2002). *The Competent Organization: A Psychological Analysis of the Strategic Management Process*. Buckingham: Open University Press.

Hodgkinson, G. P. and Thomas, A. B. (eds) (1997). Thinking in Organizations. *Journal of Management Studies*, **34** (special issue), 845–952.

Hodgkinson, G. P., Tomes, A. E. and Padmore, J. (1996). Using consumers' perceptions for the cognitive analysis of corporate-level competitive structures. *Journal of Strategic Marketing*, **4**, 1–22.

Hodgkinson, G. P. and Wright, G. (2002). Confronting strategic inertia in a top management team: Learning from failure. *Organization Studies*, 23, 949–977.

Hofstede, G. W. (1980). *Culture's Consequences: International Differences in Work Related Values*. London: Sage.

Huff, A. S. (1982). Industry influences on strategy formulation. *Strategic Management Journal*, 3, 119–130.

Huff, A. S. (ed.) (1990). *Mapping Strategic Thought*. Chichester: Wiley.

Huff, A. S. (1997). A current and future agenda for cognitive research in organizations. *Journal of Management Studies*, 34, 947–952.

Huff, A. S. and Fletcher, K. E. (1990). Conclusion: Key mapping decisions. In A. S. Huff (ed.), *Mapping Strategic Thought* (pp. 403–412). Chichester: Wiley.

Huff, A. S. and Huff, J. O. with Barr P. S. (2000). *When Firms Change Direction*. New York: Oxford University Press.

Huff, A, S. and Jenkins, M. (eds) (2002). *Mapping Strategic Knowledge*. London: Sage.

Huff, J. O., Huff, A. S. and Thomas, H. (1992). Strategic renewal and the interaction of cumulative stress and inertia. *Strategic Management Journal*, 13, 55–75.

Hunt, M. S. (1972). Competition in the Major Home Appliance Industry. Unpublished doctoral dissertation, University of Harvard, US.

Ilinitch, A. Y., Lewin, A. Y. and D'Avini, R. A. (1998). Introduction. In A. Y. Ilinitch, A. Y. Lewin and R. A. D'Avini (eds), *Managing In Times of Disorder: Hypercompetitive Organizational Responses*. London: Sage.

Irwin, J. R. and Jones, L. E. (1998). SINDSCAL source weight transformations are not always necessary or desirable: Reply to Hodgkinson. *Journal of Behavioral Decision Making*, 11, 79–84.

Irwin, J. R., Jones, L. E. and Mundo, D. (1996). Risk perception and victim perception: The judgment of HIV cases. *Journal of Behavioral Decision Making*, 9, 1–22.

Jackson, S. E. (1992). Consequences of group composition for the interpersonal dynamics of strategic issue processing. *Advances in Strategic Management*, 8, 345–382.

Jackson, S. E. and Dutton, J. E. (1988). Discerning threats and opportunities. *Administrative Science Quarterly*, 33, 370–387.

Johnson, D. R. and Hoopes D. G. (2003). Managerial cognition, sunk costs and the evolution of industry structure. *Strategic Management Journal*, 24 (Special Issue), 1057–1068.

Johnson, G. (1987). *Strategic Change and the Management Process*. Oxford: Blackwell.

Johnson, G. (1988). Rethinking incrementalism. *Strategic Management Journal*, 9, 75–91.

Johnson, G., Melin, L. and Whittington, R. (2003). Micro strategy and strategizing: Towards an activity-based view. *Journal of Management Studies*, 40 (Special Issue), 3–22.

Johnson, G. and Scholes, K. (1993). *Exploring Corporate Strategy* (3rd edition). London: Prentice-Hall.

Johnson, G. and Thomas, H. (1987). The industry context of strategy, structure and performance: The UK brewing industry. *Strategic Management Journal*, 8, 343–361.

Johnson, P., Daniels, K. and Asch, R. (1998). Mental models of competition. In C. Eden and J.-C. Spender (eds), *Managerial and Organizational Cognition: Theory, Methods and Research* London: Sage. pp. 130–146.

Jones, C. L. (1983). A note on the use of directional statistics in weighted Euclidean distances multidimensional scaling models. *Psychometrika*, 48, 473–476.

Joreskog, K. G. and Sorbom, D. (1993). *LISREL 8: Structural Equation Modelling with the SIMPLIS Command Language*. Hillsdale, NJ: Lawrence Erlbaum Associates.

Kagono, T., Nonaka, I., Sakakibara, K. and Okumura, A. (1985). *Strategic vs. Evolutionary Management: A US-Japan Comparison of Strategy and Organization*. Amsterdam, North Holland: Elsevier Science Publishers.

Kelley, H. H. (1967). Attribution theory in social psychology. In D. Levine (ed.), *Nebraska Symposium on Motivation* (Vol. 15, pp. 192–240). Lincoln, NE: University of Nebraska Press.

Kelly, G. A. (1955). *The Psychology of Personal Constructs* (in 2 volumes). New York: Norton.

Key Note (1986). *Key Note Report: An Industry Sector Overview – Estate Agents*. London: Key Note Publications Ltd.

Key Note (1987). *Key Note Report: An Industry Sector Overview – Estate Agents*. London: Key Note Publications Ltd.

Key Note (1989). *Key Note Report: An Industry Sector Overview – Estate Agents*. London: Key Note Publications Ltd.

Key Note (1990). *Key Note Report: An Industry Sector Overview – Estate Agents*. London: Key Note Publications Ltd.

Key Note (1992). *Key Note Report: An Industry Sector Overview – Estate Agents*. London: Key Note Publications Ltd.

Kiesler, S. and Sproull, L. (1982). Managerial responses to changing environments: Perspectives in problem sensing from social cognition. *Administrative Science Quarterly*, 27, 548–570.

Knight, D., Pearce, C. L., Smith, K. G., Olian, J. D., Sims, H. P., Smith, K. A. and Flood, P. (1999). Top management team diversity, group process, and strategic consensus. *Strategic Management Journal*, 20, 445–465.

Kruskal, J. B. and Wish, M. (1978). *Multidimensional Scaling*. Sage University Paper Series on Quantitative Applications in the Social Sciences, 07–011. London: Sage.

Lakeoff, G. (1987). *Women, Fire and Dangerous Things: What Categories Reveal About the Mind*. Chicago, IL: University of Chicago Press.

Langeheine, R. (1980). *Approximate norms and significance tests for the Lingoes-Borg Procrustean Individual Differences Scaling (PINDIS)*. Tech Rep No 39. Kiel: Institut für die Pädagogik der Naturwissenschaften, Universität Kiel.

Lant, T. K. (1999). A situated learning perspective on the emergence of knowledge and identity in cognitive communities. *Advances in Management Cognition and Organizational Information Processing*, 6, 171–194.

Lant, T. K. (2002). Organizational cognition and interpretation. In J. A. C. Baum (ed.), *The Blackwell Companion to Organizations* (pp. 344–362). Oxford: Blackwell.

Lant, T. K. and Baum, J. C. (1995). Cognitive sources of socially constructed competitive groups: Examples from the Manhattan Hotel Industry. In W. R. Scott and S. Christensen (eds), *The Institutional Construction of Organizations: International and Longitudinal Studies*. Thousand Oaks, CA: Sage.

Lant, T. K. and Phelps, C. (1999). Strategic groups: a situated learning perspective. *Advances in Strategic Management*, 16, 221–247.

Lant, T. K. and Shapira, Z. (2001a). Introduction: Foundations of research on cognition in organizations. In T. K. Lant and Z. Shapira (eds), *Organizational Cognition: Computation and Interpretation* (pp. 1–12). Mahwah, NJ: Erlbaum.

Lant, T. K. and Shapira, Z. (2001b). New research directions on organizational cognition. In T. K. Lant and Z. Shapira (eds), *Organizational Cognition: Computation and Interpretation* (pp. 367–376). Mahwah, NJ: Erlbaum.

Lant, T. K. and Shapira, Z. (eds) (2001c). *Organizational Cognition: Computation and Interpretation*. Mahwah, NJ: Erlbaum.

Lau, R. and Ware, J. (1981). Refinements in the measurement of health-specific locus of control beliefs. *Medical Care*, **19**, 1147–1158.

Laughlin, R. C. (1991). Environmental disturbances and organizational transitions and transformations: Some alternative models. *Organization Studies*, **12**, 209–232.

Lawrence, P. R. and Lorsch, J. W. (1967). *Organization and Environment: Managing Differentiation and Integration*. Boston, Mass.: Harvard University Press.

Lenz, R. T. and Engledow, J. L. (1986). Environmental analysis: The applicability of current theory. *Strategic Management Journal*, **7**, 329–346.

Levenhagen, M., Porac, J. F. and Thomas, H. (1993). Emergent industry leadership and the selling of technological visions: A social constructionist view. In J. Hendry and G. Johnson with J. Newton (eds), *Strategic Thinking: Leadership and the Management of Change* (pp. 69–87). Chichester: John Wiley & Sons.

Lewis, P. and Thomas, H. (1990). The linkage between strategy, strategic groups, and performance in the UK retail grocery industry. *Strategic Management Journal*, **11**, 385–397.

Lingoes, J. C. and Borg, I. (1976). Procrustean individual differences scaling. *Journal of Marketing Research*, **13**, 406–407.

Lingoes, J. C. and Borg, I. (1978). A direct approach to individual differences scaling using increasingly complex transformations. *Psychometrika*, **43**, 491–519.

Luffman, G., Sanderson, S., Lea, E. and Kenney, B. (1987). *Business Policy: An Analytical Introduction*. Oxford: Blackwell.

Lussier, R. N. (1990). *Human Relations in Organizations: A Skill Building Approach*. Homewood IL: Irwin.

MacCallum, R. C. (1977). Effects of conditionality on INDSCAL and ALSCAL weights. *Psychometrika*, **42**, 297–305.

March, J. G. and Simon, H. A. (1958). *Organizations*. New York: John Wiley & Sons.

Markoczy, L. (1997). Measuring beliefs: accept no substitutes. *Academy of Management Journal*, **40**, 1228–1242.

Markoczy, L. and Goldberg, J. (1995). A method for eliciting and comparing causal maps. *Journal of Management*, **21**, 305–333.

Markus, H. (1977). Self-schemata and processing information about the self. *Journal of Personality and Social Psychology*, **35**, 63–78.

Markus, H. and Nurius, P. (1986). Possible selves. *American Psychologist*, **41**, 954–969.

Markus, H. and Wurf, E. (1987). The dynamic self-concept: A social psychological perspective. *Annual Review of Psychology*, **38**, 299–337.

Mason, E. (1957). *Economic Concentration and the Monopoly Problem*. Cambridge, MA: Harvard University Press.

Maule, A. J. and Hodgkinson, G. P. (2002). Heuristics, biases and strategic decision making. *The Psychologist*, **15**, 68–71.

Maule, A J, Hodgkinson, G. P. and Bown, N. J. (2003). Cognitive mapping of causal reasoning in strategic decision making. In D. Hardman and L. Macchi (eds), *Thinking: Psychological Perspectives on Reasoning, Judgment and Decision Making* (pp. 253–272). Chichester: Wiley.

McGee, J. and Thomas, H. (1986). Strategic groups: theory, research and taxonomy. *Strategic Management Journal*, **7**, 141–160.

McNamara, G., Deephouse, D. L. and Luce, R. A. (2003). Competitive positioning within and across a strategic group structure: The performance of core, secondary and solitary firms. *Strategic Management Journal*, **24**, 161–181.

McNamara, G., Luce, R. A. and Tompson, G. H. (2002). Examining the effect of complexity in strategic group knowledge structures on firm performance. *Strategic Management Journal*, **23**, 153–170.

Meindl, J. R., Stubbart, C. and Porac, J. F. (eds) (1994). Cognition. *Organization Science,* 5 (Special Issue), 288–477.

Meindl, J. R., Stubbart, C. and Porac, J. F. (eds) (1996). *Cognition within and Between Organizations.* Thousand Oaks: Sage.

Meyer, J. W. and Rowan, B. (1977). Institutionalized organizations: Formal structure as myth and ceremony. *American Journal of Sociology,* 83, 340–363.

Miles, R. E. and Snow, C. C. (1978). *Organizational Strategy, Structure and Process.* New York: McGraw-Hill.

Miller, C. C., Cardinal, L. B. and Glick, W. H. (1997). Retrospective reports in organizational research: a reexamination of recent evidence. *Academy of Management Journal,* 40, 189–204.

Miller, D. (1983). The correlates of entrepreneurship in three types of firms. *Management Science,* 29, 770–791.

Miller, D. Kets DeVries, M. F. R., and Toulouse, J. M. (1982). Top executive locus of control and its relationship to strategy-making, structure and environment. *Academy of Management Journal,* 25, 237–253.

Miller, D. and Toulouse, J. M. (1986). Chief executive personality and corporate strategy and structure. *Management Science,* 32, 1389–1409.

Mintzberg, H. (1994). *The Rise and Fall of Strategic Planning.* London: Prentice Hall.

Mitroff, I. (1988). *Break-Away Thinking: How to Challenge Your Business Assumptions (and Why You Should).* Chichester: John Wiley & Sons.

Morecroft, J. D. W. (1994). Executive knowledge, models and learning. In J. D. W. Morecroft and J. D. Sterman (eds), *Modeling for Learning Organizations* (pp. 3–28). Portland, OR.: Productivity Press.

Murphy, P. R., Mezias, S. J. and Chen, Y. R. (2001). Adapting aspirations to feedback: The role of success and failure. In T. K. Lant and Z. Shapira (eds), *Organizational Cognition: Computation and Interpretation* (pp. 125–146). Mahwah, NJ: Erlbaum.

Newman, H. H. (1978). Strategic groups and the structure-performance relationship. *Review of Economics and Statistics,* 60, 417–427.

Nicholson, N. (1991). Organizational climate and organizational performance. Paper presented to the 5th European Congress on the Psychology of Work and Organization, Rouen, France.

Nicholson, N. and Brenner, S. O. (1994). Dimensions of perceived organizational performance: Tests of a model. *Applied Psychology: An International Review,* 43, 89–108.

Nunnally, J. C. and Bernstein, I. H. (1994). *Psychometric Theory* (Third Edition). New York: McGraw-Hill.

Odorici, V. and Lomi, A. (2001). Classifying competition: An empirical study of the cognitive social structure of strategic groups. In T. K. Lant and Z. Shapira (eds), *Organizational Cognition: Computation and Interpretation* (pp. 273–304). Mahwah, NJ: Erlbaum.

Osborne, J. D., Stubbart, C. I. and Ramaprasad, A. (2001). Strategic groups and competitive enactment: A study of dynamic relationships between mental models and performance. *Strategic Management Journal,* 22, 435–454.

Osgood, C. E. and Suci, G. J. (1952). A measure of relation determined by both mean differences and profile information. *Psychological Bulletin,* 49, 251–262.

Osgood, C. E., Suci, G. J. and Tannenbaum, P. H. (1957). *The Measurement of Meaning.* Urbana: University of Illinois Press.

Oster, S. (1982). Intraindustry structure and the ease of strategic change. *Review of Economics and Statistics,* LXIV, 376–384.

Oster, S. M. (1990). *Modern Competitive Analysis.* Oxford: Oxford University Press.

Palinscar, A. S. (1998). Social constructivist perspectives on teaching and learning. *Annual Review of Psychology*, **49**, 345–375.

Peteraf, M. and Shanley, M. (1997). Getting to know you: a theory of strategic group identity. *Strategic Management Journal*, **18** (Summer Special Issue), 165–186.

Pettigrew, A. M. (1973). *The Politics of Organizational Decision Making*. London: Tavistock.

Pettigrew, A. M. (1985). *The Awakening Giant: Continuity and Change in Imperial Chemical Industries*. Oxford: Blackwell.

Pettigrew, A. M, Ferlie, E. and McKee, L. (1992). *Shaping Strategic Change*. London: Sage.

Pettigrew, A. M. and Whipp, R. (1991). *Managing Change for Competitive Success*. Oxford: Blackwell.

Pfeffer, J. (1981a). Management as symbolic action: The creation and maintenance of organizational paradigms. In Cummings, L. L. and Staw, B. M. (eds), *Research in Organizational Behavior* (Vol. 3, pp. 1–15). Greenwich, C.T: JAI Press.

Pfeffer, J. (1981b). *Power in Organizations*. Marshfield, MA: Pitman.

Pfeffer, J. and Salancik, G. R. (1974). Organizational decision making as a political process: The case of a university budget. *Administrative Science Quarterly*, **19**, 135–151.

Phares, E. J. (1976). *Locus of Control in Personality*. Morristown NJ: General Learning Press.

Phillips, E. M. (1989). Use and abuse of the repertory grid: A PCP approach. *The Psychologist*, **2**, 194–198.

Phillips, M. E. (1994). Industry mindsets: Exploring the cultures of two macro-organizational settings. *Organization Science*, **5**, 384–402.

Porac, J. and Rosa, A. (1996). Rivalry, industry models, and the cognitive embeddedness of the comparable firm. *Advances in Strategic Management*, **13**, 363–388.

Porac, J. F. and Thomas, H. (1987). Cognitive taxonomies and cognitive systematics. Paper presented at the Annual Meeting of the Academy of Management, New Orleans, August.

Porac, J. F. and Thomas, H. (eds) (1989). Managerial thinking in business environments. *Journal of Management Studies*, **26** (Special Issue), 323–438.

Porac, J. F. and Thomas, H. (1990). Taxonomic mental models in competitor definition. *Academy of Management Review*, **15**, 224–240.

Porac, J. F. and Thomas, H. (1994). Cognitive categorization and subjective rivalry among retailers in a small city. *Journal of Applied Psychology*, **79**, 54–66.

Porac, J. F. and Thomas, H. (2002). Managing cognition and strategy: Issues, trends and future directions. In A. Pettigrew, H. Thomas and R. Whittington (eds), *Handbook of Strategy and Management* (pp. 165–181). London: Sage.

Porac, J. F., Thomas, H. and Baden-Fuller, C. (1989). Competitive groups as cognitive communities: The case of Scottish knitwear manufacturers. *Journal of Management Studies*, **26**, 397–416.

Porac, J. F., Thomas H. and Emme, B. (1987). Knowing the competition: The mental models of retailing strategists. In G. Johnson (ed.), *Business Strategy and Retailing*. Chichester: John Wiley & Sons. pp. 59–79.

Porac, J. F., Thomas, H., Wilson, F., Paton, D. and Kanfer, A. (1995). Rivalry and the industry model of Scottish knitwear producers. *Administrative Science Quarterly*, **40**, 203–227.

Porac, J. F., Ventresca, M. J. and Mishina, Y. (2002). Interorganizational cognition and interpretation. In J. A. C. Baum (ed.), *The Blackwell Companion to Organizations* (pp. 579–598). Oxford: Blackwell.

Porter, M. E. (1979). The structure within industries and companies' performance. *Review of Economics and Statistics*, 61, 214–227.

Porter, M. E. (1980). *Competitive Strategy: Techniques for Analyzing Industries and Competitors*. New York: Free press.

Porter, M. E. (1981). The contributions of industrial organization to strategic management. *Academy of Management Review*, 6, 609–620.

Porter, M. E. (1985). *Competitive Advantage: Creating and Sustaining Superior Performance*. New York: Free Press.

Prahalad, C. K. and Bettis, R. A. (1986). The dominant logic: A new linkage between diversity and performance. *Strategic Management Journal*, 7, 485–501.

Ramsey, J. O. (1978). *MULTISCALE: Four Programs for Multidimensional Scaling by the Method of Maximum Likelihood*. Chicago: National Educational Resources Inc.

Reger, R. K. (1987). *Competitive Positioning in the Chicago Banking Market: Mapping the Mind of the Strategist*. Unpublished doctoral dissertation, University of Illinois at Urbana-Champaign, USA.

Reger, R. K. (1990a). Managerial thought structures and competitive positioning. In Huff, A. S. (ed.), *Mapping Strategic Thought*. Chichester: John Wiley & Sons, 71–88.

Reger, R. K. (1990b). The repertory grid for eliciting the content and structure of cognitive constructive systems. In Huff, A. S. (ed.), *Mapping Strategic Thought*. Chichester: John Wiley & Sons, 301–309.

Reger, R. K. and Huff, A. S. (1993). Strategic groups: A cognitive perspective. *Strategic Management Journal*, 14, 103–124.

Reger, R. K. and Palmer, T. B. (1996). Managerial categorization of competitors: Using old maps to navigate new environments. *Organization Science*, 7, 22–39.

Rindova, V. P. and Fombrun, C. J. (1999). Constructing competitive advantage: The role of firm-constituent interactions. *Strategic Management Journal*, 20, 691–710.

Rosch, E. (1975). Cognitive reference points. *Cognitive Psychology*, 7, 532–547.

Rosch, E. (1978). Principles of categorization. In E. Rosch and B. B. Lloyd (eds), *Cognition and Categorization* (pp. 27–48). Hillsdale, NJ: Erlbaum.

Rosch, E., Mervis, C. B., Gray, W. D., Johnson, D. and Boyes-Braem, P. (1976). Basic objects in natural categories. *Cognitive Psychology*, 8, 382–439.

Rotter, J. B. (1966). Generalized expectancies for internal versus external control of reinforcement. *Psychological Monographs: General and Applied*, 80: Whole No. 609.

Rotter, J. B. (1990). Internal versus external control of reinforcement. *American Psychologist*, 45, 489–493.

Rousseau, D. (2001). Schema, promise and mutuality: The building blocks of the psychological contract. *Journal of Occupational and Organizational Psychology*, 74, 511–541.

Schiffman, S. S., Reynolds, M. L. and Young, F. W. (1981). *Introduction to Multidimensional Scaling*. New York: Academic Press.

Schneider, B. (1987). The people make the place. *Personnel Psychology*, 40, 437–453.

Schneider, S. C. and De Meyer, A. (1991). Interpreting and responding to strategic issues: The impact of national culture. *Strategic Management Journal*, 12, 307–320.

Schoemaker, P. J. H. (1993). Multiple scenario development: Its conceptual and behavioural foundation. *Strategic Management Journal*, 14, 193–213.

Schwenk, C. R. (1984). Cognitive simplification processes in strategic decision making. *Strategic Management Journal*, 5, 111–128.

Schwenk, C. R. (1986). Information, cognitive biases and commitment to a course of action. *Academy of Management Review*, 11, 298–310.

Senge, P. (1990). *The Fifth Discipline: The Art and Practice of the Learning Organization*. London: Century Business.

Sheldon, A. (1980). Organizational paradigms: A theory of organizational change. *Organizational Dynamics*, **8**, 61–80.

Siegel, S. (1956). *Nonparametric Statistics for the Behavioral Sciences*. New York: McGraw-Hill.

Simon, H. A. (1947). *Administrative Behavior*. New York: Macmillan.

Sims, H. P. and Gioia, D. A. (eds) (1986). *The Thinking Organization: Dynamics of Organizational Social Cognition*. San Francisco: Jossey-Bass.

Slater, S. (1984). *Corporate Recovery: A Guide to Turnaround Management*. London: Penguin.

Slater, P. (ed.) (1976). *The Measurement of Intrapersonal Space by Grid Technique: Vol. I – Explorations of Intrapersonal Space*. Chichester: Wiley.

Slater, P. (ed.) (1977). *The Measurement of Intrapersonal Space by Grid Technique: Vol. II – Dimensions of Intrapersonal Space*. Chichester: Wiley.

Smith, M. and Gibson, J. (1988). Using repertory grids to investigate racial prejudice. *Applied Psychology: An International Review*, **37**, 311–326.

Smith, M., Hartley, J. and Stewart, B. (1978). A case study of repertory grids used in vocational guidance. *Journal of Occupational Psychology*, **51**, 97–104.

Smith, M. and Stewart, B. J. M. (1977). Repertory grids: A flexible tool for establishing the contents and structure of a manager's thoughts. In D. Ashton (ed.), *Management Bibliographies and Reviews*, **3**, 209–229.

Sparrow, J. (1998). *Knowledge in Organizations: Access to Thinking at Work*. London: Sage Publications.

Sparrow, P. R. (1994). The psychology of strategic management: emerging themes of diversity and cognition. In C. L. Cooper and I. T. Robertson (eds), *International Review of Industrial and Organizational Psychology- Vol. 9*. (pp. 147–181). Chichester: Wiley.

Sparrow, P. R. (2000). Strategic management in a world turned upside down: the role of cognition, intuition and emotional intelligence. In P. C. Flood, T. Dromgoole, S. Carroll, and L. Gorman (eds), (2000). *Managing Strategy Implementation* (pp. 15–30). Oxford: Blackwell.

Spector, P. E. (1982). Behavior in organizations as a function of employees' locus of control. *Psychological Bulletin*, **91**, 482–497.

Spector, P. E. (1988). Development of the work locus of control scale. *Journal of Occupational Psychology*, **61**, 335–40.

Spector, P. E. (1992). A consideration of the validity and meaning of self-report measures of job conditions. In C. L. Cooper and I. T. Robertson (eds), *International Review of Industrial and Organizational Psychology – Vol. 7* (pp. 123–151). Chichester: Wiley.

Spencer, B., Peyrefitte, J. and Churchman, R. (2003). Consensus and divergence in perceptions of cognitive strategic groups: Evidence from the health care industry. *Strategic Organization*, **1**, 203–230.

Spender, J. C. (1989). *Industry Recipes: The Nature and Sources of Managerial Judgement*. Oxford: Basil Blackwell.

SPSS (1990). *SPSS Reference Guide*. Chicago, IL: SPSS Inc.

Starbuck, W. H. (1976). Organizations and their environments. In M. D. Dunnette (ed.), *Handbook of Industrial and Organizational Psychology* (pp. 1069–1123). Chicago, IL: Rand McNally.

Stewart, V., Stewart, A. and Fonda, N. (1981). *The Business Application of Repertory Grids*. London: McGraw-Hill.

Stopford, J. M. and Baden-Fuller, C. (1990). Flexible strategies: The key to success in knitwear. *Long Range Planning*, **23**.6, 56–62.

Stubbart, C. I. (1989). Managerial cognition: A missing link in strategic management research. *Journal of Management Studies*, 26, 325–347.

Sutcliffe, K. M. (2001). Commentary: Motivational preconditions and intraorganizational barriers to learning in organizational settings. In T. K. Lant and Z. Shapira (eds), *Organizational Cognition: Computation and Interpretation* (pp. 147–153). Mahwah, NJ: Erlbaum.

Sutcliffe, K. M. and Huber, G. P. (1998). Firm and industry as determinants of executive perceptions of the environment. *Strategic Management Journal*, 19, 793–807.

Tajfel, H. and Turner, J. C. (1979). An integrative theory of intergroup conflict. In W. G. Austin and S. Worchel (eds), *The Social Psychology of Intergroup Relations* (pp. 33–47). Monterey, CA: Brooks/Cole.

Tajfel, H. and Turner, J. C. (1986). The social identity theory of intergroup behavior. In S. Worchel and W. G. Austin (eds), *Psychology of Intergroup Relations* (second edition) (pp. 7–24). Chicago, IL: Nelson-Hall

Takane, Y., Young, F. W. and De Leeuw, J. (1977). Nonmetric individual differences multidimensional scaling: An alternating least-squares method with optimal scaling features. *Psychometrika*, 42, 7–67.

Tang, M. and Thomas, H. (1992). The concept of strategic groups: Theoretical construct or analytical convenience? *Managerial and Decision Economics*, 13, 323–329.

Thomas, H. and Venkatraman, N. (1988). Research on strategic groups: progress and prognosis. *Journal of Management Studies*, 25, 537–555.

Tolman, E. C. (1932). *Purposive Behavior in Animals and Men*. New York: Century.

Trice, A. D., Haire, J. R. and Elliott, K. A. (1989). A career locus of control scale for undergraduate students. *Perceptual and Motor Skills*, 69, 555–561.

Tsoukas, H. (1992). Ways of seeing: topographic and network representations in organization theory. *Systems Practice*, 5, 441–456.

Tuma, N. B. and Hannan, M. T. (1984). *Social Dynamics: Models and Methods*. Orlando, FL: Academic Press.

Turner, J. C. (1985). Social categorization and the self-concept: A social cognitive theory of group behaviour. In E. J. Lawler (ed.), *Advances in Group Processes* (Vol. 2, pp. 77–122). Greenwich, CT: JAI Press.

Turner, J. C., Hogg, M. A., Oakes, P. J., Reicher, S. D. and Wetherell, M. S. (1987). *Rediscovering the Social Group: A Self-Categorization Theory*. Oxford: Blackwell.

Tushman, M. L. and Anderson, P. (1990). Technological discontinuities and dominant designs: a cyclical model of technological change. *Administrative Science Quarterly*, 35, 604–633.

van der Heijden, K. (1994). Probabilistic planning and scenario planning. In G. Wright and P. Ayton (eds). *Subjective Probability*. Chichester: Wiley.

van der Heijden, K. (1996). *Scenarios: The Art of Strategic Conversation*. Chichester: Wiley.

van der Hiejden, K., Bradfield, R., Burt, G., Cairns, G. and Wright, G. (2002). *The Sixth Sense: Accelerating Organizational Learning with Scenarios*. Chichester: Wiley.

Wack, P. (1985a). Scenarios: Uncharted waters ahead. *Harvard Business Review*, Sept–Oct, 73–90.

Wack, P. (1985b). Scenarios: Shooting the Rapids. *Harvard Business Review*, Nov–Dec, 139–150.

Wallston, K. A. and Wallston, B. S. (1982). Who is responsible for your health? The construct of health locus of control. In G. S. Sanders and J. Suils (eds), *Social Psychology of Health and Illness* (pp. 65–69). Hillsdale N.J.: Erlbaum.

Wallston, B., Wallston, K., Kaplan, G. and Maldes, S. (1976). Development and validation of the health locus of control (HLC) scale. *Journal of Consulting and Clinical Psychology*, 44, 580–589.

Walsh, J. P. (1995). Managerial and organizational cognition: notes from a trip down memory lane. *Organization Science*, **6**, 280–321.

Walton, E. J. (1986). Managers' prototypes of financial firms. *Journal of Management Studies*, **23**, 679–698.

Weick K. E. (1969). *The Social Psychology of Organizing*. Reading, MA: Addison-Wesley.

Weick (1979), K. E. *The Social Psychology of Organizing* (2nd edition). Reading, MA: Addison-Wesley.

Weick, K. E. (1995). *Sensemaking in Organizations*. Thousand Oaks: Sage.

Wenger, E. (1998). *Communities of Practice*. Cambridge: Cambridge University Press.

Wheelen, T. L. and Hunger, J. D. (1989). *Strategic Management and Business Policy* (3rd edition). Reading Mass.: Addison-Wesley.

Whitley, R. (1987). Taking firms seriously as economic actors: Towards a sociology of firm behaviour. *Organization Studies*, **8**, 125–147.

Whitley, R. (1992). The social construction of organizations and markets: The comparative analysis of business recipes. In M. Reed and M. Hughes (eds), *Rethinking Organization: New Directions in Organization Theory and Analysis* (pp. 120–143). London: Sage.

Wholey, D. R. and Brittain, J. W. (1986). Organizational ecology: findings and implications. *Academy of Management Journal*, **11**, 513–533.

Wish, M., Deutsch, M., and Kaplan, S. J. (1976). Perceived dimensions of interpersonal relations. *Journal of Personality and Social Psychology*, **33**, 409–420.

Wood, D., and Letak, J. (1982). A mental-health locus of control scale. *Personality and Individual Differences*, **3**, 84–87.

Wood, R. and Bandura, A. (1989). Social cognitive theory of organizational management. *Academy of Management Review*, **14**, 361–384.

Wooldridge, B. and Floyd, S. (1989). Strategic process effects on consensus. *Strategic Management Journal*, **10**, 295–302.

Wright, G. and Goodwin, P. (1999). Future-focussed thinking: combining scenario planning with decision analysis. *Journal of Multi-Criteria Decision Analysis*, **8**, 311–321.

Zajac, E. J. and Bazerman, M. H. (1991). Blindspots in industry and competitor analysis: implications of interfirm (mis)perceptions for strategic decisions. *Academy of Management Review*, **16**, 37–56.

Index